Close Writing

Close Writing

Developing Purposeful Writers in Grades 2–6

Paula Bourque

STENHOUSE PUBLISHERS
PORTLAND, MAINE

Stenhouse Publishers

www.stenhouse.com

Credits

Figure 4.4: "Ordinary" from WONDER by R. J. Palacio, copyright © 2012 by R.J. Palacio. Used by permission of Alfred A. Knopf, an imprint of Random House Children's Books, a division of Penguin Random House LLC. All rights reserved.

Figure 4.5: From ONE FOR THE MURPHYS by Lynda Mullaly Hunt, copyright © 2012 by Lynda Mullaly Hunt. Used by permission of Nancy Paulsen Books, an imprint of Penguin Young Readers Group, a division of Penguin Random House LLC.

Figure 4.17: Artwork © 2013 Neil Cohn. Used with permission.

Figure 4.18: Captain America and all other Marvel characters: TM & © 2015 Marvel Entertainment, LLC and its subsidiaries. All Rights Reserved.

Library of Congress Cataloging-in-Publication Data

Names: Bourque, Paula, 1963- author.
Title: Close writing : developing purposeful writers in grades 2-6 / Paula Bourque.
Description: Portland, Maine : Stenhouse Publishers, [2016] | Includes bibliographical references and index.
Identifiers: LCCN 2015026478| ISBN 9781625310538 (pbk. : alk. paper) | ISBN 9781625310545 (ebook)
Subjects: LCSH: Composition (Language arts)--Study and teaching (Elementary) | Composition (Language arts)--Study and teaching (Middle school) | English language--Composition and exercises--Study and teaching (Elementary) | English language--Composition and exercises--Study and teaching (Middle school)
Classification: LCC LB1576 .B5327 2016 | DDC 372.62/3--dc23
LC record available at http://lccn.loc.gov/2015026478

Cover design, interior design by Blue Design, Portland, Maine (www.bluedes.com)

Manufactured in the United States of America

PRINTED ON 30% PCW
RECYCLED PAPER

23 22 21 20 19 18 17 16   9 8 7 6 5 4 3 2 1

Dedicated to the close writers in our Augusta schools: students, teachers, and administrators. We are all learners for life.

CONTENTS

PART 1: GUIDING PRINCIPLES

PART 2: CLOSE WRITING LESSONS

PART 3: CLOSE WRITING WITH AUTHORS

Acknowledgments

My story is really the collective story of the dedicated teachers I am so lucky to work with in Augusta, Maine. I am forever grateful to Haley Duncan, Andrea Bryant, Kelley Capen, Dan Johnston, Guy Meader, Paige (Dyer) Knowlton, Luanne Phair, Amber Davis, Becky Foster, Jessica Walling, Marcia Hughes, Elizabeth Chadwick, Caroline Eldridge, Katie Dutil, Samantha Simmons, Erika Meiler, Alice Drummond, Moe Heikkila, Nicole Clark, Janet Frake, Valerie Sugden, Brandi Grady, Meagan Mattice, Jenna Sementelli, Jennifer Veilleux, Maureen Cooper, and Renee Henry for welcoming me into their classrooms and for sharing their brilliant teaching (and their students) with me and with my readers. Coming into school each day never feels like work when I can collaborate with these and so many other amazing educators and administrators. I work in five schools, and I hope the students and teachers know how much I admire and appreciate them all.

A special thank-you to my coaching partner and friend, Jessica West, who supported and encouraged me more than she'll ever know, and to my fellow coaches and Maine Literacy Council colleagues: Erika Turner, Jennifer Felt, Georgia Vallee, Heidi Goodwin, and Natalee Stotz, who read through my drafts and gave me feedback that lifted my thinking.

I am forever grateful to my "ELL mentor," Carol Kalajainen. Our conversations over the years have been insightful, inspiring, and invaluable in supporting not only English language learners but also all students. I am blessed to have such gifted friends.

This opportunity to share my story would not be possible without the encouragement of fellow coach and author Jennifer Allen. She is a true literacy leader who always inspires me. I promise you, I *will* pay it forward!

I could not have asked for a more supportive team than the staff at Stenhouse who guided me through this new writing process. My gifted editor, Maureen Barbieri, has been a mentor, an adviser, and a friend every step of the way. Louisa Irele, Chris Downey, and Jay Kilburn responded to every question and request, no matter how trivial, as if it were the most important pending matter of the day. My copyeditor, Andre Barnett, read this text more closely than anyone ever will, helping me be a closer writer. To those of you whom I've not yet met but who worked to put this book together, you have my deepest gratitude and respect.

Last, I dedicate this book to the most important people in my life. My incredible husband, Jim, supported me each day and long night and picked up the slack my writing took away from our family life. I don't know how I got so lucky! To my daughter, Bailey, and my son, Casey, my love for you is overwhelming! You make me want to be a better person every day, and I definitely became a wiser teacher when I became your mother. And to my first and best teachers, my parents, Ron and Carolyn Ingham, who are always encouraging every step I take.

Introduction

Close Writing: Cultivating a relationship between the writer and his or her writing through mindful and purposeful rereading, reflecting, and revising.

This book is a story. My story and the story of the teachers and students I am so fortunate to work with. It is our story of fostering close writing. Thousands of stories are happening each day in classrooms across the world. Why would anyone want to read this one? I cannot answer that with certainty, but I know that when I read the stories of fellow teachers, such as Aimee Buckner (*Notebook Know-How: Strategies for the Reader's Notebook*), Franki Sibberson and Karen Szymusiak (*Still Learning to Read: Teaching Students in Grades 3–6*), Jennifer Allen (*Becoming a Literacy Leader: Supporting Learning and Change*), Donalyn Miller (*The Book Whisperer: Awakening the Inner Reader in Every Child*), Linda Rief (*Read Write Teach: Choice and Challenge in the Reading-Writing Workshop*), Kelly Gallagher (*Write Like This: Teaching Real-World Writing Through Modeling and Mentor Texts*), Jennifer Jacobson (*No More "I'm Done!" Fostering Independent Writers in the Primary Grades*), and many others, I can see myself in their words and in their classrooms. I "watch" them think, learn, and teach with their students, and I feel empowered. Their story becomes my story, with scene and character variations (and personal plot twists). I would like for readers to see themselves in my story and then create their own.

Thomas Newkirk describes it well in his book *Minds Made for Stories: How We Really Read and Write Informational and Persuasive Texts.* "We are caught in time, we experience our lives as a movement through time, and we tell stories to give shape and meaning to this passage. That is the human condition. Our understanding of history, science, our national identity, the very 'selves' we have developed, rests on an accounting of time—the stories of our lives become our lives" (Newkirk 2014, 5). This book is my movement through time as a teacher and literacy coach in five schools in Augusta, Maine. It is the story of several second- through sixth-grade teachers helping students develop a relationship with their writing. It is our lives as teachers, students, and writers.

The child "characters" in my story have pseudonyms to protect their identities and to respect that their stories cannot be as accurately told by me with my singular perspective. I use the pronoun he or she interchangeably when discussing anonymous or hypothetical characters. The teacher "players" in my story are all real, and are all amazing. Their willingness to let us peek inside their classrooms to share their stories, not only with me but also with unknown readers, is selfless and courageous. Imagine undergoing a formal observation or evaluation every time a teacher or administrator visits your classroom. That's what is happening as you read this book! We usually want to cry "Mulligan!" and get a do-over to fix something we've said or done. The lessons teachers share here will never be the same again; they continually reflect, refine, and evolve with their growing experience. However, they are frozen in time in this text, offering a snapshot of their teaching lives. I truly respect the fearlessness and generosity of these educators.

We are living and working in an age of constant reform. Teacher bashing and blaming are not only acceptable but often policy. Our schools and the teaching profession are judged and defined by people whose only educational experience may be that they once attended school. We teachers need to take a more active role in shaping the narrative. We need to celebrate our successes and encourage one another in our struggles. We need to tell our stories. And so, I share mine with you and hope that it may help you to shape and share your own.

But, why *this* story? What compelled me to focus more intently on this chapter of my teaching life? Over the past few years, I have become increasingly concerned with how disconnected many students seem to be from their writing. Despite incredible teaching, some students were so detached they couldn't recognize or read their own work. Some repeatedly fell into ineffective and inhibiting writing patterns. Some were unable to transfer learned skills from one piece of writing to the next. Most troubling was how few students thought of themselves as writers. And then it hit me, "Do I see *myself* as a writer?"

I truly believe that writing is a way to share our thinking, but it is also a way to shape our thinking. To learn more about our writers, I needed to be a writer. Writing is how researchers pull together their observations, reading, and experience into a cohesive hypothesis. Without the writing, it is just some deep thinking. The writing facilitates the connections, causal relationships, and patterns of thought. It provides a repository for those ideas to be examined by others and re-examined by ourselves. My writing would help me research my concerns.

Perhaps, more importantly, by becoming a writer I would be walking the talk. What better way to gain insights into the thinking of our writers than to immerse myself in the act of writing? I have always written, but I have not really considered myself a writer. How would my concept of writing expand or change faced with similar deadlines and accountability as my students? Would increased empathy lead to valuable insights? What would I discover about my own writing identity that could inform my teaching? This writing would help me fathom what it means to be a writer.

I shared my thinking with fellow educator, coach, and writer Jennifer Allen. She encouraged me to begin my writing journey. I will forever be grateful to her for that nurturing nudge. Little did either of us know that the conversation we engaged in was just a scratch on the surface of this writing tale. My original thesis, to teach students to read their own writing closely, has evolved into a premise that we can foster deeper relationships between the writer and the writing through close reading, purposeful reflecting, and mindful revising.

And thus began my story, *Close Writing*. I offer to you these chapters of that story, knowing there is no end. Each year brings new students, new teachers, new thinking to my story. I can truly appreciate that writing is a process and not simply a product. I humbly encourage you to step into this story and cast yourself as any character. When you step away, I urge you to write your own new and improved story!

PART 1

Guiding Principles

CHAPTER 1

Learning to Look

The best teachers are those who show you where to look, but don't tell you what to see. —Alexandra K. Trenfor

My story as a teacher began twenty-seven years ago, a long time by many people's standards. Yet with each approaching school year I often feel like a novice. The more I know, the more I know I *don't* know! The more I look, the more I see. I see new ways to reach struggling readers and writers. I see innovative approaches from colleagues that make me wonder, "Now why didn't I think of that?" I see each student interaction as a unique opportunity for me to grow in my own understanding of learning. I see new literacies emerging as technology takes a greater role in our lives. I see patterns that I would not have noticed if hadn't kept looking.

When I took on the role of literacy coach, I felt like a kid in a candy shop. It has been such a treat to be welcomed into dozens of classrooms, where there's always so much to see. One minute I am in a sixth-grade class helping students develop thesis statements for their essays; the next, I am in a kindergarten helping students stretch out words to write what they hear. I get to witness the developmental continuum of literacy from preschool on up, not just read about it. I am blessed to work with such collaborative teachers who invite me in and share their insights about teaching and learning. They help *me* to look, and I help *them* to look, and together we see more than either of us could alone.

> **The moral of this story:**
> Close writers develop a self-extending system in which they learn to look and look to learn.

This particular story began over the past several years, as I have worked hard at learning to look. I have shifted most of my focus from looking at the teacher to looking at the students. That is not to imply that I do not notice the teacher or that she is not important. On the contrary, I can witness just how important she is when I see the results in the work and behavior of her students. I used to come in to observe and discuss instructional approaches and decisions. Now, I focus in on how the students respond to these instructional techniques. This information can be incredibly valuable when it comes to understanding the needs of (and next steps for) our students.

The shift in focus from teaching to learning may seem trivial, but it is everything to my latest thinking. I can coach teachers on all the best practices we know, but if it doesn't result in better student outcomes, we are wasting precious time. My goal in the classroom is to collaborate so that we all grow. It requires that we learn to look, and I believe that many can see more than one.

Learning to Look at Writers

So while learning to look, I began looking to learn. What could I learn from the hundreds of students I observed writing? Their strengths and their needs were on display each day for all to learn from—if only we looked. I began to look closely at student work and student behavior during the writing workshop. What did I notice about those students who appeared to be successful writers? What did I notice about those who seemed to struggle? No two children approach writing in the same way, but the following observation reflected a typical pattern of behavior for students on either end of the writing spectrum.

PEEK INSIDE A CLASSROOM: A TALE OF TWO WRITERS

Haley Duncan has just finished the mini-lesson on dialogue in her fourth-grade classroom and invites the children to begin working on their pieces (see Figure 1.1). On one side of the class, Tavia lays her papers out on her desk and puts them in order. She grabs a pencil and starts reading through her story. She stops occasionally to write something on her paper. She pauses to answer a question from another student sitting at her table, looks around the room briefly, and then goes back to reading. After two or three minutes, she begins writing quite quickly, pausing from time to time to look at what she has written. By the end of writing workshop, she has almost two pages. She is asked to share some of the dialogue she has written, and though she is shy, can read it with prosody and fluency.

Figure 1.1
Haley Duncan's fourth-grade class

On the other side of the same classroom, Justin places his notebook on his desk and begins to search for a sharp pencil. When that proves unsuccessful, he walks over and grinds his nub down to a more sharpened point. He winds his way around several tables on the route back to his seat. He begins to pull papers out of his desk. Mrs. Duncan comes over to encourage him. "You need to get started, Justin."

"I'm looking for my paper." He pulls more papers and books out of his desk.

"Which paper? Here's your narrative." Mrs. Duncan shows him his notebook and flips it to where he had previously written.

"Never mind, it was something else," he says and replaces the papers in his desk.

"You all set?"

"Yup." Mrs. Duncan steps away but keeps a close eye on Justin. He watches her and starts writing on his paper. Within a few moments, he stops, looking around the class. He makes eye contact with me and then begins writing again. His teacher checks in several times during the workshop to observe and encourage. By the end of the period, he has a handful of sentences. He has not attempted dialogue in his piece.

I am reluctant to draw big conclusions on single observations, but in this classroom, I have seen this scenario play out many times. Conversations with the teacher confirm that these behaviors are consistently typical. As I observed, what did I see? What can I learn about these writers?

TAVIA	JUSTIN
Began right away, had a plan and an established routine for writing, eager to begin	Had trouble getting started, did not have an effective routine, reluctant to begin
Started by closely reading what she had previously written	Started writing without reading what he had previously written
Engaged in the writing, able to get back on task when distracted	Not engaged with writing, needed prompting to begin and encouragement to continue
Fluent writing, drafted quickly and at length	Disfluent writing, slow letter and word formation, few sentences written
Paused to read what she had written before continuing	Did not appear to reread his writing
Incorporated teaching points from the mini-lesson into the day's writing	Did not attempt to incorporate teaching point into the day's writing
Volume of writing was high	Volume of writing was low

I am sure most of us can see these students sitting in our classrooms. The students who are stronger writers enjoy writing, and so write a great deal. The more they write, the more opportunities they have to encounter different techniques, genres, vocabulary, punctuation, and dialogue. The weaker writers do not enjoy writing and avoid it. It is more difficult to improve because they practice less. As they fall behind, they become more reluctant to engage with their writing. Their level of enjoyment and level of skill are so entwined it is difficult to discern which influences their engagement. As a teacher, I know I must approach these two writers differently. Perhaps that seems obvious, but designing instructional practice to meet the needs of diverse writers is easier said than done. We can't tease out their needs until we look to learn.

WRITING WORKSHOP	TAVIA	JUSTIN
During Mini-Lesson	Partner her in turn-and-talk with a writer who may need support or is a patient listener.	Partner him in turn-and-talk with a writer who can express thoughts and ideas well.
Independent Writing	Allow her maximum time to write uninterrupted.	Start him off with small-group instruction to scaffold his needs. Invite him to briefly doodle or draw to spark or explore ideas.
Conferring	Conference with her to continue to lift her level of writing skill; continue to foster a growth mindset.	Set very clear and achievable short-term expectations. Share the pen between Justin and a partner or teacher to increase the volume and encourage ideas. Invite him to reread previous work to get into the flow and reflect on his intended message. Prompt strategies of rereading and oral rehearsal to guide him when he is stuck. Provide targeted, positive feedback and a focused teaching point; do not attempt to address all needs, prioritize.
Share	Provide opportunities to share with strong writing partners as well as striving writers. Share process/thinking.	Make sure he gets the support he needs to share quality work with partners and class. Needs to be seen as a writer in his own eyes.

This differentiated approach is not unique or revolutionary; it goes on every day in classrooms everywhere, including in the classrooms where I work. It requires that we give ourselves permission to pass up too many "teachable moments" and have patience to let some things go, for the time being. We feel so time compelled with a sense of urgency to teach hard, and set high expectations. The best teachers I know are the ones who understand that sometimes we have to slow down for students to accelerate. Taking the time to look and learn helps to slow us down, focus our efforts, and help students build momentum.

Helping Students to Look

Because I really want the focus to shift from teaching to learning, it isn't enough to be satisfied that we teachers are learning to look; the students themselves must learn to look. If the teachers and I are the ones doing all of the noticing, we will create students who depend on us for their learning. Our students are the ones doing the writing; they are the ones who need to monitor how it is going. We cannot possibly teach them everything they will need to know to grow as readers and writers. To become close writers, they need to develop a self-extending system in which they learn how to learn. To do this, they first need to learn how to look.

I began to ask teachers whether they thought their students were closely reading their own writing. We began to observe the routines and behaviors of the writers in our classrooms. We found that many students did not return to their writing to reread; those who did reread were still not reading closely. I asked teachers whether not reading closely had an effect on their students' writing ability. Here's what some of them told me:

> *"The result of them not closely reading is obviously that when I meet with students their stories are incomplete, missing chunks that they do not even realize, or that they do not say what they intend to say."* —Rachel Toner, third-grade teacher

> *"Before we started working together, I believe my students hardly ever read their writing closely. In fact, the revising and editing stages of the writing process were ones I dreaded teaching. I basically went over a checklist for each stage (check for spelling, check for sentence variety, capitalize, etc.), and the students went off with their draft and checked things off in about five minutes. It frustrated me that they completed these stages so quickly and made hardly any changes."* —Haley Duncan, fourth-grade teacher

> *"Many students don't closely read their own writing. I know even when I make them read it to me, they say stuff that is not there or they can't read it because it makes no sense to them, so I guess they have to fill in. For the kids who don't closely read, it's obvious what they really want to say is not being communicated to the reader. They also either end up just rewriting what they wrote the first time or make only a few changes but usually not correct ones. Lots of them don't put punctuation in, so that makes it confusing for the reader and for them when they attempt to reread. I find a lot of kids still have trouble deciding if something is a sentence. So for the kiddos who don't closely read, it affects staying on topic, organization, and maybe even learning to like writing."* —Kathi Toothaker, fifth-grade teacher

> *"Based on my experience for the last few years, I don't think a lot of my students really read their own writing in a meaningful way (they often look at length or number of*

words but not a great focus on the content of the writing). I think this does impact their writing because when they conference with me after doing a self-revision session, they often will say they didn't see that or didn't think that it sounded like that when they wrote it. I think most often, the flow or logic of a story gets twisted up, and they don't catch it themselves, as they are not really reading their own pieces for understanding, as opposed to mechanics." —Guy Meader, sixth-grade teacher

Many teachers I work with echo these sentiments. A common concern is that students' writing often seems incomplete or confusing and that writers did not seem to notice until they read their work with the teacher. The teacher has twenty to twenty-five students in a classroom. We cannot be the sole impetus, encouraging students to closely read a body of writing. It's ineffective for achieving the growth in writing we are aiming for. We need to teach our students to take on this responsibility.

A key element in close writing is *learning to look and looking to learn* by closely reading our writing. Students often look at their writing through a single lens that reflects the limits of their experiences as writers. They cannot contemplate the possibilities and potential in their writing if they cannot envision them. They cannot consistently build on strengths that they are not aware of. They might be content or complacent with their skill level in writing because they cannot see how it could be better or different. They all too quickly declare, "I'm done."

When we help them to look at their writing through a variety of lenses, they begin to envision the possibilities. They can try out new ideas and reflect on their effectiveness. They can recognize their habits and methods of writing and build on them. We can heighten their awareness of the qualities of good writing and give them opportunities to incorporate those qualities into their own writing. We can help them monitor habits or patterns that may detract from the ideas they are trying to convey.

We cannot address what we cannot see. As teachers, we can help students to notice aspects of their writing to progress in their writing competence. We can hone our skills at observing and evaluating writing to create more efficient scaffolds and lessons to drive our teaching prowess. Then, ultimately, we want to create the conditions in which our students take on ownership for perceiving, analyzing, evaluating, and refining their writing. When they can clearly see what *is* and can envision what *could be*, we open up new possibilities for our students as writers. It is my hope that through this story you will help your students discover where to look but not what to see.

How Could This Story Help You?

Some of you may remember a commercial with the tagline "At BASF, we don't make a lot of the products you buy. We make a lot of the products you buy *better*." This story is a lot like that commercial. It isn't going to teach you how to set up a writing workshop or provide you a scope and sequence for your curriculum. It isn't going to tell your students what to write about. What it could do, if you use it to create your own story, is help make the lessons or the structures you use *better*. And by better I mean that students take on more awareness, ownership, and responsibility for their growth as writers.

You might find my story helpful:

- if you feel as if you've taught your students lessons on writing that are not being reflected in the work they produce;

- if you find students don't consistently go back in and reread or reflect on the writing they've done;

- if you have students who wait for you to tell them how to "fix up" their writing before they attempt revision;

- if you have students who consistently think that their writing is done and can't imagine how it could be better;

- if you have students who aren't aware of the patterns, techniques, or craft elements they use or neglect in their own writing;

- if you want to help your students build stamina for working on a piece of writing over time;

- if you want to learn how to look better at student writing to analyze needs and celebrate successes; or

- if you are looking for ways to help students be more mindful and purposeful during writing.

How Does This Story Work?
PART 1

I begin with a summary of the theories that have influenced my teaching. As professionals, it is critical that our instruction reflects the research and methods that are reliable and valid best practices. I highlight the people, books, and research that have shaped this story.

PART 2

Writing is not linear or step-by-step, but many teachers are accustomed to teaching writing in five basic stages: prewriting, drafting, revising, editing, and publishing (see Figure 1.2). We help our students become close writers when we encourage them to be mindful and purposeful, as they work within each stage. I have used this structure as a framework to tell the heart of my story, but not to suggest a direct progression.

I help you peek inside the classrooms of our dauntless teachers and share the work of our budding authors. I then provide a bit more focus for our English language learners. Our schools, like so many others, are seeing a greater influx of ELL students each year, and we are continually looking for ways to support their adjustment and literacy development. Each chapter starts with my discoveries about close writers (Moral of This Story) and ends with a brief summary of key ideas (The Gist of the Story) followed by an invitation to reflect and plan (Drafting Your Story). Additional resources, photos, and templates for each section can be found online at www.stenhouse.com/closewritingbook.

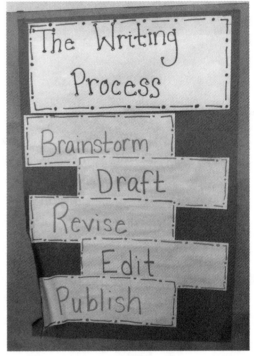

PART 3

Finally, I offer a section of interviews with a group of authors with whom I have connected on this journey. They are truly close writers from whom I have learned so much. It is my hope that their stories will enrich your story as well.

Figure 1.2: **One version of the writing process**

REFERENCES/RESOURCES

All cited texts, videos, or websites can be found in the reference section. To the best of my ability, I have tried to offer the origin for all quotes used in this story; however, with the proliferation of information on the Internet, I have occasionally had to rely on secondary sources when the primary source was inaccessible. The recommended resources are not all directly referenced in this text but have had a profound influence on my thinking and teaching. I think they would be an invaluable support to any writing classroom.

Suggestion

My advice to you is to use this book as a rough draft, or "discovery draft," of your own story. Mark it up and annotate it the way you would initial versions of the stories you write. Make revisions to create a story that is relevant to you. Add your own ideas and anecdotes to illustrate the thinking. Collect your own resources, quotes, and references and add them to the inside covers. Share your story with others. Have fun!

Drafting Your Story

You are the sum total of everything you've ever seen, heard, eaten, smelled, been told, forgot—it's all there. Everything influences each of us, and because of that I try to make sure that my experiences are positive.—Maya Angelou

At the end of each chapter, I will invite you to think about your own teaching, your own students, and your own story in light of what you've just read here. It is easier to synthesize incoming information with our existing schema while it is fresh in our minds. This conscious combination helps us to refine our thinking and teaching, sometimes challenging, sometimes reinforcing, and occasionally raising new insights.

- How closely do your students read their writing? What are the implications you have observed for those who do and for those who don't?

- How closely do you read *your* writing? Can you think of a time when you needed to?

- What concerns do you have for your students' writing? Are they shared concerns?

CHAPTER 2

Close Reading: The Key to Close Writing

Books can truly change our lives: the lives of those who read them, the lives of those who write them. Readers and writers alike discover things they never knew about the world and about themselves.—Lloyd Alexander

One of my favorite summer traditions with my kids is lying out in the hammock on a summer night during the Perseid meteor showers. We snuggle together under a few blankets and settle in to observe the night sky. It's usually not long before one of us cries, "Did you see that?" Chances are, we didn't. We refocus our eyes on another section of the night sky and wait.

"Whoa! Did you see that one?" "What one? Where?" I'll train my eyes in the direction of my son's pointing hand or my daughter's fixed gaze. It goes on like this for an hour or more as we each spy a trail of light race across the black; sometimes we see the same streak or catch one out of the corner of our eye. We understand; it is an enormous sky. We cannot possibly see it all in a single glance. We are looking at the same sky, but we all have different views and experiences.

> **The moral of this story:**
> Close writers use close reading strategies on their own texts to take an authorial stance and develop new understandings of their writing.

What Is Close Reading?

I observe a similar phenomenon happening in classrooms quite frequently. When I drop in on literature discussion groups, I often hear conversations like this sixth grade one discussing *Joey Pigza Loses Control* (Gantos 2001). "Wait, I thought he was mad that he had to go to his dad's."

"No, remember, he convinced his mom to let him go. He got mad at his dad later when he took away his meds. Well maybe not mad, but more like scared."

"Oh. Maybe he was just scared to see his dad."

"He probably was, but he was also kind of excited."

It is clear that these students read the same text but came away with different experiences (views, remembrances, or opinions). They encountered that book the way my kids and I experienced skywatching: they were looking intently but not always at the same place with the same focus.

When I hear teachers respond to students' comments about their reading with, "Where did you first notice that Joey's dad might not have changed? Show me" or "What do you think Joey's mom was feeling as she was driving him to his dad's? What did she say or do that makes you think that?" I know that those students will revisit the text and come away with deeper or different views and richer experiences. Inviting students to reread with purpose is the heart of close reading.

STANDING ON THE SHOULDERS OF GIANTS

If I have seen further it is by standing on the shoulders of giants.—Sir Isaac Newton

I am grateful for the modern-day giants in the world of literacy who have helped shape my understanding of close reading and begin to contemplate its application beyond the reading workshop. One of these giants is Dr. Douglas Fisher. In an interview about his definition of close reading, Fisher responded, "A close reading is a careful and purposeful reading, well, actually it's rereading. It's a careful and purposeful rereading of a text . . . When we have students really read carefully, they pay attention to the words, the ideas, the structure, the flow and the purpose of that text" (Fisher 2012).

Fisher's definition got me wondering about the rereading students do of their own writing. Is it a purposeful encounter? How carefully do they pay attention to the words, ideas, structure, and flow of their own texts? If we are asking them to reread other authors' texts, why not their own?

My story is also influenced by Kylene Beers and Robert Probst, who expand the idea of close reading a little further in their book *Notice and Note: Strategies for Close Reading*. "Close reading should suggest close attention to the text; close attention to the relevant experience, thought, and memory of the reader; close attention to the responses and interpretations of other readers; and close attention to the interactions among those elements" (Beers and Probst 2012, 37). They contend that meaning cannot be derived simply from the reading presented "within the four corners of the page" (2012, 35)—that what the reader brings to the text will shape his or her understanding of the author's words.

Their contention got me considering the interaction of elements when the reader is also the writer. Can being the reader of our own writing bring us new insights? Can we derive deeper meaning when we read what we have written within the four corners of the page?

And still my story was influenced by Christopher Lehman and Kate Roberts in their book *Falling in Love with Close Reading*. "Close reading is something we should teach students *to do*, rather than something we just *do to* them" (Lehman and Roberts 2014, 4). They suggest establishing a three-step ritual for teaching students to read closely:

1. Read through lenses.

2. Use lenses to find patterns.

3. Use patterns to develop a new understanding of the text.

This sounded a lot like our desired approach to revision. How could we establish a ritual for reading our writing with a variety of lenses to develop a new understanding or even new versions of our texts? Could I help my students to fall in love with their writing?

As great as these influences are to my story, I recognize that they also stood on the shoulders of giants to build their working theories and instructional techniques. One of the biggest giants was Louise Rosenblatt. She proposed a transactional theory of reading in which the reader and the text were both important elements in the creation of meaning. In her view, "the text is simply ink on paper until a reader comes along" (Rosenblatt cited in Probst 1987, 1). I began to wonder whether our student writers understood this.

She contends that the same text can be read in different ways, ranging from an efferent stance (to gather information or to analyze elements of text) to an aesthetic stance (personal response and experience of emotions from text). By closely reading a text with different lenses or stances, we can create new experiences when rereading and uncover new understandings and appreciation for what we read. I started thinking about the implication of this for our writers.

Comprehending the meaning of close reading and how it is done is only part of the practice. Knowing when to implement it is equally relevant. Not every text requires a close reading or a rereading. Imagine if we consumed every meal with a similar approach; chewing on each bite until we unlocked every nuanced flavor and revisiting that same menu offering until we could deeply appreciate the complexities of that given fare. I am sure we could write some fantastic food reviews as we grow in our appreciation for fine cuisine, but sometimes we are ravenous and want to devour the meal quickly and contemplate flavor later. Sometimes we want to sample a variety of bites to merge flavors and textures. Sometimes we just want to nibble or munch on junk food to bring us pleasure. Reading can be seen much the same way. Sometimes we devour books for pure enjoyment, digging in voraciously. Sometimes we sample books to skim and scan purposefully. Sometimes we just need to snack on our beach books, trashy novels, or pop culture reads to bring us personal pleasure. We don't want to confuse one strategy for reading with a systematic approach for reading. Understanding purpose goes a long way in determining process.

What Is Close Reading for Writers?
Not all readers are writers, but all writers are readers.
—Ralph Fletcher

In 2000, many communities and organizations around the world created time capsules to commemorate the millennium. Coordinators had to determine what was important to them, what would represent life as they knew it, and place representative artifacts into the container to be opened and analyzed by future generations. The National Millennium Time Capsule in Washington, DC, contains items of historical significance from the past 100 years, including a helmet from World War II, Louis Armstrong's trumpet, a piece of the Berlin Wall, a cell phone, and a Hostess Twinkie. A great deal of thought went into composing these collections, and then they were sealed up to await the day when they will be rediscovered. The creators hoped they would convey ideas, concepts, and emotions to the discoverers that tell the story of who we are and who we were.

Writing is a similar transaction. We organize what is important to us onto the page: the ideas, concepts, and emotions that reflect our current thinking in that moment. When we are finished, we close it up and wait for it to be discovered by a reader. In both cases, the creators have no guarantee of how their work will be received, interpreted, or valued. We can only hope with our careful choices during creation that we have clearly conveyed an engaging story. But we need to keep in mind that the reader's/discoverer's experiences may differ from those of the creator. Their understanding and appreciation of our collection will depend on and be shaped by those experiences.

That may seem like an overwhelming responsibility for young writers. Many children do not write with a reader in mind. It is all they can do to get an idea from their head, down their arm, through the pencil, and onto the paper. Many are exhausted by that effort; they do not have the stamina to revisit those squiggles on the paper. Because they do not yet understand that those squiggles need to be read and understood by others, they cannot anticipate what the needs of those readers might be.

As a consequence, the piece may be difficult to read and understand, even by the author himself! These writers see writing as a one-way process and not a transactional process between the author and the reader. They need to be taught to *closely read* their own writing with the eyes and ears of a reader. They need to put themselves in the role of the intended reader.

PEEK INSIDE A CLASSROOM: UNDERSTANDING INTENDED AUDIENCE

You might see evidence of this in your own classroom as I did when I was working in Paige Dyer's third grade one morning. The students were surprising Miss Dyer with birthday cards and letters while she was out of the room. I observe Asher rubbing his eyes and laying his head on his desk. I approach him and ask, "How's it going?" He lifts his head and shrugs. I encourage him with, "Let's see what you have so far." He picks up his paper and holds it out to me.

"Here." He thrusts the paper toward me without glancing at it.

"Can you read it to me?" I ask. "I like to hear readers share their own writing."

He sighs. "I can't think what else."

"You can't think of anything else to say?" I try to clarify.

"I think I'm done," he answers.

"OK. Let's see what you have. Sometimes when you read it to yourself it helps you to think of other ideas." He glances down at his paper and starts reading his piece, several sentences describing what he likes about his teacher and an accompanying picture. I notice he is using the pronoun "she" several times.

"When Miss Dyer reads it, will she know it's for her?" I ask. He gives me a quizzical look. I keep probing, "If I were Miss Dyer and I read this (modeling my best impersonation of Paige's reading, emphasizing the pronoun *she*) would I know you are writing it for me?"

"Yeah, because I started it *Dear Miss Dyer*," he answers.

Asher did not yet understand how to write to an intended audience. He knew that a letter needed a salutation to determine the recipient, but the body of the letter did not attempt to connect with that person. He could not picture his teacher reading that piece as the *she* in the letter. Asher needed more support to write for an intended reader. He needed to see his writing as a transaction between himself and Miss Dyer.

READING AND WRITING AS A TRANSACTION

I have kept a daily journal for most of my adult life. Each night, I recount the events of my day and include photos that capture some of those moments. A few years ago I looked through some of the journals and began to wonder, who was the intended audience? I was writing them for myself, in the moment, but hadn't really thought much about who the future reader would be. It really wasn't for my children or my husband or even some museum in the future. It was just for me. That night I decided I would more consciously write for my future me, perhaps the Paula with an imperfect memory or who might long for some snippets from the past. I started to include more photos, a snapshot of my activity for that day, and some insight into the thoughts and ideas I experience at this age. I wanted the Paula of my future age to be able to glance at a page and be transported back to that time. I was making a transaction between my current self and my future self.

Most writing, however, especially writing that is done in our schools, does have an anticipated audience: a teacher, peers, parents, or the community. I have noticed that many students do not internalize this concept. To them it makes sense and seems good enough. They do not yet empathize with the needs of the reader to interpret their writing or to make meaning from it. They do not grasp that the pictures or ideas in their own heads could be dissimilar from those of the readers. (See Figure 2.1.)

TAKING A STANCE AS A READER

One of my all-time favorite books is Harper Lee's *To Kill a Mockingbird*. I can recall reading by the fire but feeling like I was in Maycomb, Alabama, and seeing the injustice of prejudice and fear through the eyes of Scout Finch. I was caught up in the rhythm of the language and the innocence of Scout's perception of the world. This is described by Rosenblatt's transactional theory of reading (Rosenblatt 1994) as taking an aesthetic stance (personal response and experience of emotions from text). But I can also remember reading the text in an American Literature course and teasing out the themes by finding examples of prejudice or redemption or courage. Rosenblatt's theory would frame this as taking an efferent stance (gathering information or analyzing elements of text).

The reader's stance can fluctuate, depending on purpose and their interaction with the text, but meaning is made from what the writer *and* reader bring to the experience. The reader does not transact directly with the author, only through the words of the author in the text.

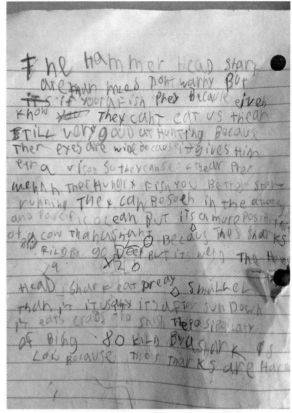

Figure 2.1: **Lacks empathy for needs of the reader**

TAKING A STANCE AS A WRITER (AUTHORIAL READING)

However, when the reader *is* the writer, Rosenblatt proposes two other reading stances that might be exercised. She calls these authorial stances (Rosenblatt 1988). Sometimes when I am reading my writing, I want to make sure that it makes sense, fits with what I have previously written, and continues to meet my purpose. Rosenblatt defines this as Authorial Reading I. At other times, I attempt to look at my story through the eyes of potential readers and consider the meaning they might make. This would be considered Authorial Reading II. She believes that writers need to approach the writing task with both authorial stances. "The emerging text must be read in the light both of what others might make of the text and also how that fits the writer's own inner sense of purpose. Rereading the text at intervals, the writer may alternate the two kinds of inner criteria, or if sufficiently expert, may merge them" (Rosenblatt 1988, 10). She contends that writers need to have a good hold on the first stance before they can effectively carry through the second.

Asher was looking at his letter to Miss Dyer with an Authorial Reading I stance. It made sense to him, and he liked what he had to say. However, he was lacking the Authorial Reading II stance. He wasn't able to consider how it would be received or understood by his teacher. He wasn't able to put himself in the place of the intended reader and see it through her eyes.

How could these stances help our writers, like Asher, closely read their work with purpose and intention? By following the first reading stance, they could closely read their work to make sure it reflects what they intended. I call this Read for Me. For many students, Read for Me may be the sole focus of their close reading, as it might be an entirely new approach for them. I may encourage other students to take the second reading stance, which I call Read for You. They closely read their work to anticipate the needs of a reader. I think about possible questions they can ask themselves to adopt the appropriate reading stance as they closely read their writing (see Figure 2.2).

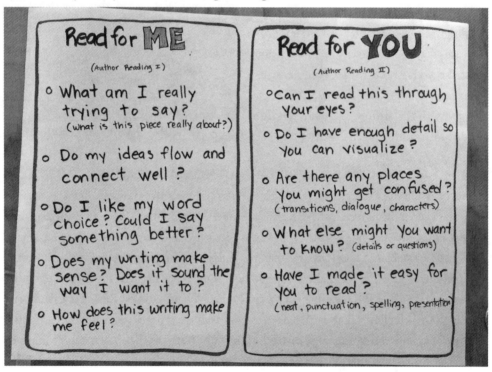

Figure 2.2
Authorial reading chart

If students closely read their work with these questions in mind, they could rely less on teacher feedback and more on their own agency as writers. Students like Asher could begin to see their writing as a transaction between themselves and their intended audience. They can take steps to analyze, evaluate, and revise their writing in a more self-regulated manner. This is the heart of the close writing approach.

Students can make notes in the margin or use Ask the Author thought bubbles (found online at www.stenhouse.com/closewritingbook) to ask themselves questions from each stance. They can then make a plan for revision that will strengthen the writing for themselves and for other readers.

Use these questions to prepare for a writing conference with teachers or peers.

AUTHORIAL READING: READING LIKE AN AUTHOR

Louise Rosenblatt proposed that writers can take authorial reading stances when they approach their own work. A stance is a position or an attitude you adopt when you are facing something.

With Authorial Reading I, we will ask ourselves these questions:

- How does what I am writing fit in with my original idea, or what am I really trying to say here?
- Do my ideas flow together well?
- Do I like my word choice? Could I say something in a better way?
- Does my writing sound the way I want it to?

With Authorial Reading II, we will ask ourselves these questions:

- Does my writing have enough detail to help the reader visualize (character, setting, main idea, etc.)?
- Are there any places in my writing that might confuse a reader (transitions, dialogue, etc.)?
- What questions might a reader ask me about my writing? What else might they want to know?

READING-WRITING RECIPROCITY

Reading and writing are reciprocal processes. In its simplest terms, we learn more about reading by writing, and we learn more about writing by reading. We can develop a greater appreciation for the author's writing craft when we analyze their moves and choices while reading. We can use that new appreciation and understanding from what we read and try out in our own writing.

The more students read and become aware of an author's craft, the more we see them using these techniques in their own writing. The more they write, the greater their appreciation for the choices the authors make in the books they like to read. Most teachers will attest to the observation that their students who read the most are often their strongest writers. This is not a random coincidence.

This young writer has clearly internalized the structures of nonfiction texts from his reading (see Figure 2.3). His understanding of how nonfiction books are organized and presented is evident in his own writing. This is a classic example of the actualization of reading–writing reciprocity by this writer. When we take the time to look and closely read our students' writing, we will begin to find evidence of this awareness throughout their work.

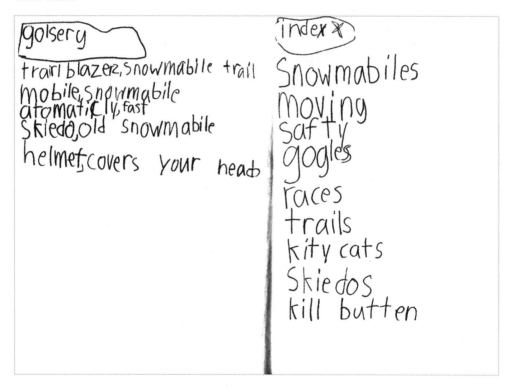

Figure 2.3

Second-grade nonfiction student mentor text

As teachers, we are constantly encouraging our students to read, to reread, and to comprehend texts written by others. We invite them to revisit texts to look for evidence, to analyze information, or to think about the author's ideas in new ways. How could I use a similar framework to apply to the students' writing? These questions could help writers take an authorial reading stance with their work.

WHEN READING OTHERS' TEXTS...	WHEN READING THEIR OWN WRITING...
Ask them to consider the author's message.	**Ask them to consider their message.**
What is the author trying to say?	What are you trying to say in this piece?
What does the author want you to think about?	What do you want the reader to think about or notice?
Why did the author write this?	Why did you write this?
Ask them to analyze the author's craft to unpack deeper meaning.	**Ask them to analyze their craft to unpack deeper meaning.**
What mood is the author trying to create in this piece?	What mood are you trying to create?
How does the author introduce the character to the reader?	How do you introduce the character to the reader?
	What do you think the reader is visualizing here?
Ask them to evaluate the work of others.	**Ask them to evaluate their work in a variety of ways.**
How does this book compare to other works by this author?	How does this piece compare to other pieces you have done?
Would you recommend this book to others? Why or why not?	Would you recommend this to others? Why or why not?

I started listening more closely in classrooms to observe how frequently I heard these questions being asked of our young authors. Were they asking these questions of themselves? Teachers were asking wonderful questions to bring out the best in their writers, but still many students were not making strong reading–writing connections. They weren't making the connection that the same questions asked of them in their reading, they could ask of themselves in their writing.

Close writing would promote this kind of self-reflection and analysis by inviting readers to closely read their writing with specific focuses, lenses, or stances to help them answer these questions. Close writing can help writers not only reflect on and revise the current piece of writing with which they are engaged but also shape their thinking when it comes to composition of future pieces of work. This is the goal most teachers have for their students; what can I learn today that will help me tomorrow (or every day)? In other words, what can I learn as I write and read this piece that will make me a stronger writer with any piece?

Observing Close Reading in Writing

As I walk through a fifth-grade classroom, I notice one writer particularly engaged in his work (see Figure 2.4). His pencil is feverishly moving across the paper, and then it stops. The student sets down his pencil and flips his paper over to the other side. His eyes continue to move across the page. He pauses for a moment and looks out into the space beyond the classroom walls, his lips move in response to his thinking. Within a few moments, he picks up his pencil, and the words begin to flow from it once again.

Figure 2.4
Student close reading

This is what close reading looks like in one writing workshop. Without prompting, the student stops writing to go back and reread what he has previously written, revises quickly, and then continues composing; building from the ideas on which he stopped to reread and reflect. This student understands that closely reading his work will create a more seamless composition that flows for the reader. He is using his eyes and ears as a reader to strengthen his skills as a writer.

Another scene reveals a student staring blankly down at his paper and gazing around the room for inspiration. "I'm thinking," is his response to prompting from his teacher. He looks around at the papers of fellow students and then at the clock before continuing with his piece. He writes for a minute or so before repeating the process. I approach him, "Let's hear what you have so far."

It's clear that he has not reread his work. "Oh, I meant to start it here." He points to the third line. He begins to read and notices words that have been left out or that he cannot decipher. He occasionally reads through punctuation or does not notice missing punctuation. There is no prosody in his reading, no attempt to interpret or illuminate the meaning with his voice. When he finishes he looks up at me, "Am I done?"

You probably have versions of these students in your own classrooms and countless variations in between these extremes. Everyone approaches writing quite individually, with varying degrees of efficiency and skill. Observing and implementing practices and procedures that will best support our diverse writers is a key task in our role as writing teachers. When we want to know how to do something well, we watch someone who is doing it well. What routines, habits, and techniques do our strong writers employ that support their success? My observations over the past several years have revealed that students who reread, revisit, and reflect on their writing with frequency are our strongest writers. Close reading, as part of the writing process, has been an integral structure to their success in becoming close writers.

SOME CHARACTERISTICS OF CLOSE WRITERS

- Have many ideas to write about, often engaged in multiple ideas or pieces of writing
- Have developed stamina to write for long stretches of time
- Are prolific readers, who often incorporate ideas and techniques of their favorite authors
- Choose to write when it isn't assigned, at home, during choice time, or recess
- Frequently reread their own writing with a variety of purposes or lenses
- Reflect on their writing for strengths as well as needs
- Develop an awareness of their writing identity

THE WRITING JOURNEY

Writing is like driving at night in the fog. You can only see as far as your headlights, but you can make the whole trip that way.—E. L. Doctorow

Writing is like a road trip. We can ramble around feeling somewhat lost, sometimes enjoying the sights, sometimes feeling confused and frustrated. We can drive the whole way never deviating from the map and never stopping to take in the views along the way. The teacher is the driver, and the students are often along for the ride. What kind of a road trip do we provide for our students? Do we know where we are going? Do we have a good sense of direction? How fast do we go? How smoothly do we steer? Do the students have some say in our itinerary?

The most successful writing workshops have a road map for teaching and learning that serves as a guide. The map may be crafted from an adopted curriculum, a set of standards, writing programs, and/or a teacher's experience, but we have a clear understanding of where students need to go as writers to improve. Teachers frequently take short side trips to address student needs and teachable moments, but they don't lose sight of their destination. This ride slows down occasionally and takes time to focus in on one aspect of writing at a time, like a unique roadside attraction. Then the trip continues with new insights and experiences that make it a richer journey. Knowing when, where, and how frequently to stop (and closely read) are indicators of a skilled teacher and writer.

Teaching for Transfer

Give a man a fish and you feed him for a day; teach a man to fish and you feed him for a lifetime.—Proverb

I am working in a fourth-grade classroom with some students, creating picture books about Maine. Reading through a student's draft, I notice that many of the proper nouns are not capitalized. I broach this during a writing conference. "I notice that you didn't capitalize 'Augusta' in this piece. What do you know about capitalizing the names of places?"

The student looks a little confused and then responds, "Oh, I was just thinking names—like for people—not names like for towns. It's like for all names?"

Transfer means to apply what is learned in one context to other contexts. This student did not transfer his understanding of capitalizing characters' names from one lesson to capitalizing city names or other proper names in other pieces of writing. This happens frequently with learners—they compartmentalize skills or understanding to a limited situation. It's hard to anticipate when that will happen, but awareness of this could help shape our language and choice of examples.

Learning is more powerful when it is generative. What I learn about writing in today's lesson could help me during tomorrow's lesson or any lesson, if I am taught to make that connection. When educators are teaching how to transfer during writing workshop, they focus on improving the writer and not on fixing up any one piece of writing. Scaffolds that allow students to transfer skills and strategies from one context to another create self-regulated learners.

Central to nurturing close writing is encouraging our writers to think strategically about using close reading skills on their own writing, not just applying close reading during a class activity. There is a big difference in autonomy between the writer who will go back and reread for clarity when the teacher tells him to and the writer who monitors his writing by frequently rereading and reflecting. This requires students to develop metacognition (the ability to understand and analyze one's own learning or thinking processes). This will require teachers to be mindful of how much we are doing *for* our students and observing how much *they* can do independently. We scaffold students' ability to transfer skills to a variety of contexts and then gradually remove those scaffolds as students become more self-regulated.

Before we examine scaffolds for transfer learning, let's begin by looking at the simple but key differences between skills and strategies. These terms are often used interchangeably, but understanding how they differ has helped me see why transfer doesn't always happen automatically.

Think of a skill as a particular ability that one has acquired or learned, for example, dribbling a basketball or shooting a jump shot. A player can develop these skills to varying degrees based on the amount of practice and coaching she has experienced. A strategy, however, is the awareness, understanding, and implementation of a skill to achieve a goal. For a basketball player, knowing when and where to dribble and when and where to shoot would demonstrate a basketball strategy.

In the writing classroom, how to look up words in a dictionary or a thesaurus is a frequently taught skill. A strategy might be to develop an awareness of when more precise words would clarify the piece of writing and then use the appropriate tool (such as a dictionary or a thesaurus) to find them. Oftentimes, students appear to learn skills in isolation and lack the understanding for when they should apply the skill or how that skill might help them in other situations. Just knowing how to use a thesaurus does not necessarily translate into a lexicon-rich piece of writing.

When we teach for transfer, we attempt to make those connections clear for students with explicit language and modeling. We can consider the circumstances before, during, and after lessons to reinforce the learning:

Before a writing lesson, I consider what has been taught previously or demonstrated by students and look for ways to connect those skills or concepts. I will generally develop a learning target to go along with the lesson that helps students reflect on expectations and their own abilities with regard to expectations. I need to decide: Will I write my own examples in front of them? Will I share some student work? Do I have a video or mentor text that would be helpful? What language will I use to make the teaching stick and help it to transfer to other contexts?

During a writing lesson, I use explicit language and models to show how to transfer a skill from one situation to another. I will create anchor charts with the students or use

Figure 2.5
Modeling a graphic organizer during writing workshop

graphic organizers to help the students visualize and internalize the concepts (see Figure 2.5). Creating the charts with the students helps to shape and reinforce their understanding and offers an anchor for them to reference. I provide opportunities during guided practice to let students try out the skill with a different example or model than the one I shared and then invite the students to try it out in their writing that day.

After a lesson, I will observe students' application of the skills and conference with them, focusing on mindfulness. I encourage them to closely read and analyze their writing to consider next steps. During the share, we show multiple examples so that the variety of uses and strategic choices become apparent to students. I think about ways to connect this lesson with future lessons to make the connections visible for students.

When I create focused lessons that build on students' strengths with a consistent and supportive framework and emphasize the transfer of skills to a variety of contexts and circumstances, I am laying the groundwork for self-regulated learners (close writers) to develop. I try to think about how the lesson I am teaching today will help to make them stronger writers tomorrow. What can these kids do better now than before I taught this lesson? If I can't tell, I need to reassess what I am doing, reflect on what the students need, and keep trying.

The Gist of the Story

Close reading is at the heart of close writing strategies. We can take what students have learned about closely reading the texts of others and apply it to their own writing. This essential skill will help them build a relationship with their writing. When they read their work with focused lenses they can better reflect, evaluate, revise, and share their writing. We can help our students with this process by doing the following:

- Reinforcing the reading–writing reciprocity and raising students' awareness of how they support one another.

- Helping our students understand that writing is a transaction between the writer and the reader so they can take an authorial stance to reflect on their work.

- Capitalizing on close reading opportunities throughout each phase of the writing workshop to support our close writing instruction.

- Teaching for transfer so today's lessons can be used in many contexts and future pieces of writing. (Focusing on the writer, not just the current piece of writing.)

Drafting Your Story

Taking some time to reflect on our teaching in terms of where we have been and where we want to go can be helpful. On your own or with some colleagues, you might want to reflect on the following questions:

- What does close reading mean to you? What does it look like for your students?

- Who are some of the giants on whose shoulders you stand? What theories have influenced your teaching?

- How could you help your writers take on an authorial reading stance?

- What are some ways that you could teach for transfer in your own classroom?

PART 2

Close Writing Lessons

CHAPTER 3

Close Listening: Developing Our Writer's Ear

Words mean more than what is set down on paper.
It takes the human voice to infuse them with deeper
meaning. —Maya Angelou

When they were very young, both of my children learned to play the violin. They learned to play "Twinkle, Twinkle Little Star" by listening to a more skilled musician perform the song and then playing it themselves, with support and feedback. They learned music by ear as they attempted to re-create what they heard. They were immersed in the sounds long before they were expected to read any lines or pages of music, developing an ear for music before they developed an eye for it.

Some of our strongest writers have an ear for writing. They understand that language should flow and that text should have rhythm. They know that the words they write on the page will need to be lifted and read, as a musician raises a song from the notes on paper. Sadly, many of our students do not have an ear for writing. They give little thought to how their words will sound when read aloud. Many

> **The moral of this story:**
> Close writers internalize
> the sounds of our written
> language so that they
> can create and monitor
> their own writing more
> mindfully.

mumble and stumble when asked to read their work. Others race to get it over with or read it with a lifeless delivery.

Every day, teachers read aloud and share the music of books as they exuberantly bring the words to life on the page. Why doesn't this immersion transfer into students' reading of their own written words? What elements helped make Bailey and Casey become skilled musicians? Listening and playing. They had to play around with the sounds and compare those sounds to the expectation of the more skilled version through practice and reflection. How could we incorporate those elements into our writing workshops to immerse our students into the *musical* expression of their written words?

First, students must develop a habit of regularly reading their writing. Many students approach writing as a one-way process; the words go from their heads to the paper, where they stay. These students do not reread their work unless they are asked to read it; otherwise, they announce, "I'm done."

How could I get my students to develop the close writing habit of reading (or rereading) their work and reflecting on it? I would have to establish the expectation, model the process, and help them to understand the purpose. Changing behavior takes a conscious effort, and we cannot change what we are not aware of. A first step in the close writing process would be to raise awareness of the importance of closely reading our writing.

Fast-Forward Versus Play

If you are old enough to remember cassette tape players, you might recall the fast-forward feature. You could stop the tape and advance to a point farther along, or while the play button was still engaged, you could press fast-forward and hear a speedy distortion of the recording. It was a quick way to get from one point to another on the recorded piece. Often, when students are reading their writing to themselves or to others, their reading sounds like a fast-forward recitation. Their mumbled, garbled, speedy reading is moving them along without regard to sound quality. Fast-forward reading of our writing just gets us *through* a piece; it doesn't get us *into* a piece.

By contrast, students who read their writing with the pace and prosody that reflects intention, mood, and meaning are "playing" their reading. They are trying it out to either share with others or to reflect on their work. This is not a typical approach to reading written texts for many students, especially in the drafting phase. How would the writing experience change if students closely read their work with a "play" rather than the "fast-forward" technique? Does it matter *how* our students read their own writing?

Rereading without an authorial reading stance (no purpose or attention) offered little support to our writers. The fast-forward reading of their work simply got them through their writing, offering few insights into how complete or engaging it would be for other readers. They did not give themselves an opportunity to notice whether their writing was clear or confusing, repetitive or sparse, or reflected their intended ideas and message. They were not close writing.

Some teachers and I wanted to change this, so we first had to create an expectation that reading is an effective strategy in all steps of the writing process. Then, in each phase of the writing workshop, we needed to teach the strategies of authorial reading. We couldn't ask students to read or reread their writing and expect their approach to be more play than fast-forward. We had to model, to teach, and to prompt for authorial reading. This interpretive style of reading would allow them to slow down, notice their writing, and reflect on what they want to say.

WHEN STUDENTS READ THEIR WRITING . . .

- What have I noticed, documented, or given them feedback on?
- When and why do they read, and with whom?
- Do they read with the same expression and emphasis that I model?
- Do they make it easy for other students to notice and appreciate their ideas, their craft, and their voice?

Writer Reading

The ear is the only true writer and the only true reader. I know people who read without hearing the sentence sounds and they were the fastest readers. Eye readers we call them. They get the meaning by glances. But they are bad readers because they miss the best part of what a good writer puts into his work.—Robert Frost

I thought about how we share great writing with our students when we use mentor texts. We show them the books of beloved authors and examine authors' techniques and craft to create powerful stories. We don't just hand students a book or show them the pages. We read it to them. We interpret the pages with our reading style. We emphasize what we want them to notice by *how* we read the text. We make it easy for them to recognize and appreciate an author's craft. We want them to notice the best parts of what a good writer has put into his work.

Then I thought about the notion that *my* reading of the text is *my* interpretation of the story. Maybe the author would have chosen other aspects to emphasize. Maybe he or she would have evoked a different mood or pace or conveyed the character's dialogue with a different emotion. I wondered what they would consider the best parts of their work to be.

I was fascinated at finding examples of authors' readings and with a few Internet searches found plenty (see "Recommended Resources"). I listened to the stories unfold through their voices and found a renewed appreciation for their work. They were lifting the words off the page and breathing life into them. I wanted these mentor authors to be mentor readers for our students.

PEEK INSIDE A CLASSROOM: LISTENING TO AUTHORS

The importance of writers interpreting their words for others is demonstrated as I work in Andrea Bryant's fifth grade near the beginning of the school year. Students had been working on biography poems as a way to get to know one another. As I conference with the children, I ask each to read what they have written. Nearly every student uses a fast-forward approach to share his or her poem. There is no prosody, no emotion, even though they write of joys, hopes, and fears.

I ask one writer, "Which of these lines is your favorite?" Her lip puckers and she looks back at the piece. I press on, "Which of these ideas seems most important to you, that really reflects *you*?" She shrugs, "I don't know. They're all kinda important." To her, they all may seem equally important, but her reading sheds no light on that.

Many of Andrea's students put a lot of thought and consideration into their poems, but the reading does not convey the emotion or the importance of their ideas. Andrea shares that many of her students don't seem to be reading their writing, let alone reading it with expression. She laments that this is sometimes a problem; students don't notice omissions or errors or get confused by what they have written. They do not engage other listeners and often they are not engaged themselves.

We decide to focus on how mentor authors read their work, and I come back to her classroom later that morning. I bring a clip of Neil Gaiman reading his book *Coraline* but only share the audio (https://www.youtube.com/watch?v=4bghlhgKnm0). I tell them to listen to how he reads and share what they notice.

"He pauses a lot," Aaron responds.

"He wants you to think about it," replies Jack.

"Do you think he is giving you time to picture what is going on?" Nods and a chorus of yeses show agreement. "So if *you* pause when *you* are reading, do you think it will give others or even yourselves a chance to get a picture of what is going on?" Again the students seem to agree. "What else does he do?" I ask.

Hands fill the air. Devon offers, "He uses different voices for his characters. He makes Miss Spink talk kinda silly, and Coraline is all serious."

"So why do you think he changes his voice for his characters? Is that something you could do with your characters when you write dialogue?" I ask.

"He wants you to get to know the characters better. Like I think the man upstairs is Russian or something. He's got an accent," she replies.

"Could you tell he was Russian if you didn't hear Neil Gaiman reading?" I ask.

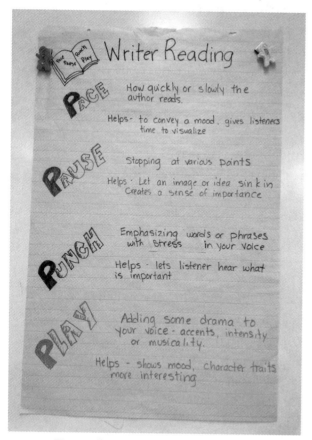

Figure 3.1: **Writer reading anchor chart**

"Not really, but he says the words kind of mixed up, like he wasn't good at English maybe."

"So if you write dialogue, do you think it is important to think about how the characters would say it?" I ask. "Do you think when Neil Gaiman wrote that dialogue he was thinking about how the characters would say it?" So far, no dissenting opinions.

"He read some parts kinda slow and stopped sometimes," answers Connor.

"How fast or slow you read something is often called the *pace*. He wasn't racing through his story, was he? He was reading it at a slow enough pace and pausing so that you could picture what was going on. If you want the picture in *your* head to be the same picture in the *readers'* heads, you have to make sure you give them enough details and enough time to create that picture. When you slow down, you have time to ask yourself, '*Did what I write make sense? Did it have enough information or details? Did I miss something?* If you read your writing too quickly, you don't have time to think about those things."

I write a few words on the board. *Pace. Pause. Punch. Play.* (See Figure 3.1.) "Sometimes it is helpful to group what we notice into categories to help us think about the qualities or traits of their reading. Here are some traits of reading that I have noticed authors using to share their writing with others. You picked up on some of these with Neil Gaiman. We talked about his pace being slow enough to help the reader visualize what was going on. We talked about the way he would pause so the reader could make a picture in his of her head. We mentioned that he was kind of dramatic and used different voices for the characters. I call this *play*. He played with his voice for effect."

"We didn't yet mention *punch*. This isn't a physical punch; it means the reader emphasizes some words with a little stress in his or her voice. You know how sometimes when you see bold words in a book you are supposed to emphasize them a bit more with your voice? Words aren't always bolded, but readers are continuously making choices about which words to stress for emphasis."

WRITER READING

PACE, PAUSE, PUNCH, AND PLAY

The way an author reads his or her writing helps the listener to interpret the story. The listener can hear what the author thinks are important ideas, what the mood is supposed to be, and how the characters talk to one another.

PACE	PAUSE	PUNCH	PLAY
How quickly or slowly authors read their writing gives some insight into the mood they are trying to create.	When authors pause for a certain length of time, it helps us to stop and consider important ideas, images, or words.	What words or phrases authors choose to emphasize in a sentence helps the reader to think about ideas in a specific way.	The dramatic quality to the author's voice helps the reader to think about the writing in a specific way.
How this works:	How this works:	How this works:	How this works:
Slow reading may create tension or suspense. Fast reading may show chaos, confusion, fear, or joy.	A pause allows the listener to stop and think, let something soak in, or create an image that lingers.	You *can't have that.* You *can't have* that. The words readers emphasize help create specific meaning.	A silly voice evokes happiness, a sinister voice evokes fear or suspense, and a regional accent gives you a hint at the characters.

I want to bring it a little closer to home. I pull out my writer's notebook and read about the first time my daughter tried to eat a Cheerio (see Figure 3.2)—a simple event from our lives, but in my voice, I try to build the anticipation of that first successful nibble. I pause at various points to give the listeners time to picture what was happening. I use emotion to express the confusion, frustration, and excitement that Bailey had been feeling.

After I finish, I ask, "Can you picture yourselves sitting there in our kitchen while this was going on?" Yeses and nods. "Could you sense how we were feeling or how Bailey was feeling?"

"Yeah, like she was happy when she did it."

"You did a show-don't-tell at the end, too!"

I ask, "Would you have the same pictures in your head if I read it like this . . .?" I give my best fast-forward reading style with no pauses, no emotion, and no punches. My voice is monotone and quick. I look up for their reaction.

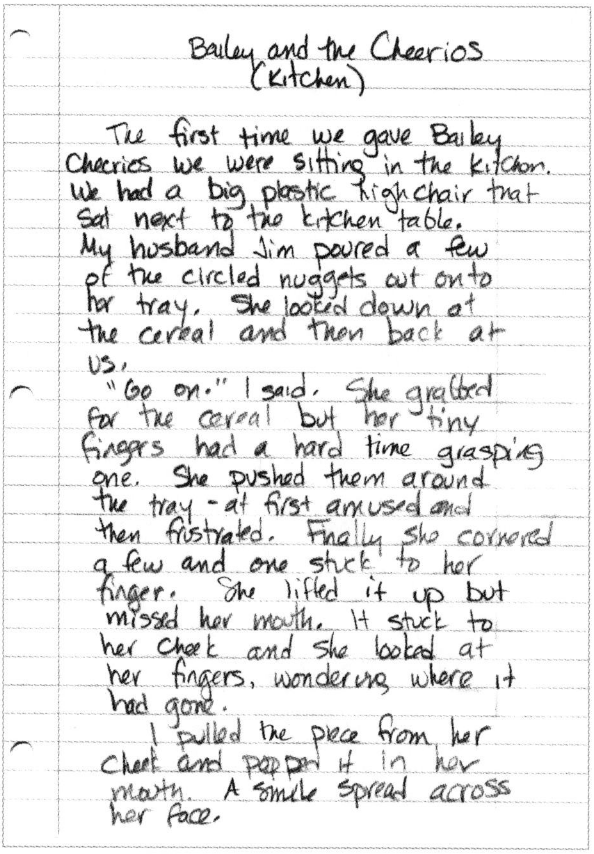
Bailey and the Cheerios
(Kitchen)

The first time we gave Bailey Cheerios we were sitting in the kitchen. We had a big plastic highchair that sat next to the kitchen table. My husband Jim poured a few of the circled nuggets out onto her tray. She looked down at the cereal and then back at us.

"Go on." I said. She grabbed for the cereal but her tiny fingers had a hard time grasping one. She pushed them around the tray - at first amused and then frustrated. Finally she cornered a few and one stuck to her finger. She lifted it up but missed her mouth. It stuck to her cheek and she looked at her fingers, wondering where it had gone.

I pulled the piece from her cheek and popped it in her mouth. A smile spread across her face.

Figure 3.2

Sharing my personal narrative with fifth graders

"You didn't have any feeling."

"You didn't slow down so we could think about it."

"So if I didn't show any feeling, and I didn't slow down or pause, does that affect how you understand my story?" Nods. "When I am writing, I want to make sure my story expresses what I am thinking or feeling or experiencing. If I read it to myself, I want to make sure I read it in a way that I can relate to, to help me think about it. If I read it like this . . . [*fast-forward* version of a few sentences], I'm not really getting *into* my story. I'm just getting *through* my story. It doesn't help me to think about what to say next or what I might want to add. Reading it with pace, pause, punch, and play will help me do that more than some speed reading."

Andrea and I invite the students to practice reading their biography poems to themselves or to a partner using their best writer reading. We can hear them slowing down, punching different words, and generally having some fun with these poems. We know it will take more than one practice session to help them internalize a writer reading habit, but we've taken our first steps.

Cranium Reading

The next week I am in Kelley Capen's fifth grade next door. I share my writer reading lesson and the students share similar responses as their neighboring class. This time, when we invite the students to try it out, we recognize that having an entire class reading aloud simultaneously can become problematic, so I introduce them to a technique to help them hear their writing more easily. I call it Cranium Reading. I want them to notice how our voices sound different to us "inside our head" and use this to help them tune in to their reading.

CRANIUM READING

GETTING INSIDE THE WRITER'S HEAD

We've looked at the benefits of reading our work aloud, but sometimes students are not able to work with a partner or would benefit from working on their own. In these instances, we've used a strategy called Cranium Reading.

- Explain to students the science of the two ways we hear our own voices, the first being through your ears as the sound waves travel through the air and the second through the vibrations in your skull, or cranium. Clarify that we will be practicing the second way with today's lesson.

- Invite the students to try saying a few short phrases while tightly covering their ears and to notice the sound differences. Most notice that their voice sounds different to them when they muffle their ears.

- Share the following insight with students: "Sometimes when things are different, we tend to pay more attention to them. Today, we are going to pay attention to our reading more carefully as we use our craniums to help us listen in."

- Ask students to use their writer reading techniques and to read to themselves. What do they notice? How does it help their authorial reading?

Kelley's students promptly begin to read their latest pieces of writing. As I walk about the room listening in, I notice some students slipping back into their fast-forward mode of reading, and I remind them of our writer reading lesson (pace, pause, punch, and play). For most, a tap on the shoulder and pointing to our anchor chart on the board is all the reminder they need. They are all listening to their reading with focus and purpose (see Figure 3.3).

Figure 3.3
Students engaged in Cranium Reading

I wanted our students to have some practice and skill with reading their writing to themselves and to others before expecting them to take an authorial stance to listen for specific aspects of their writing. It's like having the basic mechanics in place before perfecting the form. My children couldn't play songs on the violin before they had learned to hold the instrument, slide the bow, and grasp the fingerings. Once they didn't have to focus so much attention on the rudiments of the violin, they could focus on the quality of their playing. When our students have developed a habit for some basics of reading their writing, they can be freed up to focus on the quality of the writing and are better able to listen for it.

Prewriting: A Writer's Ear for Oral Rehearsal

Once students internalize the poetic rhythms of writer reading, they can use it to help compose their ideas through oral rehearsal. When I worked with Reading Recovery students, I found that a simple concept such as "Think It, Say It, Write It" was a great scaffold for novice writers. It helped them to organize their ideas and to hold onto them as they dipped down to the letter and word level for transcribing. Rehearsing and repeating what they wanted to write helped them create a memory trace for the ideas when they needed to divide their attention between sounding out individual phonemes and returning to the sentence they were trying to remember.

Lucy Calkins's strategy of telling a story across your fingers or tapping a page and telling the story were scaffolds for primary writers to construct small moment narratives with a partner (Calkins and Smith 2003). It helped many young writers to sequence ideas and to remember events with a beginning, a middle, and an end format.

When I began working with older students who were less fluent writers or were English language learners (ELL), I found the same principles applied. Rehearsing the sentences they wanted to write provided a scaffold when they needed to stop and work on individual words. They could then remember and return to the bigger idea after completing work at the word level. They could play with their ideas and make changes before they invested a lot of effort into writing them down.

I started thinking how oral rehearsal could be a close writing strategy that could help any student become a stronger writer. Talking out ideas, playing around with the possibilities, evaluating options, and verbally revising can be much easier before writing ideas down rather than after a story has been written. Students are often reluctant to make changes when they have put in a lot of effort and parts of themselves into their writing. While oral rehearsal won't eliminate the need for revision, it could cut down on some obvious mismatches, omissions, or confusions.

Hearing their words can help a writer think about what they want to say and how they want to say it. Lester Laminack, author of such books as *Saturdays and Teacakes* and *Three Hens and a Peacock*, once told me: "I need to hear the music of language. I say things aloud often before writing, or at least I say it in my mind. After each paragraph or scene I read aloud, I know that rhythm has to be present." Several authors told me that it was important to them to practice dialogue between characters aloud before writing it. Lynda

Mullaly Hunt, author of *One for the Murphys* and *Fish in a Tree*, shared the following: "I sometimes practice conversations between my characters." Cynthia Lord, author of *Rules, Hot Rod Hamster, Half a Chance*, and more, said, "I also often say dialogue aloud as I'm writing it, when I'm alone." These authors are able to find those just-right words by rehearsing and listening with an author's ear.

If published authors are finding success with this strategy, why not share it with our students? We can encourage them to reflect on and evaluate the words before writing them down. We can tweak the Think it. Say it. Write it. approach to Think it. Say it. Like it? Write it. technique.

THINK IT. SAY IT. LIKE IT? WRITE IT!

Sometimes there is a breakdown between thinking and writing. Students have a general idea of what they want to say, but when they go to write it, there are gaps, confusions, or unclear language. Opportunities to practice and listen to the words before committing them to paper could help with the drafting process.

- Model oral rehearsal for your students using the same writer reading techniques (book-talk language) they have learned previously. We want the rehearsal to sound as close to the finished work as possible to help them evaluate it effectively and adjust it accordingly.

- Be sure to *think aloud* your evaluation of ideas. *"I don't really like how that sounds, maybe I could say..."* or *"Oh, I like that. I think it will help set the mood."*

- Partner students to *story tell* their ideas before writing. Encourage them to use the book-talk language. Don't tell what the story is about; tell the story itself.

Sometimes dialogue doesn't sound natural or real in student writing. Encourage students to practice those conversations aloud. Record the rehearsed conversations with a phone or computer app to help them to listen and reflect on how authentic they think they sound. Then they can simply transcribe the conversations they play back.

CLOSE READING PICTURES IN OUR MIND

When students are beginning a writing piece we often encourage them with comments such as "picture a small moment" or "picture a time when…" If students seem to be stuck at points in their writing we often encourage them with "Picture what you think will happen next" or "What do you picture that character saying?" We sometimes encourage them to sketch out an idea or create a storyboard. We know that visualizing a scene or a story in our minds is a helpful way to create, to expand, to refine, and to organize our ideas into a richer story. This strategy has helped many writers flush out the details of their story quite successfully.

But what about our writers who seem genuinely perplexed by picturing an idea and translating that idea into writing? Our prompts to encourage visualizing their stories are sometimes met with shrugs and blank stares. Because we can't get inside of their heads, we don't know what they might be noticing. I engage them in conversation to create a tentative theory of what they might be thinking or visualizing, but without the language to transfer those images, it is often difficult. How we could make that process more visible?

We could teach our students to "closely read" those pictures in their head to create more vivid and detailed stories. We could model the process with an actual photo, a drawing, or a painting to make it more tangible. Would close reading of this visual information help with the written information students are expected to compose?

PEEK INSIDE A CLASSROOM: A PICTURE PAINTS A THOUSAND WORDS

Alice Drummond's fifth-grade students had just finished a fall writing prompt. They were given the choice of three paintings from which to create a narrative. While some told a story, others wrote descriptions of or reactions to the works. We wanted to see whether we could encourage the students to look more closely at pictures, visual information, or the world around them to extract those stories waiting to be told.

To help students closely read a picture, we need to demonstrate the difference between glancing and reading the image. We choose an illustration by Norman Rockwell that is a strong example of a story waiting to be told. In *The Runaway*, a young boy is seated at a diner counter next to a police officer. His hobo bag on a stick lies at his feet. I project the image on the board for about five seconds. "What did you notice?" I ask.

The students respond. "There was a boy and a guy at a restaurant."

"It wasn't really a restaurant, one of those places you sit at a counter."

"A diner. It was like a diner."

I press them. "What else did you notice?"

"I think there was a sign."

"I think there was a waiter." Their responses lack confidence.

"So in five seconds you just got a glance at the picture. You weren't really able to *read* the picture. Let's look at it a little longer so you can closely *read* the image." I put the illustration back on the screen. The students are able to describe the picture in great detail. Some begin to conjecture about the people.

"I think he ran away. Maybe he's lost or something."

"The cop is probably going to help him."

"So you are already starting to pull a story out of this picture! You are thinking about the characters and the plot, and you have already described the setting. Some of you are thinking about the problem and maybe even what the solution will be. These are all story elements. I write on the board:

Characters

Setting

Problem

Solution

"Now, we are going to try closely reading the picture again, but this time with purpose. This picture is going to tell us a story, and we are going to use a different lens each time we read it. The lenses are going to be each of these story elements. Let's start with characters. Read this picture and tell the story of these characters. What do they look like? What do they sound or talk like? What are they thinking? What do you infer about their personalities? What do you imagine is the backstory?"

The students begin to develop the characters from the image, and I write down their ideas.

"Well, the police officer's name is Bob."

"Yeah and he's really serious, but he's smart. He thinks the boy ran away."

"The boy's name is Max."

"I think he's like six, and his mom is rude to him."

They continue to unpack the characters, and then, we move on in a similar way to the setting, problem, and solution. I want them to see there is not one right story but that they have the power to create the story they want. I capture many of their ideas on a chart (see Figure 3.4).

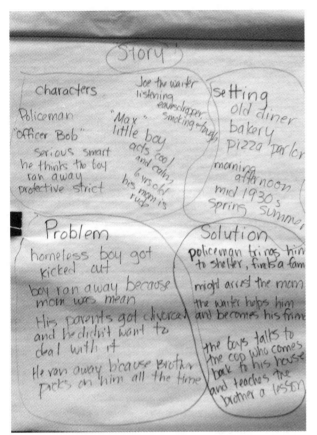

Figure 3.4

Class story map from closely reading the painting *The Runaway*

"So each time we went back to closely read this painting, we were using different lenses to look and notice. Each purpose for reading (in this case, narrative elements) is like a different lens to help us see. We can see more when we look more. Going back and looking, thinking, 'reading' is a powerful strategy.

"You can do this when you have somebody else's picture, but you can also think about how this might work when that picture is in your head. Use that picture; read it the way you did here today. That will help you to put more interesting details into your story. You want to make sure the picture that you have in *your* mind is the picture that your reader will have in *their* mind, and the only way to convey that picture is through the words you choose."

We give students time to create a story from the story web on the chart or to create their own story. The students give the characters names, detailed physical descriptions, incorporate dialogue, and create realistic problems and solutions for the story (see Figures 3.5 and 3.6). Many are similar but different enough for students to see how one picture can tell two dozen different stories.

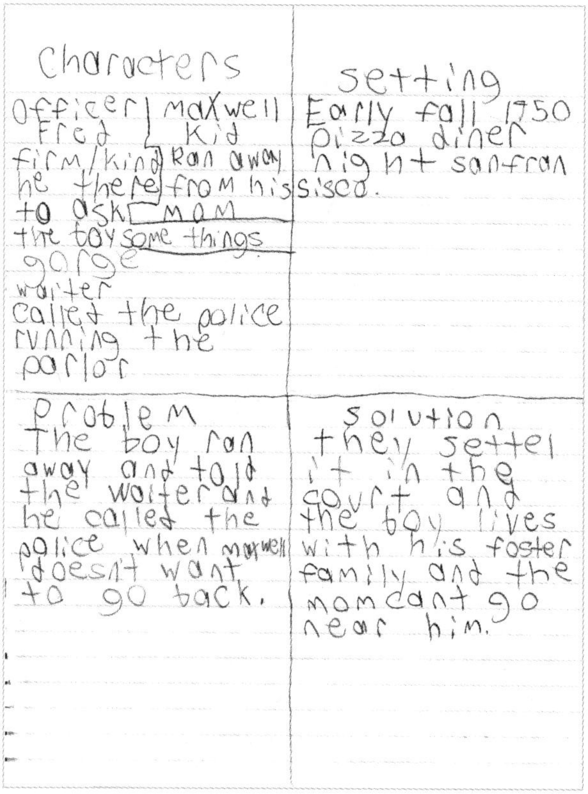

Characters

Officer | Maxwell
Fred | Kid
firm/kind Ran away
he there from his
to ask Mom
the boy some things
gorge
waiter
called the police
running the
parlor

Setting

Early fall 1750
pizza diner
night san-fran
sisco.

Problem

The boy ran
away and told
the waiter and
he called the
police when maxwell
doesn't want
to go back.

Solution

they settel
it in the
court and
the boy lives
with his foster
family and the
mom cant go
near him.

Figure 3.5

Map from close reading of *The Runaway*

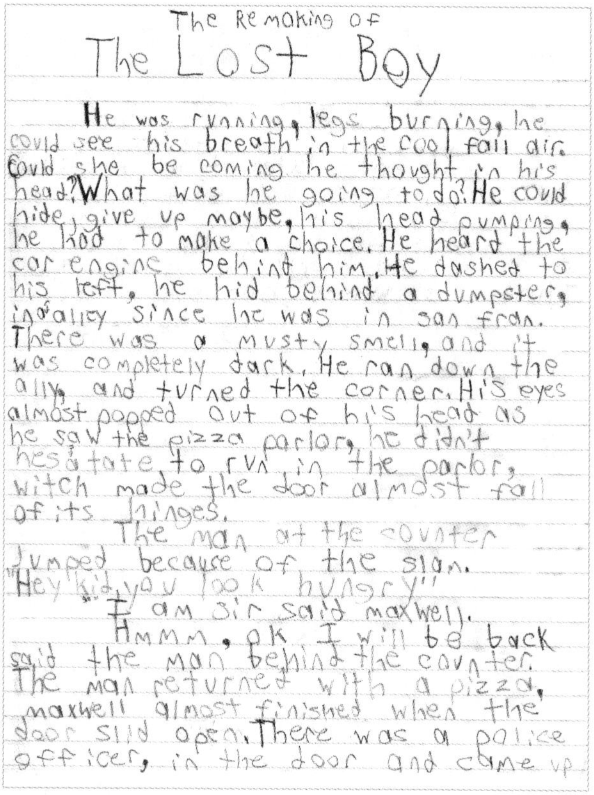

The Re making of

The Lost Boy

He was running, legs burning, he
could see his breath in the cool fall air,
could she be coming he thought, in his
head? What was he going to do, He could
hide, give up maybe, his head pumping,
he had to make a choice. He heard the
car engine behind him. He dashed to
his left, he hid behind a dumpster,
in alley since he was in san fran.
There was a musty smell, and it
was completely dark, He ran down the
ally, and turned the corner. His eyes
almost popped out of his head as
he saw the pizza parlor, he didn't
hesitate to run in the parlor,
witch made the door almost fall
of its hinges.
    The man at the counter
jumped because of the sign.
"Hey kid, you look hungry"
    I am sir said maxwell.
    Hmmm, ok, I will be back
said the man behind the counter.
The man returned with a pizza,
maxwell almost finished when the
door slid open. There was a police
officer, in the door and came up

Figure 3.6

Story from close reading of *The Runaway*

READING A PICTURE

PREWRITING ORAL REHEARSAL

To help students write from the pictures they have in their heads, we can begin by teaching them to write from a photograph, a painting, or another visual image.

- Choose a painting that invites viewers to wonder or to create.

- List the story elements you would like them to incorporate in their telling or writing.

- Invite them to read the picture with a different purpose (element) each time and consider questions to help them develop each element with details.

- Create a story map or web of these elements.

- Provide an opportunity for students to share their stories so that students notice the variation.

Try out this strategy with pictures in their heads. Invite them to reflect on how it is similar? How is it different? How could it help you as a writer?

Visual Rehearsal: Drawing or Doodling the Pictures in Our Minds

Although this chapter focuses on the listening aspect of close writing, I think it is important to discuss the strategy of visual rehearsal for some writers. Some students may not be able to directly translate the pictures in their minds to words on paper. Being able to sketch out important ideas and details as a part of the drafting process could be a helpful scaffold. In her book *The Doodle Revolution: Unlock the Power to Think Differently* (2014), Sunni Brown advocates allowing students multiple pathways to learning, including doodling and drawing. She notes, "The seemingly small act of using our hands to create something not only gets us reliably unstuck but also changes the way we look at and understand the world" (24). Allowing our writers to draw or doodle as a strategy for thinking and creating could be just the thing to unlock ideas and invite creativity in their work.

As teachers, we look to expand and not limit the strategies available to our students that support their successful writing and learning. We want our students to explore and utilize those strategies and determine which work best for their style and needs. As you share any of these lessons or activities with your students, invite them to reflect on which approaches they find most helpful and to think about how they can make it a strategy. This is part of what it means to be a close writer.

Considerations for English Language Learners

For students who are just learning English, there is very little connection between those symbols on the page and the sound of the language they represent. I am reminded when I look at Arabic script and wonder what sounds might match up with those symbols. Reading aloud the squiggles we put down on the page helps to map sounds to those symbols for our students. By incorporating lessons on writer reading, we are providing a reason for oral reading that gives our students purposeful practice.

Oral rehearsal can be especially helpful for our ELL students. Playing around first with their ideas orally helps them try out words or ideas before committing them to paper. All languages have their own rhythm and cadence, and even within the same language, there are differences between a conversational voice and a reading voice. They can practice the book-talk language of writing to help them compose their desired message.

Visual rehearsal may also be a powerful tool for communicating ideas that these students may not yet have the vocabulary to convey. By sketching out the pictures in their minds, they can think about what it is they really want to say. These drawings can be interpreted in any language so teachers or peers could use them to have a conversation about the topic, providing language support and vocabulary to help ELL students transcribe their ideas.

Once that message is written, reading and rereading it will give them multiple opportunities to practice fluent and prosodic reading on a text within their speaking vocabulary, because it is literally their spoken words.

Language is how we process information and remember ideas and strategies. When we discuss, label, and practice the strategies for writing and reading, we provide the academic language of literacy that helps make the invisible visible. This will help our ELL students build a stronger schema around writing and reading. It is essential that our ELL students have academic conversations with peers as well as with their teachers. Students may explain ideas or give feedback in much more kid-friendly terms, simply because they are kids!

The Gist of the Story

Developing a writer's ear isn't just a way to help us read our writing more beautifully, it's a way to help us read more purposefully. The big idea is that the more awareness we can foster in our writers, the closer the connection they will have with their writing. These techniques should not be considered isolated skills but rather strategies that students can use to become more self-regulated, reflective writers. We can help our students develop a writer's ear if

- we are clear in explaining the purposes for reading our writing (authorial reading);

- we provide good models (authors, teachers, peers) for reading our writing more mindfully;

- we give students plenty of opportunity to play with the language before, during, and after writing with rehearsal and reading;

- we establish clear expectations for orally reading their writing and find ways to monitor and provide feedback as needed; and

- we encourage oral rehearsal to plan, to practice, and to perceive the possible.

Drafting Your Story

Take a moment to think about how students read their writing in your classroom. You could discuss it with some colleagues or reflect on your own about your current thinking after reading this chapter.

- When do your students read their writing? While drafting? Revising? Conferring? When they are "done"?

- What do you notice about the way they read their writing?

- How might developing a writer's ear, or writer reading, benefit your students?

- What authors have your students heard reading aloud their work? What authors would they like to hear? What would they notice? How might it help them?

- How might oral rehearsal help your students to organize and draft?

CHAPTER 4
Close Looking: Learning from Mentor Texts

We share mentor texts by the likes of Sandra Cisneros, Cynthia Rylant or Christopher Paul Curtis, hoping that their sparkling sentences might lift the writing of our students, or at least provide scaffolding for them to build sturdier texts of their own. But as any writing teacher knows, it's not always easy. It turns out that this magical essence is not so simple to extract. And once extracted, it doesn't transfer easily to the student who reads it. —Ralph Fletcher

love to watch my daughter, Bailey, dance. She makes those graceful moves look effortless. She inspires me to want to leap, turn, and respond to the music with similar poise. But seeing it and doing it are two very different things. It is simply not within my zone of proximal development. It reminds me of how some students may have felt when I showed them the beautiful, seemingly effortless moves of a writer in a mentor text. I would attempt to inspire similar moves in their work. I would spotlight and name the technique to showcase it, and yet, many could not make that leap in their

The moral of this story:
Close writers will "try on" techniques and traits when they can envision the possibility and perceive the need in their own writing

own writing. I began thinking more deeply about my use of mentor texts in my lessons.

Writing teachers have been using mentor texts for years. We all have favorite books that we share with our students, anticipating that the exposure will translate into appreciation, experimentation, and application of techniques and craft. But as Ralph Fletcher reminds us, and we have seen firsthand, it doesn't happen easily, if it happens at all. I don't believe there is one right way to use a mentor text with young writers, but I try to approach lessons with the needs and knowledge of my writers in mind.

What Are Mentor Texts?

First, it is important to consider, What is a mentor? A mentor is someone with more experience or expertise who assists a less-experienced person in developing specific skills and knowledge. Authors can be amazing mentors to our students, but rarely are we able to bring them into our classrooms. So, by proxy, we bring their books to demonstrate and assist, and we call these *mentor texts* (see Figure 4.1). They are strong examples of good writing we would like our students to aspire to. But our students often need us to be a

Figure 4.1

Andrea Bryant shares a mentor text with her fifth graders.

mentor in analyzing and appreciating these texts. Therefore, the use of mentor texts is the collaboration of author, book, teacher, and student to share and inspire more skilled writing.

In their book *Mentor Texts: Teaching Writing Through Children's Literature*, Lynne Dorfman and Rose Cappelli explain, "Mentor texts are pieces of literature that we can return to again and again as we help our young writers learn how to do what they may not yet be able to do on their own" (Dorfman and Cappelli 2007, 3). Returning purposefully to a text is one of the central tenets of close reading. Mentor texts provide a scaffold for our young writers in their zone of proximal development, or ZPD (see Figure 4.2). That is the foundation for my choice and use of mentor texts. I try to think which books or texts will be accessible to these young writers. I question which techniques, ideas, or craft choices might be within the ZPD of their writing. The students need to somehow see themselves in that example of writing, or it will be out of their grasp, no matter how many times they revisit a text.

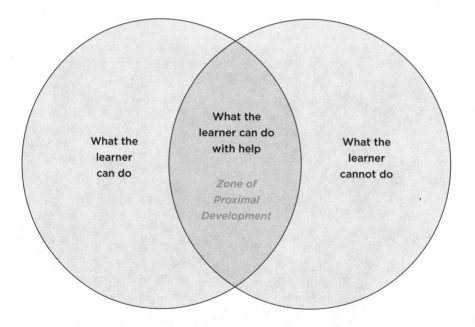

Figure 4.2

Mentoring works best in the ZPD: "The distance between the actual developmental level as determined by independent problem solving and the level of potential development as determined through problem solving under adult guidance, or in collaboration with more capable *peers*" (Vygotsky 1978, 86).

Dorfman and Cappelli go on to say, "They [mentor texts] help students envision the kind of writer they can become; they help the teachers move the whole writer, rather than each individual piece of writing, forward. Writers can imitate the mentor text and continue to find new ways to grow. In other words mentor texts help students and teachers continually reinvent themselves as writers" (Dorfman and Cappelli 2007, 3). This concept reinforces that my teaching is not about helping the student fix the piece of writing he or she is currently working on, it is about helping that student grow as a writer—on this piece and on every piece that follows. When we have students try out a technique at our request, we are practicing a *skill* with writing. When we help them to understand how and why they could use that technique, that is a *strategy*.

Writers need to be free to imitate and try on the techniques and envision their writing in new ways. Mentor texts can help students break out of patterns that they overrely on or that limit their growth as writers. Before they make those changes, however, they must see the need and imagine the benefits of trying something new. Sometimes, our students haven't read their own writing closely enough to recognize any needs or haven't yet been able to conceptualize those mentor techniques in their writing. This assumption is reflected in common utterances of, "It's fine how it is" or "I did that already" or the ubiquitous, "I'm done" without any evidence that they have attempted the mentor author's move or technique.

When I share mentor texts with my students to point out ideas or choices an author has made, I want students to understand why the author made that choice or tried that technique and consider why we might want to try it as well. This takes time and attention. Our students need multiple exposures to a text and multiple conversations about why we think the author made this or that choice. I need to give my students, and myself, permission to slow down, read closely, and think deeply so we can internalize not only the technique but also the strategic thinking that supports the use of that technique.

Categorizing Mentor Texts

Most teachers understand that mentor texts should match the intended learning, as we seek to refine or to expand a student's schema around writing. To develop that schema, we need to help students build on their prior knowledge in an organized way. Categorizing mentor texts helps group new information with prior knowledge in an organized way, making it easier to retrieve information and use it more efficiently.

Themes/ideas: The interesting ideas, perspective, or point of view presented in these books will inspire students to create their own unique ideas.	*Alexander and the Terrible, Horrible, No Good, Very Bad Day* by Judith Viorst *What events would befall you on your worst day? Your best day? Your craziest day?*
Traits: Specific craft techniques are visible in the writing and can be easily analyzed and imitated by students.	*Amos and Boris* by William Steig *What words did the author use to create precise images in the reader's mind? What words could you use in your story?*
Structure: The repetitive, predictable, or consistent structure of a text provides a framework for students to create their own versions of a story or informational text.	*Fortunately* by Remy Charlip *What adventures could you have using the "fortunately/unfortunately" pattern of this book?*

Based on work by Corbett Harrison (http://corbettharrison.com/).

Choosing Mentor Texts

One of my principal mantras is *Whoever does the work, does the learning*. When I spend hours poring through books, searching, thinking, analyzing, reasoning, evaluating, and then the student interacts with those materials for three to five minutes, I have to wonder, who has done most of the learning? I have refined and expanded my schema around writing in profound ways. I then share that example with my students and anticipate that they will build the same schema, but how could it be similar? I have done all of the critical thinking. I am the one who has noticed the patterns and moves.

What if I flipped that situation? What if I planned some opportunities for our students to discover those patterns of quality writing that emerge in the books *they* love? Perhaps this could be done during reading instruction as well as writing instruction to help make that reciprocity more apparent to our readers and writers.

Trait Mentor Texts

Early on, students may not have a complex schema around qualities of good writing. They often enjoy a book or know it is *good* but may not be able to articulate why. We can help them to recognize and identify those characteristics within the texts they read with scaffolds to help them look and read closely. I think we should use existing books the students are surrounded by, while engaged in conversations with fellow classmates. A scavenger hunt is a great way to build excitement around books and writing and to encourage engagement with copious amounts of texts.

SCAVENGER HUNT

RAISING TRAIT AWARENESS

Inviting students to analyze texts and to find examples of a trait being taught raises their awareness about the techniques as they read as well as write.

- Choose a trait, structure, quality, or style you want the students to appreciate.
- Describe this trait in kid-friendly terms and share at least one example.
- Invite students to seek and collect examples of this trait in books from their classroom library, the school library, or their personal collections.
- Collect the citations on a scavenger hunt sheet.
- Create a text collection around this trait from their choices or post examples of a trait from a variety of authors.

There are many variations to this activity. Groups of students could look for different traits. Students could have lists of multiple traits to find. This could be used as a formative assessment to provide insight into the students' level of understanding as well as a summative assessment to demonstrate knowledge of the trait. The best scavenger hunt will be tailored to your classroom, your students, and their needs.

PEEK INSIDE A CLASSROOM: ANALYZING MENTOR TEXTS FOR CHARACTER DEVELOPMENT

Andrea Bryant's fifth graders are working on character development for their narrative writing unit. Students had previously been discussing how writers show (don't tell) readers about their characters. Andrea and I want them to notice that characters are often revealed more fully over time in a story. We want them to focus on how authors first introduce a character to the reader and analyze some of their techniques.

I put a copy of the first page of *Wonder* by R. J. Palacio (2012) under the document camera. "Boys and girls, I know you have been working on character development and thinking about ways to show rather than tell about your characters. Today I want us to look at how authors first introduce us to characters, and how important that first impression is when you are getting to know a character. The authors don't tell us everything about the character at the beginning of the story; they give us just a taste. They offer hints that make us ask questions or form inferences, and over time they reveal more and more. That's the same way we make friends; first we meet them and then we get to know them better over time. So let's analyze how authors introduce their main character and see if we notice some techniques they use to do that."

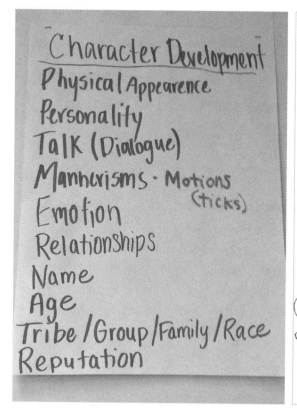

Figure 4.3

Class-created character development anchor chart

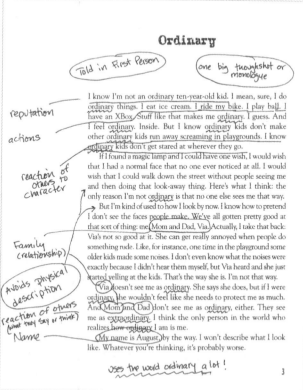

Figure 4.4

Class analysis of *Wonder*

I read the first page of *Wonder* and invite students to point out any lines that help them get to know the character. I also ask them to notice whether the story is told in the first-person or third-person perspective. They notice it is told through the eyes of the main character, August. They call out parts of the text they want me to circle or underline.

"Let's analyze what the author did with the parts we marked." They reference their anchor chart on character development (see Figure 4.3) to describe the author's techniques, such as physical description, actions, and relationships, but they find that some of our notations don't quite match the categories on their anchor chart. They notice that R. J. Palacio doesn't show us who Auggie is as much as who he isn't: "I know I'm not an ordinary ten-year-old kid." She doesn't give a physical description: "I won't describe what I look like. Whatever you're thinking, it's probably worse." The students not yet familiar with the story immediately begin to infer, predict, and question. We talk about how she has hooked us. Our discussion helps us to name the moves the author has made in this text, and we record that analysis on the projected text (see Figure 4.4).

We go on to look at character introduction from several other books. I give them first pages of *The Lightning Thief* by Rick Riordan (2005) and *One for the Murphys* from Lynda Mullaly Hunt (2012). I read the pages aloud, and then the students annotate the text with their noticings and analysis (see Figure 4.5). We share our observations and discuss techniques the authors use. We try to name the moves and consider why the author might have employed those techniques. Students are not expected to notice every craft move, but what they do notice should be within their ZPD, techniques they can apply to their own writing.

"Now that we have analyzed several texts together we are going to challenge you to collect some character introductions (see Figure 4.6) in the books that you are reading or that are in our classroom library. Find where the author first introduces

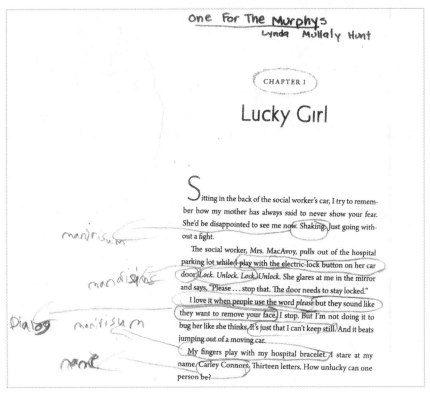

Figure 4.5

Student analysis of *One for the Murphys*

Figure 4.6
Collection of character introduction analyses

you to the character and analyze the techniques he or she uses. I want us to read these introductions closely so we can begin to see the strategies that authors use to help us get to know their characters. We can create a collection of these analyses for reference. Then I want you to think about what we have done here today when it comes to your own writing. What will *you* try in your stories to introduce us to your characters?"

The next day I invite the students to do a quick draft of a character introduction. They are not required to develop this into a complete story, just play around with techniques we've analyzed. I ask them to try some of the techniques and label them (see Figure 4.7).

Class Mentor Texts

The best mentor texts are the books we love. We are more likely to revisit them because returning to them is pleasurable. When we share these beloved books, and analyze what it is about them that we are drawn to, we can encourage students to notice more purposefully. They will be prone to reread favorite books and expand their opportunity to discover more characteristics of good writing. It is hard to see patterns with only one observation, but when we look again and again, we can often see things that were not immediately apparent.

With practice, they will have some aptitude for selecting class mentor texts. These would be books the students would most like to imitate in their writing, the books they wish *they* had written. They then analyze these books for the structure or techniques the author used, identify and label the techniques, and create anchor charts or presentations to display them.

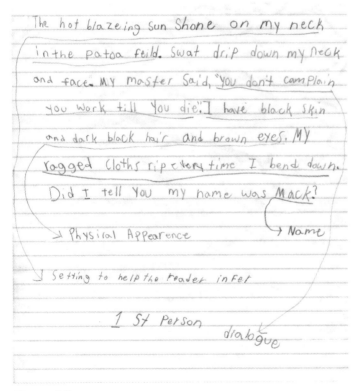

Figure 4.7

Student character introduction

CLASS MENTOR TEXTS

UNPACKING THE WRITING WE LOVE

Selecting a text that the class enjoys to revisit for multiple purposes will help students appreciate the specific qualities of writing that make the book so satisfying.

- Give students time to brainstorm and create a short list of books that they admire. These could be picture books, nonfiction, chapter books, etc.

- Categorize the books on the lists by genre or type (again classifying and creating patterns of thinking).

- Choose one book for each category for the class to analyze. This could be by popular vote or whatever method your class uses to make decisions.

- Gather multiple copies or create copies of the text (following all educational fair use copyright laws).

- Gather checklists or rubrics of traits your class has been taught to use.

- Model for the students how to analyze a part of the text with the checklist or rubric.

- Provide opportunities for students to closely read, analyze, identify, and label examples in the text of the given traits (always allow for additional analysis and observation as well).

- Create an anchor chart or display of examples of the author's use of these quality traits.

Favorite Author Study

This activity is similar to the class mentor text activity in that it involves close reading to recognize writing traits in published texts. Rather than analyzing a single text, however, we can look for some common patterns or traits that a given author uses across several texts and build schema around writing identity. Students may not have the precise language to label the move the author made, but what they notice and how they describe it can provide a teacher with some awareness of their thinking and perception.

FAVORITE AUTHOR TRAITS

DISCOVERING WRITING IDENTITY

When students see moves their favorite authors make repeated in multiple texts, they begin to see patterns emerge. They realize these are strategies the author uses on any text, and so can we.

- Choose a favorite author whose work is prolific enough and available to analyze three to five texts (a pattern often cannot be discerned from a smaller sample).

- *Open-Ended:* Invite students to look for patterns in the author's work. What are things that you notice in all or most of the texts?

  - Use sticky notes to mark evidence in the text and to describe the author's technique in their own words.

  - Create a list of common patterns for this author.

- *Focused:* Invite students to look for specific traits in each of the author's pieces.

  - Use sticky notes to mark evidence.

  - Use a checklist or form to collect examples of each technique.

PEEK INSIDE A CLASSROOM: MENTOR AUTHOR ANALYSIS

Caroline Eldridge's second-grade students have been using the work of mentor authors Kevin Henkes and Dav Pilkey during their writing workshop. Caroline and I discuss how frequently students appreciate the techniques authors use in their books but don't transfer them to their own writing. Rather than our pointing out the techniques, we wonder, "If *they* (the students) closely read some of the author's work looking for patterns, what would they notice? Would *they* then be more likely to emulate those traits in their own writing?"

We gather several of the class's favorite Dav Pilkey books (*Dog Breath, Dogzilla, Kat Kong, Dragon Gets By*) and photocopy a few pages from the beginning, middle, and end, leaving space for the students to comment. We want to see what the students notice. The children work in groups, reading and discussing their observations and then making notes on the pages. We circulate around the room to listen in and to ask probing questions, such as, "What do you notice about his characters?" or "What does he like to do as a writer?" (See Figure 4.8.) They respond with a technique or style choice they observe, "He uses *when and where* beginnings. He uses punctuation. He uses order words." We ask, "Can you show me where?" and invite them to write their observations down.

We rotate the books several times. We want the students to look for patterns of writing that they notice in Dav Pilkey's work and see what their classmates notice as well.

Figure 4.8
Mrs. Eldridge's second graders analyze Dav Pilkey books.

Whatever they notice is probably a trait or technique within their ZPD and a good place to start in their own writing.

We come back together as a class to work on a new anchor chart. I tell the students, "You guys are noticing so many things just by reading a few of his wonderful books. Let's make a list of what he taught us today that we can use in our own writing." Students eagerly share the patterns they notice in Pilkey's texts (see Figure 4.9); some are techniques that all authors use but many are characteristic of several of Pilkey's stories.

The next day Caroline reminds students of the objective: Dav can, so we can. She places her own journal under the document camera and begins her think-aloud process. "I'm going to use some of the things we noticed Dav Pilkey doing in his writing, in my own writing. Let's see, I'm going to use Dav Pilkey's Dragon as my main character. I want to start my story with a 'when and where' beginning so I need to think about my setting. We know that problems make stories more interesting, so I'm going to have Dragon eat so much food he gets sick." She pauses as she is obviously thinking. "So here it goes." She writes, *One windy day Dragon was flying a kite in his backyard while waiting for his guests to arrive. . . . It was the day of his first birthday party!*

"I want to make sure I use my order words to help me stay organized the way Dav Pilkey did. I'll probably think of some words like *first, then, next,* or *finally,* as Dav did. Now, it's your turn. Thumbs up if you will try a *when and where* beginning like Dav Pilkey today?" Thumbs shoot into the air. "Thumbs up if you are going to use order words the way Dav Pilkey showed us?" Students again respond enthusiastically. The students excitedly get to work trying out many of the techniques that they noticed in Dav Pilkey's books (Figure 4.10).

Student Mentor Texts

Sometimes the gap between published authors' work and student work is so wide that students cannot bridge it. Perhaps they cannot develop *voice* the way Ralph Fletcher does in *Marshfield Dreams* or Seymour Simon does in *Wolves.* That does not mean I shouldn't continue to share these incredible mentor texts with my students, but I am also wondering whether my examples should include student work, too.

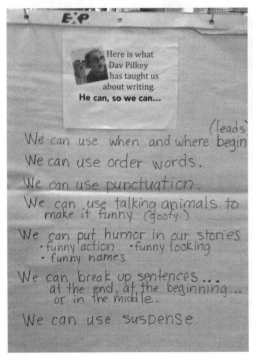

Figure 4.9

Traits we can model from Dav Pilkey books

Figure 4.10

Student tries out Dav Pilkey traits.

Figure 4.11

Collection of student-created nonfiction mentor texts

Somewhere between polished/published texts and our current student writing lay strong pieces of student writing. They often demonstrate the writing trait we encourage in our lessons. Many of us already keep samples of student work as exemplars (Figure 4.11). These can seem much more achievable to young writers than published mentor texts, because they already have been achieved by other young writers, created through the lens and experience of someone their age.

Elevating these exemplars to the status of mentor texts gives them credibility. These young writers are authors, in much the same way that Ralph Fletcher or Seymour Simon are authors. Students can see that there is a range of expertise in writing and that the goals of the mini-lesson are indeed achievable. When students utter, "I can't," they are expressing their concern that this quality of work is beyond their ability. Perhaps they can see themselves in the writing of student authors, however, and begin to believe "I can."

Frequently referencing student writing can support all students and reaffirm the student author. "Do you remember when Kady started her piece with onomatopoeia?

Her *plink . . . plink . . . crash . . .* pulled us in and made us want to read on. Think about how you will pull your readers in with your lead." Referring to Kady's piece makes the example more tangible and attainable for the students.

Once students begin to see that they have the potential to be "student-author mentors," they may begin to see their writing more purposefully. They may closely read their writing more to make sure it is accessible to other readers. They will have an authentic audience to which they will write. Trying to find opportunities for each writer to contribute a student mentor text might encourage us to look closely for the strengths of each student.

As teachers, we must also be sensitive to the fact that some students do not wish to stand out or are uncomfortable being the focus of attention. It may be better to save work from previous years to share as student mentor texts if the classroom climate is competitive or less collaborative than you would like. Knowing your students and the classroom community will help you determine the best approach for choosing and sharing student mentor texts.

STUDENT MENTOR TEXTS

EXPERTS AMONG US

The writing by peers is often easier to analyze and imitate than the work of published authors. Selecting and saving student work that exemplifies the high quality of writing we want all of our students to strive for can be an incredibly supportive scaffold.

- Collect pieces of student writing that best exemplify the focus of a mini-lesson, a writing trait, or a craft technique you want your students to work toward.

- Create a mentor text area in your classroom that contains both professional and amateur writing pieces.

- Highlight the trait demonstrated in the text. "Notice how this author uses dialogue to reveal personality traits of his characters."

- Ask students whether you can keep a copy of their work for future classrooms. Over time, you will amass a strong collection of student mentor texts. Be sure the author gets credit for his or her work.

- Refer to the student author's example when reminding students of a taught trait or move (if the student is comfortable with that attention). "Remember how Davis circled back to the beginning with his ending. He was clearly writing with the end in mind."

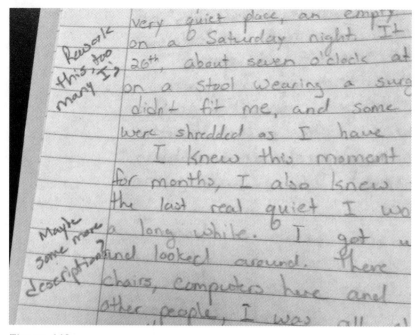

Figure 4.12

Guy Meader reflects on his teacher mentor text.

Teacher Mentor Texts

Many of us write with or in front of our students to model our thinking and writing process the way Caroline did with her Dav Pilkey-ish story. Keeping some of these pieces to revisit would be another great mentor text resource. When you think about it, we are the best mentors many of our students have for writing. The modeling we do is incredibly powerful for making the invisible visible. We show them that writing doesn't just happen (Figure 4.12). It is crafted through a series of ideas and decisions. I'll discuss the role of teacher mentors more in Chapter 5.

Having others read our writing can often make us feel vulnerable. We might think, with all of the great writing out there, what is so special about mine? That's exactly what many of our students are thinking. "Mine will never be that good." We can empathize with that. We demonstrate we are all learners throughout our lives, and embrace risk taking and effort. We are creating an authentic community of writers in our classroom.

Now that we've collected and shared mentor texts to raise student awareness of the ideas, structure, and craft of authors, how do we help them use those elements in their own writing? Will they understand not only how an author uses structures or craft techniques in their writing but also why? When they understand the purpose of those choices, will they be more mindful about their own choices?

CLOSE READING MENTOR TEXTS FOR STRUCTURE

Studying the structure of a text teaches us to think about the choices an author makes and allows us to see that in writing, as well as in life, the way we lay out a text reveals much about what we want our readers to know.

—Christopher Lehman and Kate Roberts

In their insightful book *Falling in Love with Close Reading*, Lehman and Roberts (2014) share how to make the invisible visible to readers by analyzing texts for structure. They encourage readers to analyze what the author is doing and why. Could we apply some of these close reading strategies to our mentor texts to enhance writing?

Contemplating Genre

When students are asked to write in a particular mode or genre, they should have some solid understanding of how that genre works. There is a purpose for the genre, and the structure helps to support that purpose. This understanding can help our writers begin to organize their writing before the pencil even hits the paper.

DISCOVERING GENRE PURPOSE

WHY READ IT? WHY WRITE IT?

Our students can often recognize a genre, and sometimes describe characteristics of a genre, but many haven't considered the purpose of reading or writing in that genre.

- Create a T-chart or a two-column chart with the headings: "Genre" and "Purpose." (You could add a third column titled "Structures" for future analysis.)

- Invite students to name the genres with which they are familiar and list these in the first column. You may wish to add any that you know you will work with.

- Break them into small groups or partners and ask them to identify the purpose for each genre. (Why do authors write that type of text? What is our purpose for reading them?)

- As a whole group, share responses, discuss those points, and create a class anchor chart.

PEEK INSIDE A CLASSROOM: SIXTH-GRADE GENRE PURPOSE

Near the start of their sixth-grade year, Dan Johnston's class is exploring the taxonomy of genre and brainstorm an extensive list. "Well, I call that science fantasy instead of science fiction." "I think drama is a genre, but maybe it's just a kind of fiction." "Nonfiction is really kinda big for a genre; it's got lots of different types." Dan marks off the genres he will teach more systematically this year. We divide the students into small groups to discuss the purpose of each genre. Some groups jot down general purposes (to learn, for fun) while others have more refined purposes (to connect with characters who are like you, to think about something in a different way than you usually do). Dan and I float around the room listening in, prompting, and questioning to help them think more deeply about purpose.

We create an incomplete list (Figure 4.13) of several genres and the student-perceived purposes. Though your lists may be different, the point is to encourage students to think about the types of writing they will be doing during the year and the purposes behind them. A third column could be added when beginning a unit of study on a particular genre to help students identify elements or structures that support the purpose of that genre. Close writers can use this analysis to better understand the authors' choices in the mentor texts we use.

In their book *Nonfiction in Focus*, Jan Kristo and Rosemary Bamford note, "Knowing about organizational structures is important both as a reader and a writer. When students recognize the structure, it aids in processing and recalling information, building schema or background knowledge about the topic,

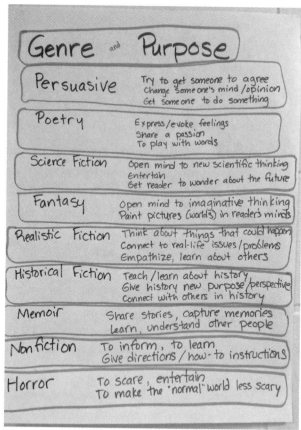

Figure 4.13

Student-generated genre and purpose chart

and even taking notes" (Kristo and Bamford 2004, 56). It also helps to provide a writing framework to organize their ideas and then share them with another reader.

Some books have multiple structures embedded within the text. It's easier to start our book analysis with an obvious structure or to analyze sections of text rather than an entire book. We can then ask, "How can we help our students to recognize and internalize those structures to support their writing?" One way would be to use close reading to answer the question, "How does this text work?"

HOW DOES THIS TEXT/BOOK WORK?

ANALYZING STRUCTURE AND TEXT FEATURES

Sometimes our students don't recognize or appreciate the intentional decisions that go into organizing the information and layout of a text. When they understand the structure, they can begin to internalize it for their own writing.

- Determine which genre and structure the students' writing will focus on.
- Collect examples of mentor texts featuring the focused structure.
- Model the thinking and close reading you want them to try out as you notice the structures and text features the author used.
- Use a sticky note to mark the text feature choices the author used and note why you think they made that choice (purpose).
- Invite students to continue this analysis on their own or in groups, noting the features and their purpose.
- Let students share what they noticed and see whether other readers noticed similar features.
- Give students a storyboard template to record their observations and notes. This will demonstrate their understanding of how the author organized the book.
- Invite students to create a similar storyboard to organize their own writing, referencing techniques, structures, and features used by the mentor author.

PEEK INSIDE A CLASSROOM: ANALYZING MENTOR TEXTS FOR STRUCTURE

Haley Duncan's fourth graders are beginning a unit of study on informational picture books. They have chosen topics of interest and will begin doing some mini-research to gather information. Students often collect a lot of information about their topic but then are unsure how to organize it. For this unit, we want them to understand how structure can help a writer think about how they want their piece to work.

We choose a nonfiction book with a common enumerative structure. Our goal is that students will look closely at how the author chose to organize the book and understand the purpose for the text features included. By analyzing the structure and features, they can begin to internalize a similar structure for organizing their writing.

To model our analysis, I project the text onto the board with a document camera. "Boys and girls, today we are going to look at some informational picture books and ask ourselves this question, 'How does this book work?' If we can see how other authors organize their ideas and present their writing, we can use that to help us write our own informational picture books."

I start with the cover and talk about the information we would find there and its importance to the reader. Students are quick to share. "The title tells you what you are going to read about." "The picture shows you what the book is about." We open the book to find a table of contents; again the students are familiar with this. "That tells you what you can read about in the book and what page it's on."

I put the word "analyze" on the board and ask them whether they know what it means. One student responds, "Study something?"

"Yes!" I reply. "It means to study something and understand it better or to see how it works. You guys are going to analyze the nonfiction book we give you, to see how it works. You already showed us that you know how the book begins, so now you are going to analyze the rest of the book. How does the author lay out the book? What text features does she use, and what are their purposes? Use a sticky note to label a text feature, write down how it helps the reader. Then, we want you to think, *How does this book work?* Look at a sample from the beginning, the middle, and the end to see how this author structures her book."

Haley and I pass out the books and sticky notes to the groups. They take turns holding and analyzing the pages and jotting down what they notice (Figure 4.14). We circulate to listen, prompt, and support their analysis. Some students are noticing that the left side of the spread is always a photo or illustration and the right side contains the text. Every text feature is discussed, from captions, text boxes, and headings to bold print words, glossary, and index. If students simply label a feature, we remind them to state its purpose. We want them to think more deeply about why a writer chooses a feature and how it helps the reader access information.

After a time, we call the students back together to share what they notice. They are building a more refined schema for how informational books could be structured. Their

Figure 4.14

Haley's fourth graders analyze a nonfiction book.

conversation gives us insight into what they already know and what they are discovering. We then give each student a template to record the structure they observed (Figure 4.15). We don't need them to document everything they noticed, only a sample from the beginning, middle, and end of the book.

After students record their observation and understanding of the structure of this nonfiction picture book, we give them a graphic organizer that looks similar to the template they used to analyze the published text (Figure 4.16). They use this as a prewriting structure, applying what they have learned from the mentor text to plan and organize their own writing.

It isn't important that students notice everything an author does in the mentor text. It is important that we heighten their awareness about structure and text elements so that they can begin to imagine possibilities and try on these moves in their writing. I cannot expect them independently to use something they don't notice or understand. We can tell our students to try out techniques, but close writers will notice what others do and

Figure 4.15
Students record their analysis on a graphic organizer.

look for ways to try it out in their own writing. I don't want writers to be good at only following directions. I want writers to be able to think strategically about how best to organize their writing.

DON'T FORGET COMICS AND GRAPHIC NOVELS

There is no denying the popularity of comics and graphic novels in the literary diet of our students these days. Because they are not often a part of our school curriculum for reading and writing, students are left to discover on their own "how these texts work." Most successfully navigate the medium and enjoy the books tremendously but may not appreciate the intentionality of the author's choices or understand how the structure supports the narrative elements. There are opportunities for applying close reading and close writing to comics and graphic novels that I want to explore with students.

Although comics are often considered a genre, the comic format can be used to write in any genre, including nonfiction, historical fiction, realistic fiction, fantasies, and mysteries.

Figure 4.16

Using mentor text analysis to plan their own nonfiction books

The unique composition of comics and graphic novels is quite different from most of the texts we teach within our classrooms.

Comics and graphic novels have their own set of text features, such as panels, gutters, caption boxes, speech and thought balloons, tails for those balloons, zip ribbons (motion lines), and sound effects that accompany pictures or icons. There are also considerations for how to navigate the layout of panels that may not be clear to a reader. The traditional left to right with return sweep (Z-path) can be complicated by the shape, overlap, or layout of panels (Figure 4.17). Comic writers often use a variety of layouts within their pieces to keep it visually stimulating, to convey time, and to emphasize elements of their

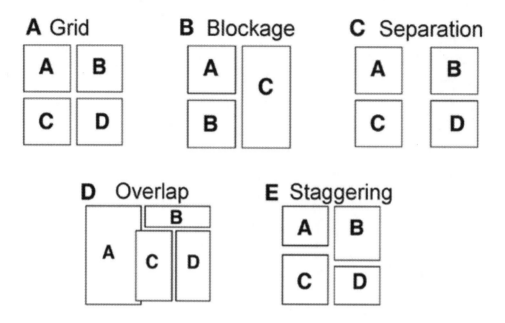

Figure 4.17
Comic grids (Used with permission © 2013 Neil Cohn)

story. Readers need to know how to navigate a diverse assortment of formats within a text (Figure 4.18).

Using a selection of comics and graphic novels as mentor texts would be a tremendous support for many students. Space is limited, and these authors need to convey their ideas with an economy of precise words, important details, thoughtful transitions of time and place, and an organized event sequence. These are all qualities of writing that we emphasize with our students. Understanding how these authors make decisions to convey their ideas in such a focused manner could easily translate to other forms of writing. (See Figure 4.19.)

Figure 4.18

From Marvel's *Captain America* by Jim Steranko

Figure 4.19

Students practice writing dialogue and description from comics.

COMIC ANALYSIS

HOW THIS TEXT WORKS

To help students create a comic with a good structure, an explicit lesson in design and format would be a good first step. Understanding the relationship between pictures and words will help them read and write their own comics more successfully. Here are some considerations for a lesson on analyzing and using comic structure.

Text features: Display a comic panel and point out to students the features and their purpose.

- Panel: the box for each scene
- Panel border: outline of the box
- Gutter: space between panels
- Caption box: for the narrator's voice
- Speech balloons: for the characters' voices
- Thought balloons: for the characters' thoughts
- Tail (to the speech and thought balloons): points to who is speaking or thinking
- Sound effects: onomatopoeia written into the panel
- Zip ribbons: the lines that depict motion
- Pictures/scenes: depict the action going on; may or may not contain much setting

---

Picture/text relationship:

Panels do not reflect all of the action; readers must infer between scenes (the importance of the gutter).

- Pictures, captions, speech balloons, and sound effects all contribute to the telling of the story with different information (the words do not often repeat what is being "said" with the picture).
- Students may need to be shown how to navigate different page layouts as they are not always a simple left to right, top to bottom (Z-path). Provide several comic layouts to demonstrate the variety.

As teachers, we may not be as familiar with this medium as we are with other writing formats. I certainly wasn't. I wanted to look more closely at this type of composition because my students were so captivated by them. I wanted to be able to discuss their importance to parents who didn't consider it *real* reading. I wanted to be able to tap into the literacy potential for engaging my students in more reading and writing. There are some wonderful books that have helped me to understand comics and graphic novels on a deeper level (see McCloud [1999] or McLachlan [2013] in "Recommended Resources") that have certainly convinced me of the value of incorporating this format into my literacy instruction.

Considerations for English Language Learners

The work we do in our classrooms around mentor texts can be incredibly helpful to our English language learner (ELL) students. Sometimes texts in their native language have different layouts, directionality, or features. Explicitly teaching them how a text works supports their reading and writing skills. Taking time to examine and discuss the structure of books, articles, comics, or other media allows me a window into what they already know and helps me to support their understanding. Most of the lessons I do around analyzing texts include multiple opportunities for shared conversations. These conversations support the vocabulary and schema around books, writing, and reading for our students.

We often use short texts and picture books for mentor texts that offer additional scaffolds to our ELL students. The illustrations in picture books offer visual support that assist students' comprehension, and the lower volume of text can make examples easier to find and notice for these novice readers. Using student mentor texts or teacher mentor texts can make those exemplars even more apparent as the authors are available to talk about their process as we examine their work.

When we work with mentor texts, we are often looking closely with a more focused lens. Letting our ELL students lead the analysis can help us assess what *they* notice and know. At other times, we direct their attention to specific aspects of writing with strong examples and clear language that can lift their level of understanding. I sometimes assume that students may see what I see in a text or can detect the intentional moves that authors make, but studying mentor texts together removes all assumptions, which can be especially helpful for my ELL students. They haven't been exposed to and immersed in these books as long as our native speakers who have internalized many of the basic structures. I cannot take for granted what students are noticing, thinking, or understanding, especially those with the least experience.

The Gist of the Story

My thinking about the use of mentor texts over the past few years has evolved as I have wondered, Why is it that some students integrate the techniques we are sharing and some do not? In my observations, I have contemplated that mentor texts *work* best if

- the shared technique or trait is within the child's zone of proximal development;

- we expand our definition and analyze our selection of mentor texts to provide greater scaffolds;

- the desired technique or approach is taught as a strategy for any piece of writing and not a skill to be practiced on the current piece of writing;

- students can envision the possibilities and recognize the need in their own writing;

- students are actively engaged in the noticing and naming of the structures and techniques;

- students have multiple opportunities to engage with a text or genre, to closely read and analyze how it works; and

- students connect with the books or the authors and desire to emulate the work.

Drafting Your Story

Take a moment to think about your own use of mentor texts in the classroom. You could either discuss with some colleagues or reflect on your own about your current thinking:

- What is your process for selecting mentor texts?

- How do you approach the teaching of the desired techniques, ideas, or structures?

- How do you know whether students have *learned* what you taught?

- Would you consider your approach more teacher directed or student directed?

- What is something you would like to try after reading this chapter?

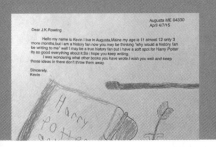

CHAPTER 5

Close Modeling: Learning from Mentor Authors

I find that teachers who write themselves, as well as write with their students, offer their students greater flexibility and understanding. —Donald Graves

love listening to authors talk about their process. I am always eager to see them speak at conferences, sign books at the local bookstores, visit our schools, or Skype with us in classrooms. I am fascinated by how they do what they do. They always seem larger than life until I meet them. Many have become dear friends. Now, I am also in awe of how "normal" their lives are. They still cook dinner for their families, cheer on their kids at sporting events, and post pictures of their cuddly dogs, the way many of us do. They are people who work hard to come up with ideas, research their topics, and then write, write, and rewrite. Once I get to know them, I feel like the curtain has been pulled back, and I can see the wizard parked in a chair, feverishly tapping away at a keyboard—professional close writers.

The moral of this story: Close writers learn from mentors all around them: published authors, teachers, peers, and even themselves.

I have the same sense of wonder many of our students have for the teacher or for strong writers in their classrooms. They ponder, "How'd they do that?" A big part of close writing is creating awareness around how writers bring their words to life on the page. Studying mentor texts helps us to see the results of that work, but interacting and learning from mentor authors helps us to see the process of that work.

It benefits students if we begin to expand our definition of an author to encompass more than published writers. An author can be anyone who writes for an audience, even if that audience is themselves. There are varying degrees of expertise, but what separates the novice from the accomplished writer is practice, practice, practice. Helping our students see that authors aren't born writers, that they work at their craft every day to improve, might help students envision possibilities for themselves as writers.

Student Authors as Mentors

As I discussed in Chapter 4, collecting and sharing student writing as mentor texts can be a great resource for other student writers. It is equally powerful to have student mentors share their process with other students. If we value the process, and not just the product, we need to look for opportunities to make that apparent. When the expertise of a mentor is too advanced for a student to emulate and aspire to (published authors or even their teachers), a closer scaffold might be to observe the writing of fellow students. These pieces are closer to being within the zone of proximal development for younger writers.

Some teachers set up a learning buddy system in which a middle-grades classroom partners with a primary classroom. Once a week, students get together to engage in a learning activity. Traditionally, it revolves around reading. The older buddy chooses picture books to share with his or her younger counterparts. Teachers are now expanding the scope of learning to include writing, which provides an opportunity for student authors to be mentor authors to others.

Writing Buddies

To become more purposeful with writing, mentor or teach someone else. Mentors have to think more intentionally about what they are doing and the choices they make. Becoming writing buddies with another student provides authentic practice in close writing strategies and in nurturing a writing identity.

KINDERGARTEN WRITERS AND SIXTH-GRADE MENTORS

Brandi Grady's kindergarten students have been reading nonfiction books about animals and writing their own. Nicole Clark's sixth graders are helping these students research information on animals by reading from a text and then talking about what was read.

Figure 5.1
Kindergarten buddies work on writing

The older buddy then helps the kindergarten student decide what sentence(s) to write (Figure 5.1). When the kindergarten writer needs help, the sixth grader may sound out words, remember the original sentence, or reread the work.

As Brandi, Nicole, and I walk around the room, we listen in to conversations. The sixth graders offer support with questions and advice.

"What do you want it to say?"

"You should leave a space after that word. You don't want to scrunch it all together."

"What else do you know about cats?"

It's obvious to the adults just how beneficial these interactions are to students. The sixth-grade mentor authors are seen as writers and experts. We want to know what the kindergarten students think about these experiences so Brandi asks how a writing buddy could help them.

"She read my cheetah book to me. It helped me because I didn't know how to read. If we knew a word, they would stop so we could say that word."

"I liked having a buddy because she was really focused."

"When I had my partner and I didn't know how to spell *snails*, she got out my book so I could look and see how to spell *snails*."

"They helped me think by going back if I didn't hear something, and they read it again."

I also want to know if the sixth graders see benefit to this. They talk about being looked up to, having fun with the "little kids," and being helpful. I ask them, "How could working with a younger buddy help you as a writer?"

Some respond, "It can help you work better with partners. Little kids can be more difficult than older kids. You have to be patient."

"They do actual research out of books; we do computers. I'm sure books hold more information that we don't know, so we could use more books and that could help us."

"It gives us a chance to see how we struggled back then and how we've improved now. A lesson we could take from working with the little kids is having more patience."

Figure 5.2
A fifth grader shares her writing with a kindergarten buddy.

KINDERGARTEN AND FIFTH-GRADE MENTOR AUTHORS

Meagan Mattice's kindergarten students love meeting with their fifth-grade buddies from Andrea Bryant's class. Today, Andrea's students are sharing the picture books they created for their buddies. The fifth graders have worked hard to create interesting stories for their pals and rehearsed them with expression. As they read, the kindergartners are mesmerized (Figure 5.2). There are frequent calls of "Read it again!"

As they create these stories, the fifth graders learn a lot about writing picture books from the mentor texts they study. They understand the importance of the visual information matching the written message, and they lay out their books with engaging formats for the younger readers. They practice reading their writing carefully, which helps them to revise and edit more effectively.

The kindergarten students are offered a clear model of the writing process from a mentor who is much closer in range to their own proficiencies. They ask questions of the author and discuss each page that is shared. They see these older students as buddies but also now as authors. The process of creating a book has become less mysterious and more possible for these young writers.

THIRD-GRADE AUDIENCE AND FOURTH-GRADE AUTHORS

Haley Duncan's fourth graders have just finished writing informational picture books. Haley wants to find a way for the students to share their work and give her students an authentic audience for their efforts. Haley's students practice using the writer reading strategies they have been taught (see Chapter 3). She invites Paige Dyer's third-grade class to a book share.

The students break into small groups. The fourth graders talk about their process before reading. Audry opens to her table of contents. "Well, I really like skiing so I wanted to write a book about skiing facts. I thought about some topics like *How to ski* and *Different types of skiing* and *How do I get up the mountain?* Then I had to do some research, and we wrote up our ideas in this outline, and then we wrote our stories from that." She opens her book and begins to read (Figure 5.3).

As I walk around the room, I hear similar conversations about why writers choose their topics and how they organize their writing before they begin to read their work aloud. Some pause between pages, and there are conversations about illustrations and questions about their subject. The fourth graders take pride in their expertise, and the third graders seem genuinely engaged with the process (see Figure 5.4). Several students declare, "I

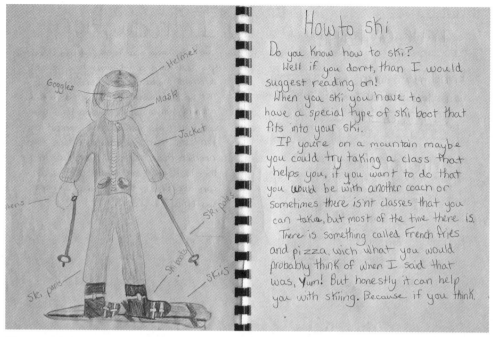

Figure 5.3
Fourth grader's student mentor text

Figure 5.4
Fourth graders read their books to third-grade neighbors.

know what I'm writing about next year!" They are obviously thinking ahead, planning their own informational books and envisioning the possibilities.

FIRST-GRADE AND FIFTH-GRADE CO-WRITERS

Maureen Cooper's first graders are getting ready for St. Patrick's Day. They are excited about the prospect of leprechauns visiting the school. Today, their fifth-grade buddies will co-write a story about catching a leprechaun. They listen to fifth-grade teacher Kelley Capen read a story about a leprechaun, and now they are working with their buddies to write their own stories (see Figure 5.5).

They start with a paper divided in half; the fifth graders will compose on the left, and the first graders will use the right. This is similar to the We Both Read series of books (Treasure Bay). Today, we are creating a "we both write" version of a story. The students talk about the ideas they want to create together. "Let's say we made a trap filled with chocolate to catch him," offers Brody.

Figure 5.5
Buddies collaborating on a story

Ray, his fifth-grade buddy, orally revises, "Yeah, but the chocolate is like gold coins. Those coins that you unwrap, and there's chocolate inside. We put those in the trap to trick him."

Brody adds on, "So he goes up to the box, and he tries to get 'em, and he falls down in this can and we trick him!"

"And he's screaming like, *You tricked meeeee!* in this little leprechaun voice. But he escapes, and the kids are like, *Hey, where'd he go?*" Brody and Ray talk a few more minutes, and then Ray begins, "So I'll start, *One windy St. Patty's day, two kids wanted to catch a leprechaun.*"

"Yeah, that's us!" says Brody. Ray models his idea orally and then slowly writes each word as he says it aloud. He helps Brody say his idea before writing and helps him spell a few words. When it is Ray's turn again, he models for Brody how to write dialogue (see Figure 5.6).

"So when the leprechaun is talking we use quotation marks (makes air quotes) around what he said, so we know he's talking. I'm making these letters uppercase 'cause he's yelling, but it's just in his tiny leprechaun voice. And like he says *me* really long so I'm making lots of *e*'s to stretch it out." Ray writes, *You TRICKED MEEE!!*

Brody is getting some important insights into how authors choose what they write and how they write it. He knows *me* is spelled M-E but accepts Ray's explanation for why he is spelling it with multiple *e*'s. He has learned when an author writes with all uppercase letters he intends for the reader to read it differently, perhaps louder or with more emphasis. He's probably heard these lessons from his incredible teacher, but hearing it from this buddy he admires as they create a story together gives him a different kind of ownership and attention to detail. He is able to see the lessons his teacher has shared being used by a real writer.

Ray is becoming more metacognitive about his process because he knows he needs to make it visible for his buddy. Articulating what he is thinking and his choices causes him to reflect on his writing process in a more purposeful way. Putting those thoughts onto paper for an audience takes on a whole new meaning. He gets immediate feedback if his writing is confusing or doesn't connect with his reader. Both students have approached the writing process more mindfully; they are becoming close writers together.

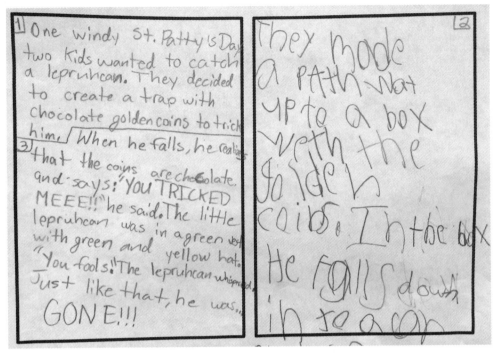

Figure 5.6
Buddies' coauthored story

FOURTH-GRADE AND FOURTH-GRADE VIRTUAL BUDDIES

Erika Meiler's fourth graders are working on historical fiction pieces. They have been using graphic organizers to help them develop their ideas on setting, characters, and plot. Erika is talking with her colleague Samantha Simmons about her trifold graphic organizer she calls a flipper. Samantha likes this, "I wish one of your students would come over and show my kids how to use it." This gets us thinking about how our students can mentor one another through some of our writing lessons. They don't have to worry about phrasing things in kid-friendly language, because that's their native tongue!

Erika knows who she'll ask, but trying to figure out a time that works out well for both is tricky. I inquire, "What if we tape one of your students explaining how to use the flipper and then Samantha can show it to her students as needed? Plus, you'll have it for next year as a mentor lesson for when you introduce the flipper again." Erika and Samantha like that idea, so that afternoon, I pull Daniel for a video session, and he explains how to use the flipper step by step. Keeping this mentor video will be a terrific resource for Erika

Figure 5.7

Farrington fourth-grade writers club

and other students. We think about other possible opportunities for archiving students mentoring students!

WRITING CLUBS

Marcia Hughes is a fourth-grade teacher with a passion for helping students channel their energy and creativity. She is the founder of the Farrington Writers Club (see Figure 5.7). A few years ago several students approached her about forming this group, and Marcia got behind their efforts. She has continued to sponsor a fourth-grade and fifth-grade club that meet at least once a month during recess or lunch to collaborate, to share, and to immerse themselves in their writing.

They support one another as writing mentors, but their influence extends beyond the group meetings. These students are role models in the eyes of their peers. They are looked up to as authors, which helps in building up their positive writing identity. What they do is seen as "real" writing because it isn't assigned or graded. It is a more authentic approach to writing, as it requires an audience of peers who are not evaluative but accepting and encouraging. The literary quality varies considerably, but the engagement, enthusiasm, and interest levels are of the highest quality. Marcia has been a true mentor to them and has helped spread the love of writing throughout our school.

Many schools sponsor reading clubs for their avid readers. It builds community around a common passion for reading and books. If your school has students with a passion for writing, encouraging the formation of a writing club will support a community of authors whose influence may easily spread beyond the group.

Teacher Authors as Mentors

I was once with a group of teachers who were asked, "How many of you consider yourselves readers?" The room was filled with raised hands and excited chatter. They were then asked, "How many of you consider yourselves writers?" Only a few hands were raised, somewhat tentatively. Some even qualified their responses with, "Well, I try" or "Just for myself," as if they needed to justify their claim as writers. How does this happen? When did this perception become the reality for so many teachers? More importantly, how can we change this?

Donald Graves has always been one of my heroes. In an interview with *Instructor* magazine, he was asked, "If you had to choose one thing teachers should do when teaching writing, what would it be?" He responded,

> Write yourself. Invite children to do something you're already doing. If you're not doing it, *Hey*, the kids say, *I can't wait to grow up and not have to write, like you.* They know. And for the short term and the long term, you'll be doing yourself a favor by writing. All of us need it as a survival tool in a very complex world. The wonderful thing about writing is that it separates the meaningless and the trivial from what is really important. So we need it for ourselves and then we need to invite children to do what we're doing. You can't ask someone to sing a duet with you until you know the tune yourself. (Graves 1995, 38–43)

So how do we prepare ourselves to sing that duet?

TEACHERS WRITE: WALKING THE TALK

Last year I joined Kate Messner's Teachers Write! virtual summer camp. She describes it on her website (www.katemessner.com/teachers-write/) as "a community of teachers and librarians who believe that people teaching writing should walk the walk." Published authors share their expertise and offer lesson ideas for teachers to try. Teachers are encouraged to practice their craft, post their writing, and receive nurturing feedback. Even when the summer camp ended, teachers and authors continued networking with one another through Twitter and Facebook to share ideas, resources, and support. It has been a powerful experience for everyone who has tried it. Kate has followed up this work with a great book for teachers, *59 Reasons to Write* (Messner 2015) filled with mini-lessons, prompts, and inspiration to get teachers started with writing.

In the fall of 2014, I invited the teachers in my district to join me in a writing group. I have always encouraged new teachers to keep a journal or to jot down vignettes from those hectic first days, months, and years in the classroom. I have worked with teachers who share their joys and struggles with parenting or with aging parents and urged them to pen some of those memories to keep them preserved. It can be hard to justify carving out time to write *about* life when we are so busy living it and dealing with it, but we do.

TEACHER WRITING GROUP: JUST DO IT

Our first-ever group meets on a rainy December afternoon at a local bookstore. There are five of us, all at different points in our careers and family lives. We each grab a coffee, find a table in the cafe, and look at one another. "Now what?" one giggles. We each pull out our writing books; there are beautiful new journals, spiral notebooks, and even scrap paper.

"What should we write about?" Jenna asks.

"Whatever it is you want to capture, remember, or create," I respond. I really want teachers to collect stories from their classrooms. We think we'll never forget, but we do. "You could write a book *for* your students. You know what they love," I add. "Or write what *you* enjoy reading. You don't have to worry about it being good, just write whatever comes to you. Write about your life. Capture a little slice of it."

Andrea starts us off, "Were we supposed to bring something to share? I've got something I could read." We all feel grateful that Andrea is breaking the ice for the group. She shares with us a poignant fictional Thanksgiving tale that leaves several of us with watery eyes. Here in our circle is writing with the power to move us. I could hug her; I am not expecting such a beautiful launch to our group.

There is a united "Wow." We ask her how she came up with her idea and why she wrote that story. She talks about wondering what Thanksgiving would be like without her mom and how sad she would feel. It opens up a conversation about family.

"I want to write for my grandson. I want to write some poems, but some other things, too," shares Luanne. Kelley talks about her very young daughter, sharing anecdotes and emotions that will inspire her writing. It is clear that the writing is going to be meaningful for each of us.

With that, we pick up our pens, look at each other with a shrug, and dive in. Occasionally, one of us thinks aloud or draws another into conversation about an idea and then retreats into the writing. I look around at these four with their heads down and their pens flying (Figure 5.8). I am so inspired. I have goose bumps.

After a time, we take turns sharing little pieces of ourselves we've inscribed on paper. One writes a poem to her grandson. Another speaks of a scary trip to the emergency room with her boyfriend and playing around with time shifts in her story. I write about my brother. It would have been his birthday today, and I am surprised by the emotion in

Figure 5.8
First Augusta teachers writing group

my voice as I talk about it. I am reminded of the power written words have to carefully hold memories for me and the teachers around me.

As we leave, I know they will see their young writers a little differently tomorrow. I am already seeing them a little differently. I have always respected these teachers so deeply, but now I also admire their courage and willingness to take a risk like this. We meet several more times during the school year again. It isn't always easy, but it is time well spent. We are appreciating the successes and empathizing with the struggles of our student writers more and more.

POWER OF THE PEN IN THE WRITING TEACHER'S HAND

So how can our writing pursuits encourage close writing from our students? Your story may be different, but in ours we found the following:

- We develop empathy for our students. We sometimes forget how difficult it can be to construct a cohesive piece of writing. Keeping those experiences fresh can help us more compassionately understand the struggles some of our students are facing.

- We help make the invisible more visible for our students. We can talk about our process and choices, and our students can see the results of that cognitive effort in the writing we share with them.

- We can try out our own assignments and see just how long they might take, how much effort is required, or how interesting they might be. Our students see that the assignments are being done *with* them and not *to* them. If we are resistant to trying out assignments, maybe we can understand some of the same reluctance of our students.

- We can share common experiences with our students when we read together and write together. We build a community of support for one another that can change the dynamic in the classroom from compliance to collaboration.

- We show students that writing truly is a lifelong skill. We won't, as Donald Graves cautioned, have students decrying, "I can't wait to grow up and not have to write, like you." They will instead witness the perpetuity of writing skills as the adults around them demonstrate their significance to school and beyond.

TEACHER MENTORS: MODELS FOR STUDENTS

Andrea Bryant wants her students to reflect on the choices they make as authors. To do this, she shares some of her thinking about her process. "I was reflecting on my writing in the past, saying, *What is it that I want to do next? What is it that I want to try?* And I was really purposeful about that. I was saying to myself, *What is it I see that good authors do, and how can I do that when I write?*

"One of the things that a good author did, that I really liked, was alternate settings. He started at one setting, and then he went to another setting, and then he went back and forth and back and forth. So in my piece of writing here, I tried to do that." She pulls out her writer's notebook. "Here's just a little bit. I can't share with you the whole thing, but I can show you what I tried to do. Maybe I didn't do it perfectly, but you can see my first attempt." She reads her piece to her students.

She continues, "So what we want you to start doing is take something that you see good authors do, and purposefully do it in your writing. Does anybody have any ideas about what they've seen good authors do that they want to try?"

Students share some examples of what they like in the books they read: stories that are letters between characters, graphic novels and comic formats, and chapters that switch perspectives. Andrea wants her students to make conscious connections between the books they read and the writing they do, and she shares how that process has purposefully shaped her writing.

Moe Heikkila has looped with her students from third to fourth grade. They are a close community of learners, partly because Moe shares her learning along with them. Today, she is revising a story she wrote to accompany the illustrations in a wordless picture book. She sets up a split screen on her SMART Board so students can see the pictures and her text (see Figure 5.9).

"So I wrote this a couple of years ago, but I have learned so much since then. I want to add some onomatopoeia and some dialogue to make it more interesting. I'm going to read through it and look for some places where I could add that. After I work on mine, I want you to work on yours and try the same thing." Moe reads through the pages, pauses to think aloud, rehearses some possibilities, and then makes some revisions. She invites her students to contribute ideas and incorporates many into her piece. This shared approach invites engagement and opportunity for students to explore writing choices with a more capable mentor.

Sixth-grade teacher Guy Meader shares a draft from his writer's notebook (see Figure 5.10). Students are hanging on every word as he takes them through his experience as a new father. He describes the birth of his daughter with detail and emotion. He wants his students to see that when you write what you care about, the ideas come more easily. As he reads, he pauses occasionally to question or revise. "I think I want to add more about

Figure 5.9
Moe Heikkila as a mentor author

those first moments. I didn't really say that much here." He adds a note in the margin: *More on the first moments*. He continues reading and then pauses again. "Wait a minute, this part about the elevator should have gone back here." He makes an asterisk to show where he will move the idea. "That's why it is important to go back and read what we write. It needs to make sense. I've read this three times, and that's the first time I caught that one." He stops in a few other spots to talk out some potential ideas and details he will probably go back and add.

"So, now I want you to go back and read your piece again. I want you to look for places where you might want to add more details or where something might be out of order and not make as much sense. It might help if you do what I did and read your story out loud so that you can hear if it's making sense, or if you are getting a clear picture in your head." The students go back to their pieces and begin rereading. Guy has provided a strong example of the writing process as well as a writing product. He helps to make the invisible visible. His writer's notebook contains many teacher mentor texts that will support his students' writing this year.

On the other side of the school, Dan Johnston shares a revised version of a memoir. He has incorporated suggestions provided by students after hearing the first draft. Because he frequently shares his writing with his students, they have learned to listen with a critical ear. They know he sees his writing as a work in progress and that he doesn't want praise; he wants analysis and feedback. He reads aloud his memoir of his fifth-grade year in school, when he was determined to reach the top of a climbing ladder in his physical education class and learned a lesson about celebrating too soon (see Figure 5.11).

As he reads, his expression captivates the students and models a strong interpretive style. They nod with satisfaction and smile at the humorous details. It is clear they appreciate this recent iteration much more. We want them to understand what it is about this piece they felt was stronger, not in generalities but in specifics. Understanding those moves is how they will begin to envision possibilities in their own writing.

Dan lets me tag in. "I want you to compare this draft of the memoir with the first, and look for specific examples of what Mr. J did differently. What revisions did he make to

Figure 5.10
Guy Meader shares his teacher mentor text.

Figure 5.11

Dan Johnston shares his teacher mentor text.

this version? Your task is going to be to highlight those specific techniques he tried and then describe what it is you think he was trying to do. Sometimes we *think* that something is better, but until we understand what makes it better, with specific examples, it is hard to try it ourselves."

Students engage in analysis and conversation about the story, the techniques, the labels they will give those moves. Dan and I move about the room, listening in and at times offering the language to capture the craft, approach, or technique. Some students have additional questions and suggestions they offer as well (see Figure 5.12). After a time, we pull the group back together to share specific evidence of revision and why they think Mr. J made those choices. The students have been given a potent example of the power of revision but also that writing is a process for their teacher as well. By sharing his work, he is one of the best mentors they will have this year for their writing.

When I asked Dan's students what it was like to have a teacher who shares his writing with them, the students had a lot to say:

"When he reads his stories out loud it helps me think of other ideas I've had or things I've written. It makes me a better writer."

"When he shares his stories, I get to know him. When I get to know what kind of person he is, it helps me be able to write better, connect better, but also know his thoughts and have him know mine. I think voicing yourself is one of the most important things you can do."

"I think it makes it easier for us to see how he thinks and for him to think about how we think, and that's really important. I've never been in a classroom where that has been as explicit, and sharing writing is one of the biggest things that can help make that happen."

Writing has become a vehicle for building community in many classrooms, certainly in this classroom. I encourage teachers to think about ways they can become a mentor writer for their students. There are benefits beyond literacy that may surprise you.

COLLEAGUE MENTORS: RESOURCES AROUND US

Tapping into the resources of the wider school community, there may be other teachers or school personnel who would be willing to share their writing and their process with our students. As a literacy coach, I am an obvious choice. I keep a writer's notebook in which I try out many of the assignments given to our students (see Figure 5.13). Students appreciate seeing someone else's version of their writing assignments, knowing that writing is not just a kid thing. I also keep some of my own writing in my personal

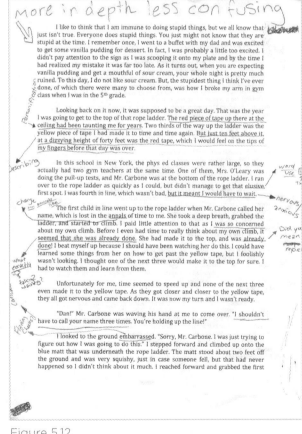

Figure 5.12

Student analysis of Dan's mentor text

writer's notebook that I share on occasion. These are collections of ideas, photos, and beginnings that I have used as fodder for my blog or other writing projects.

Students would love to have previous teachers come in and share their writing. Imagine the influence of a future teacher, administrator, or office staff on students if they came in to share writing. We can show students how writing is a way of life, not just an assignment. Maybe you have a closet writer on your staff who is waiting for an opportunity to share his or her work with an audience.

Connecting with Published Authors

When I was in third grade, I desperately wanted to meet Astrid Lindgren. I had read every Pippi Longstocking book dozens of times. I wanted to be Pippi! My teacher had no idea how to contact an author then. There was no website to visit because there was no Internet. I always hoped that one day I would meet Astrid and she would share with me some of Pippi's secrets. But the odds of running into a Swedish author in an Illinois farm town were just too great. It never happened.

Today, I think about the authors our students admire, and I know the odds are much greater that they might connect. I encourage all teachers to seek out the authors their students love. Many authors are excited to meet and talk with their readers after working long, hard hours in isolation. They want to hear what students think, and it's gratifying to hear that their work is appreciated. So, how do we connect our students with published authors?

Figure 5.13

Sharing my writer's notebook with fourth graders

VISIT AUTHOR WEBSITES

These days, nearly every author has his or her own website. This is a great place to start for biographical information, lists of published work, and frequently asked questions. Some link to video interviews or to discussions about how the books were created and insights into their writing process. Most will have some information on how to contact the author. A simple web search is a great first start to connect your readers with their favorite writers.

ATTEND BOOK SIGNINGS

Many bookstores frequently schedule author discussions or book signings to promote the release of new books (see Figure 5.14). We are lucky where we live to have independent booksellers as well as a local chain store that enjoys hosting these events, which are usually quite small and intimate. Local libraries also

Figure 5.14
Ammi-Joan Paquette at a local book signing

invite authors in to read their work. Attendees have an opportunity to listen to authors speak, engage them in conversation, and have books personally signed. Don't forget that some students might enjoy meeting authors who write outside the children's book genre. Some like to connect with others who share their passion for cooking, history, outdoor adventures, and other interests. Share these event dates with students and parents and encourage them to engage with authors who visit their community.

ATTEND AUTHOR NIGHTS

Watch for author nights sponsored by literacy organizations. They are similar to book signings, but they bring together a larger number of authors and illustrators to visit with attendees in a variety of formats. Susan Dee, a literacy coach colleague in Maine and her

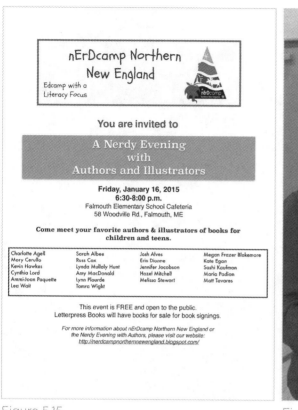

Figure 5.15
nErDy Author Night roster of talent

Figure 5.16
My first meeting with Cynthia Lord

team at nErDcamp Northern New England, set up a yearly nErDy Author Night (see Figure 5.15). They invite authors and illustrators of children's books to meet readers in one room, for a fantastic evening event. Kids, parents, teachers, and librarians go from table to table talking with their favorite authors and illustrators, getting to know the person behind the pen. Each year the event has grown in popularity and participation. Having so many talented people together gives children a real sense of the variety and styles of writing available to them as writers.

SCHOOL VISITS

When her book *Rules* first came out, Cynthia Lord visited our Augusta schools (Figure 5.16). She was a rock star to our students. Her visit was part of the Augusta Reads program in which all fifth- and sixth-grade students were given a copy of her book, and teachers used a variety of approaches to engage students with the text. Because all the students had read *Rules* and got to know the complex relationship between siblings Catherine and David, the questions were thoughtful, and Cynthia's responses were personal. She talked not only about her writing process but also about her poignant experiences raising a child with autism. That visit left an impact on a lot of students. Many could relate to having siblings with challenges and felt that she really understood their lives.

For several years, Augusta Reads has brought books and authors into our schools, and it has been an incredible avenue for building those connections between readers and writers. We have been fortunate to have many Maine authors make school visits (see Figure 5.17). The homegrown celebrity has made a particularly strong impression on our students. We have found funding available through grants, business sponsors, or parent groups to supplement tight budgets. Many schools have found this one-book, community wide approach to be a powerful shared reading experience, and bringing in the author makes it even more meaningful.

Figure 5.17
Author/illustrator Chris Van Dusen visits our schools.

USE SOCIAL MEDIA

Many authors have Facebook pages or can be found on Twitter or Instagram. They often establish public profiles and accounts to connect with their audience. Many of these platforms have age restrictions in place for children's safety, so some teachers have created classroom accounts to oversee the activity of students online. They can then follow other classrooms or authors to engage in a wider digital community. A quick tweet or photo share is relatively easy for classrooms to send and for authors to respond to. Some classrooms take screenshots of their correspondence with authors and keep these for the students as a memento of that connection. Social media have definitely made connecting writers and readers infinitely more possible.

SKYPE WITH AUTHORS

Along the lines of social media comes the use of virtual visits by authors to our schools and classrooms. Most authors will Skype with classrooms, especially if students have read their books. Authors can set up multiple visits in a single day and never have to leave their

Figure 5.18
Suzanne Selfors Skypes with Kelley Capen's fifth graders.

homes. Schools can afford the cost of bringing authors to their classrooms because they are often very inexpensive or free. Kate Messner's website offers information on authors who will Skype with book clubs or classrooms for free (see "References"). You'll need a little bit of technology to make it happen, but it is an easy and fun way to bring your students face to face with the authors they admire (see Figure 5.18).

SNAIL MAIL

Writing a good, old-fashioned friendly letter never goes out of style. I know some authors who collect letters in a notebook to give them inspiration when they need it most. Although letter writing is not as immediate as a tweet or an instant message, it is more personal to compose a letter and take the time to think about what we want to say to this person. It offers us an opportunity to be reflective and thoughtful. You can always blend two approaches by snapping a photo of the letter and posting it to an author's Twitter, Instagram, or Facebook page if you are concerned it would be lost in a stack of fan mail. When readers are determined to connect with their favorite authors, they can be pretty creative.

I've seen the enthusiasm firsthand when students meet their writing heroes. Aspirations skyrocket, the excitement over writing is contagious, and the students' confidence escalates. It is really magical for some of these kids. Their writing identities are nourished and enhanced by these interactions in immeasurable ways. They begin to feel a part of a wider writing community. Who knows, maybe one of those students sitting in our classrooms today will be the author we connect our students with in the years to come.

Part 3 of this book contains a compilation of interviews with the authors I have met over the past few years. I wanted to explore their close writing strategies and better understand their writing process. It has helped me to see that the process is similar in many ways to that of writers in our classrooms. I want our students to see that as well.

I also want to expand my connections with authors and study of work to embody more diverse books. The faces of our classrooms have changed dramatically in the past few years, and I want to make sure our students see themselves and their peers in the pages of these books and in the shoes of these authors. I want our students to experience the rich and varied approaches these diverse authors can bring to writing. The Internet and virtual literacy communities will help me to make this possible.

Considerations for English Language Learners

All kids benefit from mentors, but mentoring for our English language learner (ELL) students can provide some potent encouragement and modeling that will support their literacy acquisition. As teachers, when we share the thinking behind the writing, we demystify the process for coding our spoken language into print. When we have ELL students in our classroom, we may need to think aloud more purposefully those steps in the writing process that we take for granted and that many of our students already control.

The mentoring we do with some of our ELL students may resemble the shared writing approach in which students both observe and participate in the writing process. The teacher/author demonstrates while explaining each step of the process and may solicit student involvement to keep the writers engaged. There are often discussions about the choices and techniques used that require students to analyze and evaluate the work. The level of scaffold will vary with the needs of the students. Once the piece is completed, students can use the writing as a mentor text to support their own writing.

Encouraging some of our native English-speaking students to be mentors and models ensures that explanations and demonstrations are kid friendly. I have also seen older ELL students mentoring new arrivals or younger students in meaningful ways because they can empathize with their peers' struggles. They may have advice that we as teachers and native speakers cannot offer.

We can also think about finding mentor authors from our students' native country. Are there writers they would like to connect with? The Internet has removed many borders from our classrooms and made those connections more attainable. The ability to identify with a writer that they admire should not be limited to English-speaking authors. All students might enjoy the experience of interacting with authors from other countries, cultures, or parts of the world.

The Gist of the Story

Mentor texts play a supportive role in showing students strong writing products. We can infer the author's intention by analyzing the texts and trying out those moves in our own writing. But having the opportunity to interact and learn directly from mentor authors reveals to students the strong writing process. Both aspects can elevate a student's understanding of writing and appreciation for the choices a writer must make. We can use mentor authors when we do the following:

- Expand our definition of an author to include anyone who writes for an intended audience.

- Believe that the best teachers of writing are teachers who write.

- Become mentor authors for our students by sharing our writing and thinking.

- Find ways to help our young writers connect with published authors. Whether in person, by letter, through social media, or via virtual conferencing, we have more opportunities than ever to bring authors and students together in meaningful ways.

- Understand that mentor authors help our students envision possibilities in their own writing, enhance their writing identities, and become part of a larger community of writers.

Drafting Your Story

Take a moment to think about how you have used or might use mentor authors in your classroom.

- What mentor authors have your students had opportunities to learn from?

- How could you bring authors to your community, school, or classroom?

- How do you present your writing identity to your students? Do you consider yourself a writer? Do you feel comfortable sharing your writing with others?

- What is something you might try after reading this chapter?

CHAPTER 6

Increasing Volume and Stamina

If you write one story, it may be bad; if you write a hundred, you have the odds in your favor.—Edgar Rice Burroughs

My son, Casey, has a soccer ball by the door in our living room. Several times a day he practices step overs, stop turns, and 360 spins. He realizes the more he does it, the better soccer player he becomes. We can support him with coaching and tips or better equipment, but ultimately, it is the time and effort he puts into practicing that will make him a better soccer player.

Becoming a better writer is a similar endeavor. There are no shortcuts and quick fixes. We can teach every lesson we know, purchase the latest programs aligned to the Common Core, or design better assessments, but if our students aren't writing each day, then that stuff won't matter. The simple truth is we get better at writing by writing. If you are satisfied with your students' volume of writing, and their level of engagement, you might want to skip over this chapter. But if you would like to help your students look more closely at their volume of writing and explore any roadblocks that might hinder their volume or stamina, this chapter might provide a start to that conversation.

> **The moral of this story:**
> Close writers problem-solve obstacles to writing stamina so that they can increase the volume of writing and purposeful practice necessary to improve.

Let's first consider what I mean by these terms. *Volume* simply refers to the amount of writing the children produce. It can be measured by word counts or by pages written. It is the quantitative product of writing. *Stamina* refers to the active engagement with the writing process. It requires students to stay focused and on task for sustained periods of time. It is the quantitative process of writing. Neither of these factors guarantees qualitative writing outcomes, but in this chapter, we will explore the correlation.

Volume: The Quantitative Product of Writing

Every word a writer pens provides him or her with more writing practice. The more words you write, the more opportunities you have to practice spelling skills and word choice. The more sentences you write, the more opportunities you have to practice punctuation. The more stories you write, the more leads, characters, plots, and endings you will develop. Whatever skill or strategy you have taught will become more automatic and proficient with practice.

When I asked teachers for their input on what influences writing volume, most of their responses fell into one of these categories:

Time

Attitude

Stamina

Many of these factors are certainly correlative, and understanding how they affect our writers can help us plan more effective instruction. Even more important for close writing is helping writers see for themselves how these issues might support or prevent them from growing, so they can begin to increase their sense of agency as writers.

Time: Opportunities Outside the Writing Workshop

Time is a fixed commodity for all of us. We cannot speed it up, slow it down, or increase it. All we can do is manage it and try to spend it well. Teachers in our district have a regularly scheduled writing workshop, but many have also found ways to sneak in more writing in their day. We began to replace the word *time* with the word *opportunity* to help us reframe our approach to this common roadblock.

QUICK-WRITES

Can you find five or ten minutes in your schedule each day? Then, you've got time for quick-writes. Linda Rief, author of *100 Quickwrites: Fast and Effective Freewriting Exercises That Build Students' Confidence, Develop Their Fluency, and Bring Out the Writer in Every Student*, says, "Quickwrites offer an easy and manageable writing experience that helps both students and teachers find their voice and develop their confidence, as they discover they have important things to say" (Rief 2003, 8). Many teachers incorporate these compact bursts of writing into their daily schedule (see Figure 6.1). They are not revised or edited, and they are not graded.

Quick-writes take many formats, but the basic idea is to give students some kind of prompt or stimulus for writing. It could be a poem, a passage, or a picture. It might even be music that inspires them to write. Sometimes it is as simple as a single word. Options are limited only by our imagination.

Quick-writes are explorations, not destinations. We are not looking for polished pieces but rather a free flow of ideas. How we teachers respond to this writing is an important

Figure 6.1
Haley Duncan's daily quick-write

consideration that will set the tone and expectation. We want our comments to support the purpose, to just let ideas flow without filters or criticism. It is the effort that will be recognized, an emphasis on process over product. At first, students might be stumped or reluctant to try this on-demand approach. They might feel pressure to write something "perfect" instead of fast, but classrooms that encourage this daily writing have students who not only get used to this strategy but also look forward to it.

QUICK-WRITE IDEAS

There are many resources for quick-write ideas. An Internet search will yield many results, or you can check out some of my favorites:

- **Question of the day:** *Which book character would you like to be? Why?*
- **Poetry prompt:** Read a short poem; write whatever comes to mind or resonates.
- **Lift a line:** Choose a line from a poem or short text, write it down, and respond to it.
- **Musical notes:** Play some music for the students. What ideas does it inspire?
- **Picture this:** Share a photo, drawing, painting, etc. Write whatever this inspires.
- **Story starters:** Begin a story and invite students to continue: *I never should have said that!*
- **Title of the day:** Provide provocative or fun titles for students to write about: *The Forbidden Room*
- **With me or against me:** Give students a statement that they need to take a position on: *Recess is too long.*
- **How-tos:** Ask students to explain how to do something: *How do you make new students feel welcome?*
- **Reflection:** Invite students to reflect on some aspect of their day or learning: *Something I worked hard at this week was _____.*
- **Reviews:** Ask students to review a book, a movie, a game, etc. Can be positive or negative.
- **Days of the year:** There are many unusual celebrations throughout the year. How would you celebrate one? *January 3rd Is Fruitcake Toss Day*
- **Nonsense word of the day:** Give the students a nonsense word and have them create a definition and sentences using it: *Garbkind*
- **Class collection:** Invite students to create quick-write prompts and collect them in a jar. Choose one day of the week for student ideas.

To move quick-writes from an assignment to a strategy for drafting, students need to understand why they are doing it and how that process can help them as a writer. Talking to them about the benefits is a start, but when they can see for themselves we are enhancing their agency as writers, that is where the power lies. After students have created a body of quick-writes, engage them in some inquiry about their process and patterns.

REFLECTING ON QUICK-WRITES

WHAT DO YOU NOTICE ABOUT . . .

- How you get started?
- Which ideas are easier to write about?
- Which quick-writes you go back to explore or expand?
- How your thinking and process differs during this type of writing?
- Your volume of writing over time? Does it increase?

TRACKING VOLUME

Before students can reflect on the growth of their volume of writing, they need some way to measure it. Haley Duncan's fourth graders periodically count the words in their quick-writes to help them do this (see Figure 6.2). Haley does not have set expectation for word counts, but she invites her students to reflect on what is reasonable. They discuss and recognize numerous factors that influence the volume of a single piece of writing, and then they look for trends and patterns to reflect on in their own writing. This offers students one more "noticing" tool for becoming a close writer. Now they can answer for themselves, "How am I doing?"

WRITING ROUNDS

Many teachers have implemented some form of writing rounds as an independent work activity. Some are based on *The Daily 5* (Boushey and Moser 2006), literacy stations, or writing centers. While teachers are conferring with readers and writers or meeting with small groups, the rest of the class is engaged in independent writing. This freewriting time is a window into the skills, strategies, and concepts students carry over from mini-lessons, conferences, and direct instruction. Often, the choices they make and the work they produce are better when it is self-directed. Choice can be a powerful motivator.

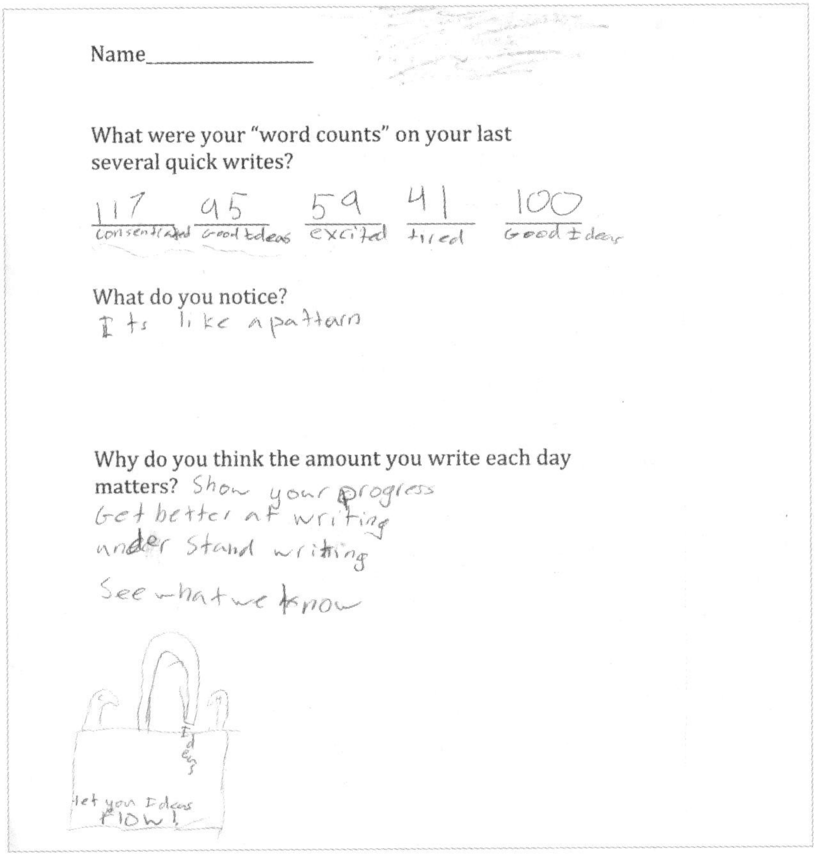

Name_____

What were your "word counts" on your last
several quick writes?

117   95   59   41   100
concentrated   Good Ideas   excited   tired   Good Idear

What do you notice?

I ts like a pattern

Why do you think the amount you write each day
matters? Show your progress
Get better at writing
under stand writing

See what we know

let your Ideas
FlOW!

Figure 6.2
Examining word count with quick-writes to reflect on volume

CONTENT-AREA WRITING

Nonfiction books, texts, and websites kids love to read should be the models for the types
of informational writing they do. Excessive research and reports have killed the passion
for many aspiring nonfiction novices. We want to tap into their natural curiosity for
the world around them and help them to see how writing to learn can be both fun and
instructional. The more opportunities they have to play, experiment, and engage with
informational types of writing, the stronger their skills become and the broader their
knowledge of the world grows.

CONTENT-AREA WRITING IDEAS

There are hundreds of writing ideas in a content area that do not involve report writing. Here is a sampling of a few.

- **ABC concept book:** Build schema around a concept or topic by encouraging students to brainstorm as many related ideas as there are letters in the alphabet.

- **Write a letter:** Choose a historical figure, scientist, or explorer and invite students to write a letter with questions they would like to pose to that person. Once they have studied or researched the person, perhaps another student could respond to the letter based on what they have learned.

- **Content comic**: Invite students to write a brief comic strip to demonstrate a concept, topic, or event. The comic should explain or demonstrate a main idea or important notion.

- **Concept poems**: Students express their understanding or interpretation of a concept in a free-form poem or by completing lines in a given template.

- **Paraphrasing:** Lift a line from a text or give a definition and ask students to rewrite it in their own words. Invite them to reword a math problem in a variety of ways. This skill can help them read more closely and demonstrate their understanding. This is excellent practice when they write informational texts.

- **Exit slips:** Students reflect on the learning, ideas, or processes used during class. They allow teachers to evaluate what the students' take-aways were or lingering questions might be. They can help students synthesize information or become more metacognitive with their learning.

  - Discuss one way you might use what we discussed today in your "real" life.

  - What title would you give today's lesson and why?

  - What questions do you still have or have you thought of during today's lesson?

- **Science journals:** Students keep track of lab experiment notes, observations, and hypotheses. This is a place for them to reflect on their thinking, wonder about their world, draw visuals of concepts they are trying to understand, and explore additional ideas.

  - What do you notice about the frog's body? What are you wondering?

  - Why do scientists need to know about the three types of rocks?

  - Create and explain a diagram of the water cycle.

- **Math journals:** Students and teachers use math journals to "show your work," but they can be insightful into students' understanding of concepts and attitudes toward math. Students can write about big ideas or individual solutions to problems in a paragraph or *mathagraph* (see Figure 6.3):

  - Why do we need to know how to use fractions?

  - When I worked on these problems today I felt _____.

- **Number of the day:** Give students a number. Each student must come up with a word problem that has that number for the answer.

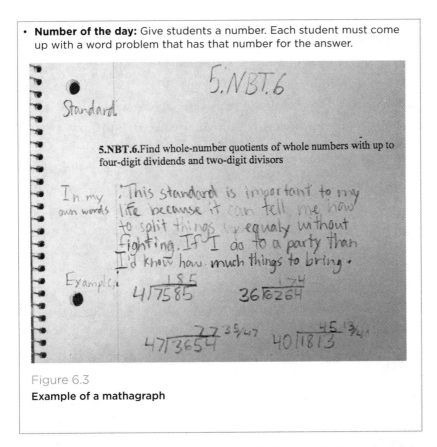

Figure 6.3
Example of a mathagraph

The idea is not to collect activities for students to do but to keep the focus on how writing can reflect and shape thinking. We want our students to write like mathematicians, scientists, or sociologists. Giving them opportunities for creative exploration can increase engagement and volume of writing, as well as deepen their thinking in all content areas.

SILENT CONVERSATIONS

In *The Best-Kept Teaching Secret: How Written Conversations Engage Kids, Activate Learning, and Grow Fluent Writers* (Daniels and Daniels 2013), Harvey "Smokey" Daniels shares a variety of options for increasing writing through written conversations. It was gratifying to see some of the work that we were already doing featured in the book, but it was also enlightening to see the positive effects touted in his research happening in our classrooms.

PEEK INSIDE A CLASSROOM: FIFTH-GRADE SILENT CONVERSATIONS

Becky Foster's fifth graders have been studying the Jamestown Settlement, reading passages that detailed many of the hardships the settlers endured. Today, they will have a silent conversation about those hardships. Becky and I introduce the activity to the students.

"You are going to have a conversation with a group of students in your class. In fact you will have several conversations, but they will be silent. Instead of talking, you'll be writing. Each of you will start a conversation by addressing this question: *What do you think would be the most difficult part of living in Jamestown? Why?* Then when we say *Pass,* you will pass your paper to the classmate on your right, read the paper you receive, and respond to it. You can agree, disagree, ask a question, give more information, or expand their idea. We'll repeat this several times."

They begin filling in the first conversation box with their thoughts (see Figure 6.4). There are some giggles and some requests for deciphering, but the classroom is calm, quiet, and busy. Once the papers have made it around the group, we ask students to take a look at the conversation they started and see what they noticed.

Figure 6.4

Becky's fifth graders have a silent conversation to discuss Jamestown.

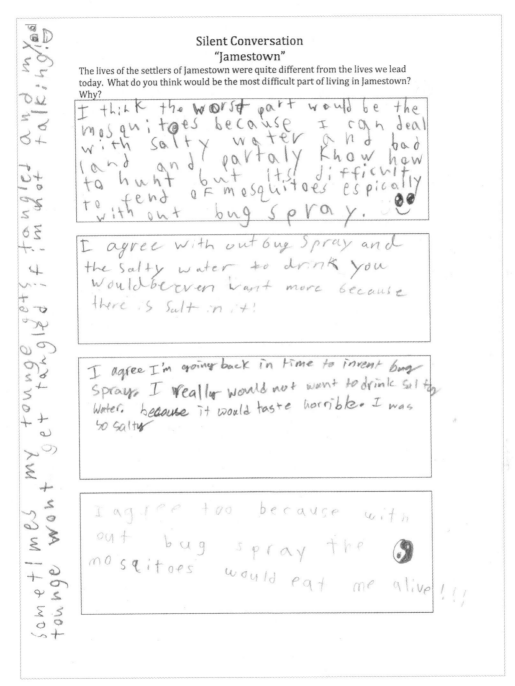

Figure 6.5

A silent conversation (and reflection in the margins) on the same topic

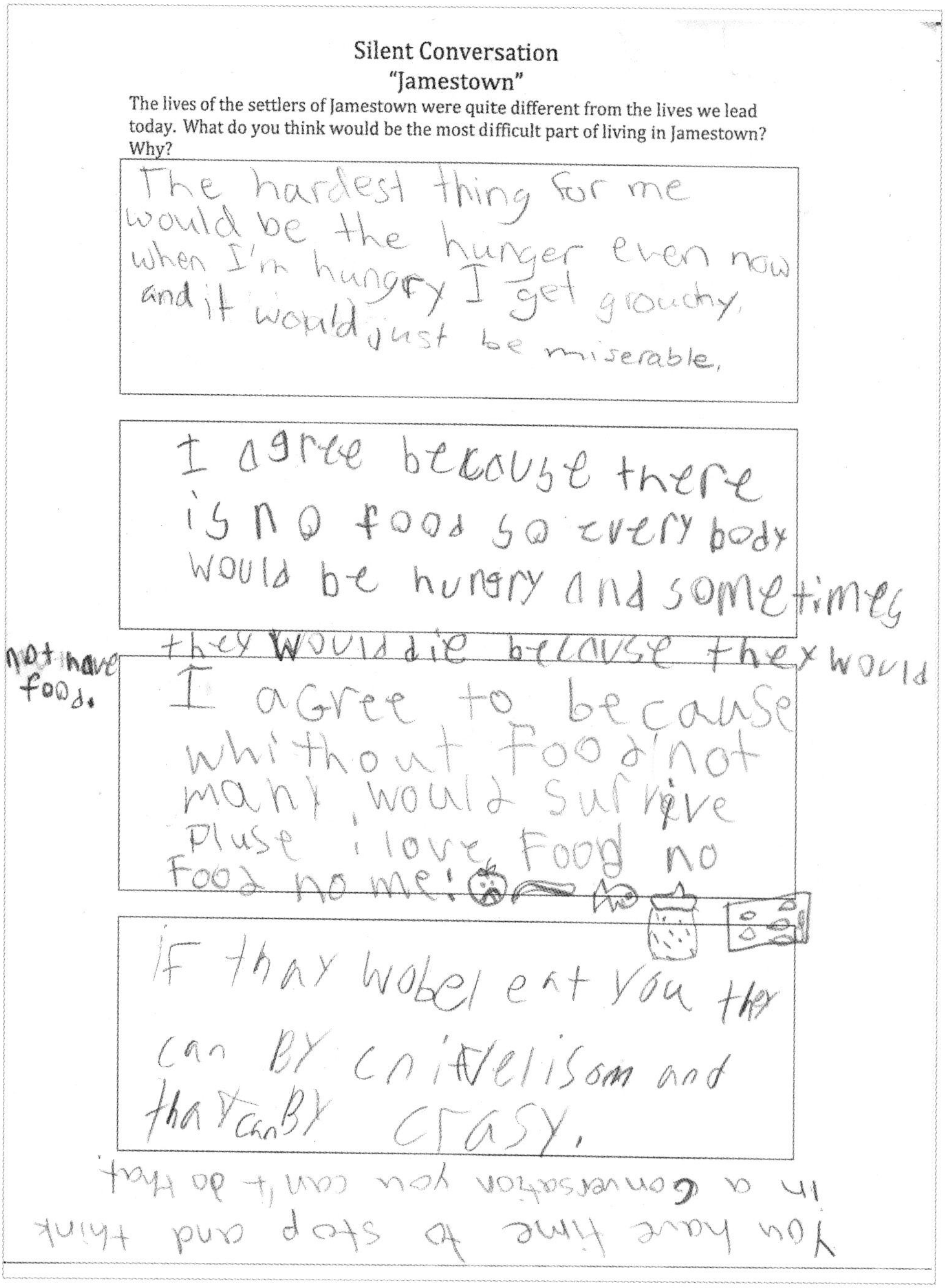

Silent Conversation
"Jamestown"

The lives of the settlers of Jamestown were quite different from the lives we lead today. What do you think would be the most difficult part of living in Jamestown? Why?

The hardest thing for me would be the hunger even now when I'm hungry I get grouchy, and it would just be miserable,

I agree becouse there is no food so every body would be hungry and sometimes they would die becouse they would not have food.

I aGree to because whithout food not many would surive pluse i love food no food no me!

if thay wobel eat you thy can BY cnivelisom and thay can BY crasy,

You have time to stop and think in a Conversation you can't do that.

Figure 6.6

A silent conversation (and reflection in the margins) on the same topic

I ask the students, "What do you think about this activity? How was this silent conversation different from a 'regular' conversation?"

Hands shoot into the air. "Usually, in a normal conversation, you have a lot of interruptions and people will come in and they don't know what you are talking about, and with this, people don't just barge in while you are saying something."

"When you're writing you have more time to think, because when you're in the middle of a conversation you don't want to stop and pause and think."

"When you're having a normal conversation everybody makes a mistake and says something they shouldn't, like when you're writing on paper you can just make a simple erase; you can't just change it when you are talking."

Becky and I are impressed with the students' engagement in the silent conversations, as well as their thoughts and reflections on the process afterward. When we look over the threads of conversations, it is clear that they are appreciating the hardships of the settlers and trying to put themselves in the shoes of the people of Jamestown (see examples in Figures 6.5 and 6.6). We are eager to try this process with other conversations.

GRAFFITI BOARDS

Cover a space with paper and provide markers for this writing activity. Invite students to write comments on a current topic such as a review of a read-aloud, opinions on an issue, or information on a subject of study (see Figure 6.7). Students can then respond to one another's comments. This can be done as a singular activity in which students take turns writing and responding in one lesson, or it can be kept up as an ongoing public writing event.

Our classrooms reflect what we value, and a classroom awash with writing in its many forms indicates that writing is revered and expected. Looking for opportunities to make it easy and acceptable for students to write will encourage engagement and volume. Not all writing needs to be long and involved. Frequent short bursts of writing are also valuable options for increasing the volume of writing across the school day.

Figure 6.7
Nicole's sixth graders share their thoughts about a book.

Time: Opportunities Within the Writing Workshop

I often work with students and teachers who are surprised at how little writing is accomplished in a thirty- to forty-five-minute workshop. It seems as though everyone is engaged and busy. So why is the volume of writing sometimes less than what we would expect? Several teachers and I explored the mystery when we closely observed the routines and structures of our writing workshops.

MINI-LESSON VERSUS MAXI-LESSON

A common remark I hear from teachers as they reflect on their instruction is regarding the length of their mini-lessons. Too often, mini-lessons can easily extend into maxi-lessons when we are not sharp and precise with our teaching. Mini-lessons are brief, focused lessons, typically no more than five to ten minutes. Model lessons, by contrast, are intentionally longer and used for introducing a technique or creating a text with or for the students. Whichever approach we use to kick off the day's workshop, we still want the majority of time to be spent on student writing. Occasionally, observing and noting the time frames of writing workshop can help us determine how much time we allocate for actual writing.

PLANNING VERSUS DISCOVERING

It is often said that you should write about what you know. I completely disagree. I get bored writing about the topics that I thoroughly understand. I find that I get better writing from—and really enjoy—writing about the things I wonder about.—Lynda Mullaly Hunt

We need to show our students that writing is a way to discover and explore ideas. This can be quite liberating for students who often exclaim, "I don't know what to write." We can model this by sharing our own struggles in coming up with ideas or topics. How do we get started? Where does our thinking take us? Too many kids think writing is complete inside the heads of the author and just comes spilling out. If they don't have a whole story or idea conceived, they often give up before they even begin.

For some of our young writers, an excessive amount of time is dedicated to planning their writing, which can shorten the amount of time available for drafting and revising. Lists, story maps, outlines, and notes should help students quickly organize the big ideas of their writing and help them focus. Students stuck in the "I'm thinking" mode are almost paralyzed by the number of choices and options that writing presents. Their planning should be a road map rather than a minute-by-minute itinerary of their writing journey.

Many students have also learned to think of writing as one and done! If they hear the phrase *first draft*, their immediate response is often, "How many drafts are we supposed to do?" To them, the ordinal number *first* signifies a predetermined number of drafts that will be required of them. They envision rewriting their work over and over, making it neater or perhaps a little longer.

The term *rough draft* is often thought of as the "sloppy copy" that is later copied onto nicer paper with neater handwriting or possibly typed. For close writers, drafts are thought of as stronger versions of their writing, shaped with new information, perspectives, ideas, or word choices, not simply the number of required times they must rewrite a piece.

DISCOVERY DRAFTS

REFRAMING THE IDEA OF DRAFTS

Donald Murray talks about discovery drafts in his classic text *The Craft of Revision* (Murray 2013). Whenever we engage in writing, we need to start somewhere. Sometimes where we end looks nothing like the way we started. The process of writing is itself a discovery. How can we uncover the story beneath the story?

- Encourage students to think about initial attempts at writing as discovery drafts.
  "Revisit and reread your writing to help you discover things about the piece of writing, as well as about yourself as a writer. Discover your likes and dislikes, your habits, your strengths, and your needs to help you grow as a writer."

- Teachers can model a think-aloud of discovery for the students.
  "I'm noticing that I haven't really described my character for the reader, I might want to add a physical description." "I like how I used a metaphor here, I want to look for some other places to help make those comparisons."

Students can either do a quick-write discovery draft or take out an older draft and reread it to see what they discover about it or within it (or about themselves as writers). Encourage students to jot down some discoveries on a sticky note, the magnifying glass notes (available online at www.stenhouse.com/closewritingbook), or in the margins.

It is difficult to say how much planning is too much, too little, or just right. The idea of close writing is to help students to become more acquainted with their writing identities and to recognize how their process affects their product. When we consistently tell them how to plan, we are removing the opportunity of discovery for them. Giving them a chance to reflect on their process is key to close writing.

Attitude

There is a complex relationship between attitude and behaviors. Sometimes we can work on adjusting our attitude to change behavior. Other times changing our behavior can often result in a changed attitude. Savvy teachers understand this dynamic and attend to the needs of their students on both fronts. They understand that they can't make a student do or like something, but they recognize there are many factors that influence attitude and behavior that we can address.

ROUTINES AND RITUALS: HABITS FOR A HEALTHY ATTITUDE

Paige Dyer is a third-grade teacher who has created an environment for her writers that triggers an almost automatic writing response. After her mini-lesson, she turns on some quiet music. Students quickly find a spot in the room and the pencils start moving. She does not answer questions or talk with students while they settle in, it is only when they are absorbed in their work that she will commence her writing conferences (see Figure 6.8). In Paige's classroom, the physical environment shapes the behavior of her students.

In classrooms with consistent routines and clear expectations during writing, students develop habits that drive their behavior. The environment influences our actions, sometimes more than our verbal directions. If we notice that our students have developed habits that are not supporting engaged writing, we can help them in two important ways. First, we can examine the environment and expectations to make sure they are more conducive to writing than any other activity. Second, we can help our students become more mindful of their behaviors and habits.

Figure 6.8
Paige confers with students while quiet music plays in the background.

A revealing method for examining both the environment and student behavior is to videotape our writing workshops and share this with our students. What do we notice? How can we create a more supportive setting? How are my behaviors (student or teacher) contributing to or detracting from writing? What is working well? What are some roadblocks we need to address?

Reflecting together removes value judgments that often come when we try to share our observations. It increases student ownership in problem solving. It fosters more self-regulation because students are not being told what to do. They can see for themselves what needs to be done. Reflecting on the effectiveness of routines and organization with our students can also help them to become more metacognitive: the heart of close writing.

THE POWER OF INERTIA

An object at rest tends to stay at rest, and an object in motion tends to stay in motion . . . —Isaac Newton's first law of motion

Habits and routines can be a form of inertia; they keep us in motion even when our hearts aren't into it. I notice this every spring when I resume a more consistent running routine. Each day that I go out creates a habit that drives my behavior. Clothes laid out, shoes by the door, and time set aside make it easy for me to go for a run. I find each day that the run seems less difficult. But if I skip a day or two, it becomes easier to make excuses not to run and harder to get back into the routine. I am beginning to see this in my own writing now. When I commit to writing each day, even just a little (a body in motion), it makes it so much easier to get back into the piece and into the swing of things. When I take a day or two off (a body at rest), I feel more disconnected from my writing and slower to get back into the flow of it.

I also see this with our students. If they don't write each day, it often takes them more time to get back into a regimen. It's less automatic and more sporadic. We teachers may recognize this, but it is more important that our students do. We can look for opportunities to raise their awareness. Celebrate those moments when kids don't want to stop writing. Recognize those times when it is tough to start writing. Sometimes students think they are alone with those perceptions. Helping them to understand that all writers experience these conditions can encourage a more mindful approach to their writing.

TUNING IN TO ATTITUDE

When students say, "I don't like writing" or "I'm not good at writing," I want to understand what it is about writing that causes them to feel that way. It is important for our writers to connect with their underlying attitudes if we want them to create a stronger relationship with their writing. Ignoring their feelings or denying their perceptions doesn't make them go away, it pushes them underground. Acknowledging our students' thoughts and feelings establishes a basis on which we can begin our work together.

We asked about a hundred students to share their attitudes or feelings about writing. Here are variations of the most common responses:

WHAT IS IT ABOUT WRITING THAT MAKES YOU FEEL GOOD?

• Writing makes me feel free and like I'm in a totally different world.

• I like to write because it tells people what I know.

• It kind of keeps me calm and it's fun.

• That you can put your feelings inside your notebook and when you have a rough day write your feelings inside the paper or the notebook.

• I love to write because I can write about fairies and it lets me be me, to be free of what's happening around me, and lets me be inspired.

WHAT IS IT ABOUT WRITING THAT DOESN'T MAKE YOU FEEL GOOD?

• I don't like how sometimes the teacher makes us write about what she wants us to write about and I just want to write freely.

• I don't like writing about fiction because I make them too funny and I get in trouble when I laugh.

• It doesn't make me feel good when I do revising because it is hard to think what I should take out to change.

• Sometimes I don't like to write because if something bothers you and you write about it, it may bother you more.

• It takes a lot of time and thinking. It's hard.

DO YOU WRITE OUTSIDE OF SCHOOL? IF SO, IS IT DIFFERENT FROM SCHOOL WRITING? HOW?

• It is different because I add lots of pictures.

• I can write in Arabic.

• No. I don't write outside of school unless I am forced to.

• Yes, it is different because I can write about anything and not have to deal with being told what to change.

• No, I don't have paper for it.

> **IF YOU COULD BE THE TEACHER . . .**
>
> - If I could teach writing I would let them do the best they can and review the mistakes later. The story could be about anything.
> - If I was the teacher I would have kids act out their stories and write comic books.
> - Let them choose what to write. Make it fun to write instead of pushing them to write.
> - If I was a teacher I would make it so you can write letters to each other.

Taking time to discover their views and perspectives with regards to writing can help us reflect on our teaching practice and environments and appreciate the wide variety of needs and perspectives. It can also help students get in touch with their writing identities, which is a critical component of close writing. What questions would you ask your students?

RECOGNIZING AND SHAPING MINDSET

Carol Dweck's fascinating book *Mindset: The New Psychology of Success* (Dweck 2006) explores the power of our perception and the way we approach our goals. She calls this *mindset* and categorized the two types as *fixed* or *growth*. Students with a fixed mindset avoided taking academic risks because they don't believe that effort plays a role in success. They believe their intelligence is fixed and talent (or lack of it) determines your success. Students with a growth mindset understand that their potential is limited only by the effort and attention that they give their work. They are motivated to try new things and reflect on their work.

The type of mindset our students identify with will influence their ability to be close writers. Students with a fixed mindset do not wish to reread, reflect on, or revise their work because they do not believe it can be improved. Getting close to their writing might shatter their notions about talent and be hard to face. They may hear comments about their writing as a judgment on how smart they are rather than as a possibility for growth and improvement. Students with a growth mindset, however, will embrace close writing strategies as an opportunity to become stronger, more reflective writers.

FOSTERING A GROWTH MINDSET

LANGUAGE TO SUPPORT CLOSE WRITING

- Set clear expectations and acknowledge that to achieve them will require effort.
  "This might be a little tricky, but I know you can do it, and I'll help you if you have any questions."

- Encourage reflection and celebrate revision.
  "Who can share an example where they closely read their story and revised it for _____."

- Reframe mistakes as opportunities.
  "So when you went back to read your story, you noticed that part was a little confusing. That is a great example of close writing."

- Give feedback that focuses on the process, not just the product.
  "You reread your story for spicy words and revised quite a few."

- Tap into the power of *yet*. It conveys your faith in their ability to accomplish something.
  "You don't have any punctuation around your dialogue; *yet*, when you do, it will be much easier for us to see who is talking."

- Encourage more effort from students who succeed with little effort.
  "Looks like you are ready for a challenge. You deserve to grow as a writer in this classroom, too."

- Reflect on your own learning and growth; make it visible for students.
  "I'm not really excited about how I started this piece. I think I want to go back and try a few other leads."

- Post "look-fors" (see Chapter 11) next to student work to focus readers' attention on growth in writing.
  "One thing I'd like you to notice is how I worked on creating a realistic setting in my story. I used to have pretty generic settings, but now I am much more descriptive."

- Share brain research with your students to help them appreciate how their thinking works.
  "The largest part of your brain is the cerebrum. It is responsible for thinking, talking, and remembering. Let's give our cerebrum a workout today in writing."

The feedback we give students can greatly shape their attitudes and mindset. One of the simplest changes I made to my language became one of the most powerful. Replacing "I like . . ." with "I noticed . . ." shifted the emphasis from pleasing the teacher to reflecting on the process. Try it out and see how much more specific your feedback becomes with a change in those two little words. Encouraging your students to use that sentence stem when giving feedback to others can help them to be more aware of specific aspects of writing.

Stamina: The Quantitative Process of Writing

Several years ago my son started running 5K races with me. We took off from the same place and needed to complete the same distance but nothing else was similar in our races. I had built up my stamina for running so that I could sustain a consistent pace, with perhaps a small kick at the end. My son had intense bursts of speed, followed by a need to rest or walk before sprinting on again. We did not have the same stamina, but we were each able to complete the task successfully.

Some writers in our classrooms have a steady, consistent stamina for engaged writing, while others move forward in fits and starts. Do we recognize the individual approaches our students may bring to the process and evaluate their effectiveness?

Figure 6.9
Resting writer

Can we broaden our definition of stamina to include variations in style? How do these differences in stamina affect our students' volume of writing, and how can we help all writers to grow stronger?

THE PHYSIOLOGY OF WRITING WORK

Walk into any classroom and you are sure to see students engaged in a variety of seated postures. Some have their entire upper body strewn across their desktop (see Figure 6.9). Some tip precariously backward, balancing on two of the four chair feet. Others sit sideways or hunched over, with notebooks in their laps. Some students tightly grasp and push their pencils across the page, whereas the timid, awkward pencil grip of other students leaves a slightly darker shade of invisible on their papers. Do all the variations of student ergonomics play a role in the stamina students sustain for writing?

When students understand some of the basic physiology of writing work, they can mindfully adjust their behaviors to support their stamina. They can see that they have some control over some of the basic aspects of their learning. For many, they do not see a correlation between their writing behavior and their writing ability. We can help them make this connection.

Over the years, I have worked with our occupational therapist, Val Sugden, to support students in classrooms. My conversations with Val and other teachers have helped me look more purposefully for conditions that support or hinder writing.

QUESTIONS TO CONTEMPLATE CONDITIONS FOR STAMINA

- What were students doing prior to writing workshop? Sitting? Moving?
- Where are students expected to work? Desks, table, floor?
- Are the desks or tables set at a height that supports writing posture or hinders it?
- What physical complaints are students describing? Sore hand? Tired?
- How frequently are the students given or allowed breaks?

Our conversations also remind me that we adults have been writing for a lot of years and probably put very little thought into the technical requirements for transcribing our thoughts onto paper. We have had time to build up the strength and attention span needed to write with almost no effort. If we wanted to develop some empathy for our students, we could do the following:

- Try writing with our nondominant hand for ten or fifteen minutes (or the length of your typical writing workshop).

- Try sitting still at a desk for the length of writing workshop.

- Try writing in a language that is foreign or new to us.

Then we can reflect on what we notice to build empathy and anticipate the needs of our striving students. Close writing isn't just for students, we can become more mindful as we teach and walk in the shoes of these young writers.

RAISING AWARENESS TO FOSTER SELF-REGULATION

Argue for your limitations, and sure enough, they're yours.
—Richard Bach

Even with the most organized and thoughtful preparation, there will still be factors that can influence our stamina for writing. At some point, we want students to recognize when they aren't as engaged as they could be and take some responsibility for adjusting behaviors that are distracting or hindering their ability to write. When we hear common complaints during writing, this can be a great teachable moment for problem solving and self-regulation.

Physical Stamina

"My hand hurts."

- Can I adjust my grip? How tight am I holding, or how hard am I pushing the pencil? Are there dents or redness on my fingers?

- Can I shake out my hand and take a few deep breaths?

- Would using a pencil grip or a pen help me?

- Have I tried giving myself a quick hand massage?

"I'm tired."

- Am I hunching over and putting strain on my neck, shoulders, and back? (Rounding the shoulders can cause compression of the chest cavity, which reduces air capacity in the lungs and oxygen intake. This can lead to lower energy levels and headaches.)

- Are the lights or the sounds in the room making me sleepy? (Sometimes an environment that fosters creative calm can contribute to fatigue. Seek student input to set up the best conditions; mix it up from time to time if there is no consensus.)

- Would a quick stamina break help me get back on track or would it distract me? (Decide on the guidelines ahead of time; the break should support writing, not avoid it.)

- Am I hungry or thirsty? (Kids who are hungry, a bit dehydrated, or sleep deprived will lack the energy required to be fully engaged in their writing. Decide on snack and water-break procedures as a class. Invite students to research the effect of sleep deprivation on learning. Awareness is the first step in changing behavior.)

"My eyes get tired."

- Am I sitting too close to the computer screen, or have I been on the computer too long?

- Have I tried a few eye exercises? (Try looking at the end of your nose and then looking out the window to a point far in the distance or move your eyes from side to side.)

- Have I talked to my parents or school nurse about any eye problems? (Students who consistently complain about their eyes should be evaluated by a school nurse or an eye doctor. However, occasional eyestrain is common when students are studying or working with computers for long periods of time or in certain lighting conditions.)

"That takes too long to write."

- Do I need more practice making my letters and words more efficiently?

- Would a pen or keyboard make it easier? (This would depend on prior approval from the teacher.)

- Could I share the pen with someone? (Co-writing with a teacher or a peer could be a preapproved option for some students. They are responsible for the ideas and get support for scripting.)

- Am I letting myself get distracted or interrupted? How can I keep myself more focused?

Mental Stamina

Stamina also requires mental focus. Writers often put a lot of themselves into their writing, and it can be emotionally or mentally draining. The topic may be difficult for the students to write about or the assignment may be challenging. We teachers cannot always anticipate how our students will react to a writing assignment, but we can recognize when students are struggling, acknowledge their challenges, and look for ways to support them. Close writers understand their emotional connection to their writing and the ramifications for how to approach it.

STAMINA BREAKS

SUPPORTING SELF-DIRECTED WRITERS

Students lack stamina for a variety of reasons. Directing them to keep writing is rarely effective in fostering quality work. Students need to understand the factors that influence their stamina and take ownership in problem solving those negative factors.

- Survey students or brainstorm for issues that affect students' ability to stay focused on their writing. Create a list.

- If possible, group and categorize the list. Perhaps you could identify teacher issues and student issues to determine who would be responsible for solving them. Another possibility is to identify physical issues and feeling issues to help them classify a physical or mental stamina cause.

- Invite students to come up with solutions or remedies that could help. Create a chart that could be referenced during writing workshop.

- Practice how these remedies might work during class to support more writing instead of avoiding writing. Will there be rules, guidelines, or protocols?

  - *Stamina break cards*. If a student needs a brief (one- to two-minute) break, they set the card on their notebook. They can then refer to an agreed on break activity, such as stand and stretch, hand or eye massage, drink or bathroom break.

- Occasionally, debrief on how these techniques are helping. Encourage students to reflect. "Who tried something today that helped them to build stamina? How did it help?"

If "solutions" do not result in more sustained and focused writing, students will need to be made aware of that and held accountable for making more effective choices.

Whatever issues our students may experience that are roadblocks to their writing can be seen as opportunities to engage in close writing conversations. Invite students to offer solutions as well as indicators for success. The ideas should lead to better, measurable writing outcomes by the teacher as well as by students. This is how we become a community of writers who support one another.

Considerations for English Language Learners

Writing is an immersion in language. The more our students write, the more immersed in vocabulary, grammar, structure, and conventions they become. Opportunities like quick-writes free up the English language learner (ELL) student from the pressures of producing perfect writing. When they can practice letting their ideas flow onto the paper, they will gain skill with automaticity. They can focus on ideas and not conventions of our language; they don't have to worry about being "right."

Content-area writing gives our ELL students exposure to and practice with the vocabulary of those subjects. The academic language they face in science, social studies, or math varies greatly from the social or literary language they encounter during writing workshop. Experiences with writing outside of the language arts block provide exposure and practice with this specific vocabulary.

Silent conversations also encourage engagement for our ELL students. Because everyone is expected to participate, they are encouraged to add their own thinking to the discussion, no matter how long or short their response may be. They can read and reread the comments of their peers at a pace that allows them to comprehend and reflect. The reading level of the written conversations should be accessible to many students because they are the words and ideas of their peers, not those of a textbook author.

Looking for opportunities when our ELL students can write in their native language could also be an accommodation that could scaffold their writing. Though this is controversial in many schools, this option may encourage our students to do more writing. Perhaps freewrites, homework, or independent projects would lend themselves to this. It might be a conversation worth having in your schools to look at the pros and cons of this approach.

The Gist of the Story

For students to develop a writing identity, they have to be writers. For students to get better at writing, they have to write a lot. For students to become close writers, they have to connect and reflect on their writing: both product and process. As teachers, we can help with this by examining and encouraging the volume of writing and stamina of writers in our classrooms. Some ways we have tried include the following:

- Helping students recognize the importance of volume and stamina for becoming stronger writers.

- Looking for opportunities to "sneak" more writing into our day.

- Fostering habits and routines that motivate and activate more writing.

- Noticing the amount of time actually spent writing during writing workshop.

- Building stamina for writing over time: both physical and mental.

- Raising students' awareness of their writing process to spark self-regulation.

- Fostering a growth mindset in our writers so that they are open to reflection, revision, and rereading as opportunities to become more skilled in their craft.

- Collaborating with students to problem-solve any roadblocks that hinder volume and stamina.

Drafting Your Story

Take a moment to think about the function of volume and stamina in your classroom. On your own, or with colleagues, reflect on your current thinking:

- What are your expectations regarding volume of writing in your classroom? How have you shared that with your students?

- What does writing stamina look like to you? What does it look like to your students?

- What factors have you noticed with your students that might be inhibiting their writing volume or stamina? How can you and your students address them?

- Can you recognize the type of mindset your students have toward learning? How have you seen it affect their writing?

- What is something you would like to try after reading this chapter?

CHAPTER 7

Rereading and Reflecting

Until children are able to reread their work critically, revision is anathema. —Donald Graves

We've probably all had those moments when we've pulled our car into the driveway, switched off the key, and then thought, *I don't really remember the drive home.* When this happened to me in the past, I would reflect on the experience and realize I was operating on autopilot. I didn't think about my choices as I drove because I wasn't anticipating any need for variation. My drive lacked awareness and deliberation because it was so habituated.

The moral of this story: Close writers closely read (reread) and mindfully reflect to discover new things about their writing and themselves as writers.

This method closely parallels the modus operandi of many of the writers in our rooms who approach their writing with the same well-ingrained habits and minimal mindfulness. If it gets them home, they have little incentive to alter their behavior or raise their consciousness. To move our writers forward, we need to modify the journey's end from the routine safety of home to a more purposeful destination.

Along the Road to Revision

Writing is such a personal endeavor. We are putting little pieces of ourselves down on the paper with each word we pen. Having to change something can feel like a personal rejection. Something wrong with my writing may feel like something is wrong with me. Having someone else point it out to me can make me wonder, *Why didn't I see that?* Students are almost always looking for approval when they hand you their work to read. "Do you like it? Is it good?" are often the first words out of a student's mouth when they hand over their papers.

Close writing encourages students to look, decide, and act by themselves when creating a piece of writing. Our role as teachers is to focus on the writer, not the writing, to help our students shift from the idea of fixing their writing to empowering the writer inside them. That may mean helping them to look but not telling them what to see. It may mean letting some things go (for now) so that the student is more in control of what and how they revise. It means celebrating progression over perfection.

Rereading
Each time you reread you see or learn something new.
—Ernest Hemingway

I am in a second-grade classroom where students have been working on writing personal narratives. A student asks if I would like to hear his story (see Figure 7.1).

"It was so cold I went home. I didn't get to fish and I went home and I went home . . . 'wait, I just said that.'" He looks a little puzzled but continues ". . . and took my—'I think that's supposed to be stuff or shoe, I got mixed up. I'll say *stuff* . . . and took my stuff off and went inside and played a game and we went to a game and my dad came home and went to the game. 'Wait, I said that again. I said, We played a game and we went to a game and my dad went to the game.'"

"Does that sound the way you want it to?" I ask.

Leon starts laughing, "No. That sounds stupid. I just kept saying it a bunch."

It can become painfully obvious at times that a student hasn't read or reread a piece of writing before they turn it in or attempt to share it with you. Like Leon, they stumble through repetitions and sentence fragments; they have difficulty deciphering their spelling or handwriting, and make comments that begin with, "Wait, that should say . . ." Often their inability to fluently read their writing takes away from the work that they put into it and obscures the message they are trying to convey.

If our students aren't naturally rereading their writing, we need to explicitly teach them and then establish that expectation (see Chapter 3). Until students can see the benefits of rereading their writing, they often won't think to do it on their own. Close writing is purposeful writing. Students need to understand why we ask them to do things, so that they can take on greater control and responsibility for the behaviors. Rereading their work is a crucial step toward this awareness so we need help them see its purpose.

I asked several published authors about their process for rereading their work. Gae Polisner (*The Pull of Gravity, The Summer of Letting Go*) talked

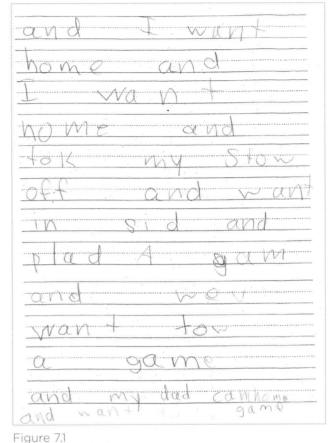

Figure 7.1

Leon makes some discoveries as he reads his draft.

about her focus when closely reading her own work. "I'm listening for a lot of things: for flow and the words to make sense out loud the way they did in my head, for cadence—a certain rhythm or poetry that works to my brain and mostly authenticity. I'm asking questions, such as *Does this feel real to me? Would my kids say this to their friends? Would I hear a kid say this to their parents?*" Authors don't reread to just look for errors; they are looking for their voice in those words.

Author Linda Urban (*A Crooked Kind of Perfect, The Center of Everything*) talked to me about her rereading. "I read my work aloud during revision. I write, often, by rhythm. The sentences have to bump and thump and clang in the right places, and I can't always tell if that is happening when I read them silently. But when I read aloud, I can hear if a sentence is too long, if you lose the rhythm of it before you get to the end. I like when sounds and words echo each other, especially in dialogue, but I want all of those echoes to be intentional." These authors know the importance of rereading with purpose. Helping our student develop habits like the mentor authors they admire can begin with some consistent expectations.

REWIND/REPLAY

REREADING TO MONITOR AND DRAFT

For some of our young writers, the writing seems confusing, disjointed, or inconsistent. They don't seem to notice that their ideas do not connect well. They may need to revisit what has been previously written before continuing on.

- If you have an old cassette tape player, the lesson will be much more concrete for the students, but the analogy is that just like a tape player, we can rewind and replay our words to make sure they are clear and say what we want them to say.

- You can model this by writing a sentence on the board under the document camera. Before going to the next sentence or paragraph, "rewind and replay" it (i.e., reread it to make sure it says what you want it to say).

  - Think aloud any changes, wonderings, or revisions to the text you would like to make before moving on.

  - Model how going back and rereading helps the writer to continue the story more seamlessly as you orally share what you would write next.

- Invite students to try the rewind and replay strategy as they are writing. Listen in/check in with students on their use of the strategy.

The frequency for rewinding and replaying will vary for writers. Some students may need to rewind after every few sentences, or a paragraph, or a page. Writers need a strategy (a habit) for monitoring what they write to clarify and/or to continue with their ideas in a more seamless way.

PEEK INSIDE A CLASSROOM: REWIND AND FIND

Andrea Bryant gives her fifth-grade students copious amounts of time to work on writing ideas and projects of their choice. Today, we will encourage the habit of rereading their writing. Students are asked to select a piece of writing they have previously written and have it open on their desks. I introduce the Rewind and Find strategy to the group.

"Today, we are going to look at a rereading strategy that you could turn into a powerful habit before you begin writing each day. I call it Rewind and Find because you back up, or rewind, and reread something you've already written, and see what you can find that might help make your writing stronger."

I write Rewind and Find on the chart paper. "You might find a sentence that was never finished, a word that doesn't make sense, or a place where punctuation is missing. You might not find any 'mistakes' [I use air quotes], but you may find a place where more details would make it better or where you thought of better word choices. I'll give you a few minutes to reread your piece and make some kind of notes to show what you find."

Andrea takes out a piece of writing she has been working on and does her own rereading. One boy sitting near her keeps looking over to see what his teacher might be discovering. Andrea thinks it's important for the students to see her engaged in the tasks she asks of them. She doesn't just want to assign; she wants to inspire.

"I noticed a lot of you reading and marking some things on your work. Who was able to rewind and find something?" Hands shoot into the air. Students find a

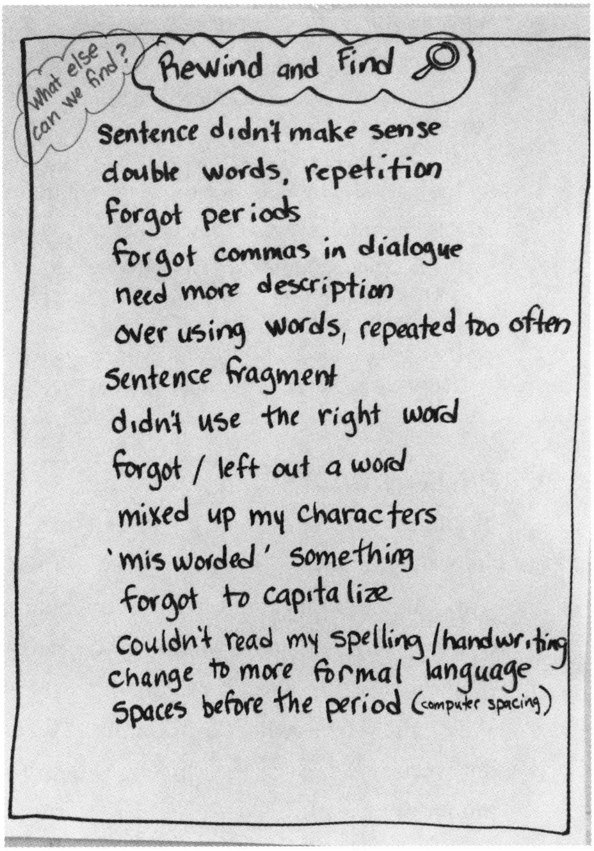

Figure 7.2
Observations from Rewind and Find

sentence that didn't make any sense, wrote the words *as* twice, forget to put commas in their dialogue, and so forth. I create a list on the chart of "finds" from their writing (Figure 7.2).

"Wow, in about three minutes of rereading our pieces, we were able to find all of these things pretty easily that we could work on to make our writing better. Imagine if you did this each day before you started writing; just go back and reread something you've previously written to see what you might find. How much stronger would your writing be by the time you were done with a story or a project?"

Andrea shares her thinking. "Do you know I've already read this piece I'm writing about seven times, and I still found some things when I reread it just now. I can't find everything if I only reread once." We leave the list posted in the classroom and invite students to add to it when they do their own rewind and find.

> **REWIND AND FIND**
>
> REREADING TO DISCOVER
>
> To develop a habit for routine rereading before writing, do the following several times a week:
>
> - Invite students to revisit a piece they are working on or even one from the past and reread for three to five minutes.
> - Ask them to see what they notice when they read closely.
> - Invite a few students to share their discoveries. Celebrate the skill as a positive strategy rather than a focus on a mistake they may have previously made.
> - List a few discoveries on a magnifying glass poster or keep an ongoing list of discoveries to encourage possible "look-fors" for other writers.

PROXY READING

Sometimes as much as we try to be observant and careful in our close reading, when it comes to our own writing, it is easy to miss things. We are so close to the ideas of the story that our brains tend to fill in the blanks if something is missing or askew. We may read over words that we we doubled, insert words we have out, or ignore the weigh we spell some words. (See, it's frequently easier to notice errors in someone else's writing!) We can help by slowing down our pace, focusing on a specific element, and even reading our work aloud. Even then, it might help to have another set of eyes or ears to help us monitor our work.

Proxy reading is an approach in which another person stands in as either the ears or eyes for the writer. It encourages greater perspective on a piece of writing and let's the writer take an Authorial Reading I stance (How does this look or sound to me?) and/ or Authorial Reading II stance (How does this look or sound to others?) This can be an eye-opener for some writers when they see how an intended audience receives and interprets their work.

PROXY EARS

With this more familiar approach, students read their piece aloud to their audience, who becomes the "ears" for the writer. The audience must listen with a specific purpose (re-petitive word choice, use or omission of transitions, dry or vivid verbs, variety of speech tags, or any recent focus of instruction). They could also retell what they have heard so that the writer can reflect on the clarity of his or her intended message.

REREAD AND REPLAY

PROXY EARS

It's one thing to read to ourselves. A piece of writing often makes perfect sense because our brains fill in the missing pieces so readily. This activity gives the writer the opportunity to share his or her work with an audience, who will listen closely and replay what they see in their minds.

- Remind *writers* that they should read at a pace and volume that helps the listener to create an image of their words. (You may wish to revisit writer reading practice in Chapter 3.)

- Remind the *listeners* that they are trying to get a clear picture in their heads of what they hear and will be sharing that with the writer.

- The writer shares a paragraph or short page of his text while the listener is trying to visualize the image those words evoke. (The writer should not share any illustrations that may trump the verbal message.)

- The listener replays the visualization to the writer. "In my mind, I see_____." "What I heard you say was _____."

- If the writer thinks the listener missed something or has a mismatched image, she should discuss this before reading on further. Are there different words the writer could have used? Would more details be helpful? Would it help the listener to hear it again?

PROXY EYES

With this approach, the writing is read aloud by a partner, who becomes the writer's eyes. This can provide a unique Authorial Reading II perspective. (How does it look and sound to others?) We can see quickly how considerate our writing is for other readers. We get immediate feedback on the legibility of our penmanship and the quality of our spelling by how easily the reader can decipher our text. If the reader is confused by run-on sentences or lack of punctuation, this becomes apparent as they stumble and backtrack.

Proxy reading isn't just an activity to find and fix mistakes. It is also a way to foster authorial reading skills. It allows writers to experience their words through the point of view of potential readers. It may not shape this particular piece of writing, but eventually it will find its way into all of their future writings once they gain that perspective.

> **LISTEN AND LEARN**
>
> HEARING OUR WRITING READ TO US
>
> We may benefit from being our own audience as someone else (teacher, partner) reads our work. The reader should not attempt to fix or alter any of the writing as he or she reads.
>
> - Partner students with a competent reader. It does not help the writer to listen to a struggling reader.
>
> - The author may listen for a specific focus (close) or with a more general stance (open). The teacher can help determine or suggest a purpose.
>
> - The reader may pause after a paragraph or page to give the writer time to process what she is hearing. Either may decide to mark sections of the text that will be revisited or revised.
>
> - When finished, invite the writer to reflect on what he learned, noticed, wondered, or discovered.
>
> A variation of this exercise would be to turn on the text to speech application if word processing. Sometimes hearing our writing in a monotone voice can help us to notice problems in our writing we might not have previously considered.

Reflecting
It's not what you look at that matters, it's what you see.
—Henry David Thoreau

When we look into a mirror, we see a reflection of ourselves. Our stance, distance, or angle dictates what we see. When we look into our writing, we see a reflection of our writing selves that is also determined by our stance. As writing teachers, we can help students hold that mirror up to their writing to assist them in seeing their writing identities more clearly. Sometimes our reflection is so familiar that we don't look closely. We need to think about varying the stances, focuses, or lenses that our students use so that they can see themselves as more mindful writers.

CHOOSING LENSES

Walking along our Maine beaches, there are so many things to see. Depending on where and how you look, you'd be amazed at the variety of sights you will find sitting on a single rock at the water's edge. With a wide lens (see Figure 7.3), you can gaze out over the waves and spot harbor seals or porpoises breaking the surface, or you can glance back over your shoulder to watch the piping plovers nesting near the dune grass. With a closer

Figure 7.3
Seeing with a wide lens

Figure 7.4
Seeing with a close lens

lens (see Figure 7.4), you can spy periwinkles making their way across the wet sand or green crabs scooting sideways among the rockweed in the tide pools. Your choice of lens (focus) dictates what you will see.

In writing, we can look with a very close lens for specific elements, or we can step back and look widely at an entire piece or even a body of work and see something entirely different. With close writing strategies, I want to give our students opportunities to vary the lenses with which they look at their writing, so they can analyze their work and enhance their perception of themselves as writers.

PEEK INSIDE A CLASSROOM: REFLECTING ON SENTENCE STRUCTURE

Haley Duncan's fourth-grade students are writing informational articles. They have conducted brief research on a self-selected topic and written an initial draft. Haley knows from experience that sometimes students' early drafts sound like lists of facts that may or may not relate to one another. They have talked about how transition words help to connect those sentences and ideas to one another. She advises the students: "Sometimes when you take notes and put them into sentences it may sound like a list of facts. *Lions are carnivores. Lions hunt animals. Lions stalk prey.* It can sound like a repetitive pattern." She taps out the cadence, *Bump, bump, bump. Bump, bump, bump.*

"I'm going to have you choose a paragraph or two and read it aloud to yourself to see if you notice any patterns. Do you think your sentences kind of flow together with some transition words, or do all sentences start the same or end the same? Can you hear if it is *bump, bump, bump* ... fact, fact, fact? Or do you use transition words from our list, such as *for example* or *however* to connect ideas together?"

The students use the Cranium Reading strategy of reading aloud the text to themselves, and then Haley gives them an opportunity to share what they notice or hear in their writing. Some comments include: "All of my sentences started with the same word." "I used transition words, but it was like the same word every time." The students are beginning to tune in to qualities of writing they hadn't considered before. They can now envision revision!

PEEK INSIDE A CLASSROOM: REFLECTING ON EFFORT

Dan Johnston is determined that his sixth-grade students become self-regulated learners. His students are struggling to get back into a routine after Christmas break; they aren't focusing as well, and the quality of their work is decreasing. As he notices what is going on, he has a class conversation about what it means to try. He gives them a writing prompt: *What does the word* try *mean to you?*

He collects and reads them over and then decides to share them with the class. He reads the prompts to the class, and they discuss their differing views. They then discuss the similarities among them. Dan decides to take a few lines from each prompt to see whether he can create a poem. He shares this mashup with the students, and they are amazed with the result.

Try

Try is more than just a word

It is the building blocks of life

Try is not to be perfect

It is to strive for your best

Try your best

Give your full effort

Only you know what your try is

It is better to try and fail than to fail to try

Trying is giving all your effort even at a cost

Try, because you never know what you are good at

Try is to go beyond what is expected of you

Try means you care

Try to be friends to those who need it

Try means doing what you think you can't

Try is a hero battling

Try, to me

Means to succeed in life

If you try your hardest

Things will be easier in the future

If you don't try in life

You'll show you died

Not trying to live

I understand try, but I

Am going to do

—Mr. J's Sixth Grade

Dan's unique approach to encouraging reflection on effort made a lasting impression on his students. They each had their own individual compositions about what it means to try, and now they have this collaborative poem that they all had a part in creating. This is an innovative example that demonstrates how writing not only reflects our thinking but also shapes our thinking. With this lesson, these students are thinking and reflecting on process as much as on product. Are there other mashup possibilities you could try with your students?

PEEK INSIDE THE CLASSROOM: REFLECTING ON OPENING SENTENCES

I am working in Erika Meiler's fourth-grade classroom. Throughout the year, Erika has been focusing in on and teaching a variety of writing traits with mentor texts and craft lessons. Today, we are looking at the leads they used in several writing pieces to help them reflect on their approach to beginning stories (Figure 7.5).

"You have done some work with writing leads this year, and I want you to have an opportunity to take a look at them, but if we look the same old way, we often see things the same old way. Let's try a new way. We are going to lift the first sentence from several different stories and create a lead-line poem. All you need to do is find your first sentence from each piece and copy it onto this new sheet, creating a list of leads. Then take a few moments to analyze and label your leads." (See Figure 7.6.)

We look at the leads anchor chart they have been using. I want the students to determine the type of lead they used rather than ask someone else for the label. Their understandings will raise awareness. Their perception is more important than the accuracy of the labels.

"If I had asked you earlier this morning, *What type of leads do you usually use in your writing?* How many of you could tell me?" No one raises a hand. "If I asked you that now, how many of you could tell me?" Most hands go up. "That's being more aware of your writer identity—who we are as writers. Understanding the choices we make when we write helps us to think about our writing identity. Awareness is one way to help us be more mindful and purposeful with our writing decisions."

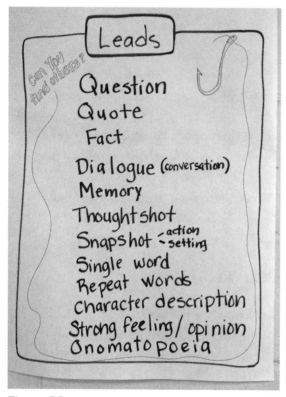

Figure 7.5

Fourth-grade leads anchor chart

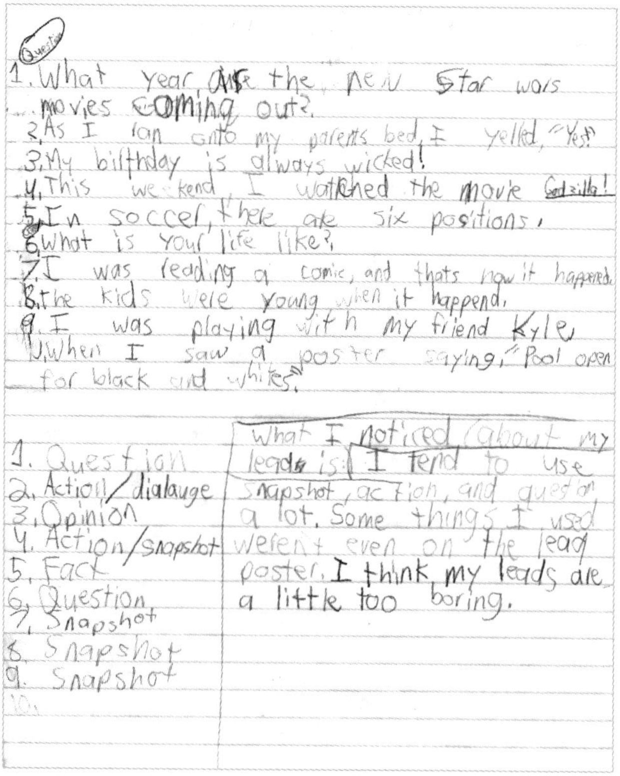

Figure 7.6

Lifting lead lines: poem and analysis

LEAD-LINE POETRY

REFLECTING ON OPENING SENTENCES

Sometimes it is easier to reflect when we look at things in different ways. This approach could be used with a variety of writing aspects (ending sentences, character or setting descriptions, dialogue). Encourage students to look for habits, patterns, or tendencies in their writing.

- Take a writer's notebook or folder that contains multiple pieces of writing students could reflect on.

- Ask the students to write down the lead sentences in a list format for eight to ten pieces of writing.

- What do they notice about their leads? Do they vary? Are they similar?

- Allow students to edit and/or revise, and then post these pieces as a compilation of their current approach to writing leads.

- Try it again several months later. Do they notice any changes in their approach to writing leads?

Here are some other close lens reflection activities. The variations are endless to help your students look but not tell them what to see.

WORD CLOUDS

REFLECTING ON WORD CHOICE

A fun way to get students to notice and reflect on their word choice is to have them create a word cloud that represents their choices. Taking the words out of context helps students to focus in and think about words in a fresh way. Many of these apps display repeated words in a larger font so that students can analyze word frequency as well.

- Choose a focus for reflection: speech tags, sensory words, first words in a sentence, adjectives, adverbs, etc.

- Choose a word cloud program (Wordle.com, ABCya.com/word_clouds, Tagxed.com, etc.).

- Students read through their pieces and pull out the targeted words. Create a list of these words.

- Type in the list or upload the entire text into the desired word cloud program. Most will depict frequently used words larger and bolder. This can help students notice the frequency of word choice.

- What do they notice about their word choice? What patterns or tendencies do they detect with their choice of words?

TITLE TALK

WHAT'S IN A NAME?

Titles are important in helping the reader anticipate and frame their reading. They can invite or dissuade potential readers from reading a piece. Titles often reflect the writer's theme or heart of their writing and provide insight into their thinking. Sometimes writers neglect to title their pieces or quickly attach a title with little thought. We can give them opportunities to be more mindful with the creation of titles.

- Invite students to pull out or look at their last eight to ten pieces of writing in their notebooks, folders, or portfolios. These could be pieces from the same or different genres.

- Ask students to list the titles for these pieces. They can use the book spine template (found online at www.stenhouse.com/closewritingbook) or simply create a list. If a piece does not contain a title, the student should leave that spot blank.

- Give the students time to reflect on what they notice. Invite them to write down their thoughts about their titles or lack of titles. Are there any titles they'd like to revise or add? Do they notice any patterns with their choices?

- Discuss why titles might be important to a writer. To a reader.

LAST LINES LINGER

REFLECTING ON ENDINGS

We often advise students to write with the end in mind or to try to create a satisfying ending. What does this mean to them? What does this sound like? Unlike revising word choice or dialogue in which you have multiple opportunities, there is only one end for each piece of writing. Reflecting on one end can limit your perspective. Reflecting on several endings, however, can shed some light on our skill or tendency at concluding our pieces.

- Take a writer's notebook or folder that contains multiple pieces of writing students could reflect on.

- Ask the students to write down the last sentences in a list format for several pieces of writing.

- Give students an opportunity to analyze and reflect on their endings. What do they notice? Do they vary? Do they leave a lasting impression in the reader's mind?

- Encourage students to craft alternative endings that could be used in comparison or as a "before revising" and "after revising" anchor chart.

- Invite students to reflect on the endings of their next several pieces. Were they influenced by this lesson to create a more satisfying ending?

WIDE LENSES ON SINGLE PIECES OF WRITING

It can be helpful to narrow our lens to analyze and reflect on writing choices. However, if the teacher consistently determines the focus, we can inadvertently limit what our students will see. We need to provide students with opportunities to use a wide lens to examine their writing. What they notice will be within their zone of proximal development and accessible for self-reflection and revision. This is an important step in becoming a self-regulated learner and an important component of close writing. If the lens is too wide, however, students may be overwhelmed by the possibilities. We can start out by reflecting on a single piece of writing as a way to keep the focus manageable.

PEEK INSIDE A CLASSROOM: NOTICE AND NEXT STEPS

The day after Haley's reflection on sentence structure I follow up with a lesson to help students plan for some revisions. I bring my own paragraph of informational writing to model the process.

"We talked about how our first attempts at writing are really *discovery drafts*. We write to explore an idea, and we reread it to think more about it and often discover what we really want to say. Yesterday, you read your pieces to listen for any patterns in rhythm and to look for transition words to connect your ideas. That is a type of discovery. Today, I'm going to do the same thing and ask you to help me. I'm going to write down what you discovered about my paragraph on this magnifying glass note. The magnifying glass reminds us to look closely at our work to help us discover."

I read my paragraph, and the students are quick to point out that my sentences start the same and sound like a list. I notice that my sentences are all about the same length. I share that writing can sound more interesting with a mix of longer and shorter sentences. I count the number of words in each sentence to make this more apparent. Then, I take my magnifying glass and jot down what they observed and what I observed. "So now I can make a plan for my next steps. I could use this to help me revise." The students help me make a list of possible revisions.

Then, the students begin reading and noticing things about their own informational articles. After a few minutes, I pass out the "next steps foot notes" (Figure 7.7). "Now think about what revisions you could make with this article after reflecting on your discoveries and jot down a few on your foot note." Everyone had at least one idea for how to make his or her pieces stronger.

PEEK INSIDE A CLASSROOM: USING PAST WORK AS MENTOR TEXTS

Caroline Eldridge's second-grade class is about to begin a new unit of study in writing. Student work on realistic fiction from the previous unit graces the hallway. Caroline expresses her hopes that they will transfer that learning to future pieces of writing, but past experience has shown that many will not.

We talk about using these last pieces as mentor texts for future pieces. Having them available for students to look back on is sometimes helpful, but we want to make the learning more explicit for the students. We make copies of the work and take some time for students to analyze and label the moves they made in this piece of writing to become mentor texts for future pieces of writing.

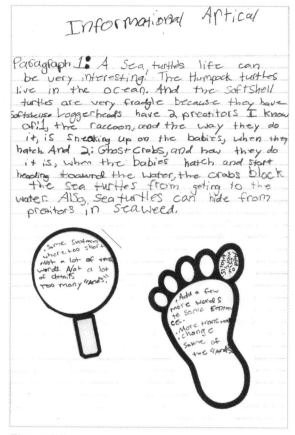

Figure 7.7

Reflecting on sentence structure

"Boys and girls, today, we are going to look back at your realistic fiction stories and notice all the work that you put into them. I made this checklist of the things we were trying to make sure we used when we were writing them. The first one says, "I have a *when and where* beginning." Remember, we started our stories with that type of lead to tell the reader *when* our story took place and *where* it happened. Who has a *when and where* lead for their story?"

The students begin rereading their stories, highlighting their leads and noting whether they have a *when and where* lead (see Figure 7.8). Some are now realizing they don't have both. A few ask whether they can add the missing element. Caroline always encourages them to make any revisions that strengthen their writing.

Caroline continues through the checklist, inviting students to closely read their fictional stories to look for examples of the taught techniques. Students share their "evidence" and then highlight and label it on their stories. Some are beginning to realize that writers can always revise, even after they think they are done. There are lots of discussions about traits and choices; it is a great way to wrap up to one unit and front-load another.

Students will keep a copy of this analysis in their writer's notebooks as a mashup of anchor chart and mentor text that will be referenced as they work on new pieces. Caroline and I want the transfer of skills to be easy for these young writers. Rereading, reflecting, analyzing, labeling, revising, and referencing these pieces of writing have offered students that opportunity.

PEEK INSIDE A CLASSROOM: ASK THE AUTHOR

Kelley Capen's fifth-grade students have just Skyped with author Suzanne Selfors. They are energized by their connection with a published author and did a great job asking her questions about her work. Kelley and I want to tap into this excitement and practice of

Figure 7.8
Second grader closely reads and analyzes her writing.

Figure 7.9
Questions students ask about my writing

questioning authors to support their own writing. To help them, we design an Ask the Author lesson in which they closely read one another's work and ask the writer some clarifying questions.

I bring out my writer's notebook and put it under the document camera. "You guys asked Suzanne Selfors some really good questions the other day. So we are going to practice asking the author today. I am going to share a piece of my writing with you, and you are going to take turns asking me questions."

I read my short piece *Bailey and the Cheerios* to the students, and they immediately begin peppering me with questions. "How old is she? What does she look like? What was Bailey thinking? Why a smile?" I jot these questions down on little thought bubble notes I created (see Figure 7.9) and set them under the document camera as well.

Then, it is their turn. "You are going to share a piece of your writing with a partner, and they'll use these yellow Ask the Author thought bubbles to ask you some questions about your writing. When you get your paper back, you can respond to the question with an orange bubble." The students are paired up and swap writing pieces with partners. They use a glue stick to attach the notes near the point of query. When they pass back the papers, students immediately begin responding to the questions (see Figure 7.10).

"How many of you were asked some questions that made you think about ways you could revise your writing?" A few hands go up, "How many of you got questions that were not helpful?" A few more hands go up. "Did reading those questions help you to think about what would be better questions to ask an author?" Lots of nods. "So this activity today could not only help you think about ways to revise your writing based on a reader's question but also help you think about good questions to ask yourself or others that can help a writer reflect more closely. Asking questions is a good strategy for reading comprehension, and it can be a good strategy for reading your own writing as well."

Figure 7.10
Students ask questions about one another's writing.

ASK THE AUTHOR

QUESTIONS TO STRENGTHEN OUR WRITING

We teach questioning as a comprehension strategy for reading, but it is also a great strategy for writing. Encouraging students to ask questions of the author invites students to approach writing with an authorial reading stance. (See Chapter 3.)

- Model this questioning strategy for students using a teacher mentor text. Read aloud and then stop to ask a question that would clarify or expand an idea.

- Write this question in the margin or in a talking bubble.

- Continue through the piece, stopping to ask several questions and jotting them down. Try to model deeper thinking and not one-word answers or simple yes-or-no questions.

- Go back through the piece and model how to include information that would answer the question. Oral rehearsal might demonstrate the possible options.

- Invite the students to try this strategy on a piece of their own writing. Keep a list of some helpful questions that students could use as stems if they are having difficulty at first.

- This could also work with peer conferences, encouraging students to ask questions of one another's work.

WIDE LENSES ON MULTIPLE PIECES OF WRITING

When we ask our students to reflect and revise pieces of writing, they are building a sense of identity as a writer. But if this is always done on a single piece of work at a time, they may not see the bigger picture. Who they are as writers is not contingent on the current project. No one piece can adequately reflect the skill or identity of a writer. I strive to remember that our focus is on developing the writer, not the current piece of writing.

Therefore, it is helpful to encourage students on occasion to reflect on a larger body of work. They could reflect on two or more pieces to look for tendencies, habits, or patterns of behavior that they can begin to recognize. This can facilitate a greater appreciation and identification of their writing identities. We can show them where to look but not what to see.

PEEK INSIDE A CLASSROOM: COMPARATIVE REFLECTION

Andrea Bryant's fifth graders just finished up a unit on memoir. She was noticing some of the writing elements the narrative unit focused on are not being carried over into their memoir writing. She wants the students to be aware of this and to understand that what they learn on one piece of writing is expected to be transferred to future pieces of writing. We decide one way to help them reflect is to ask them to compare the two pieces of writing using focused lenses on a few key traits/elements.

- Engaging leads

- Effective dialogue

- Character development

- Paragraphing structure

We make sure all students understand how a Venn diagram works as we pass out our template. "Today, we are going to compare your narrative pieces of writing with the memoir pieces you just finished. To help us, we are going to look at only one element at a time that we focused on during these writing units. Let's say when I look at my leads, I notice I used onomatopoeia to start both pieces. I would write that where the two circles intersect because it is included in both genres. If I only used that in the narrative, I would list it in the narrative circle. So closely read your leads and reflect on how you began each piece." Students begin to read and reflect while Andrea and I walk around the room, helping them to focus in on what type of lead they used. We then discuss each element one at a time and ask the students to closely read, looking only for evidence that they applied the element to their writing (see Figure 7.11).

I hold up one student's comparative reflection sheet (see Figure 7.12). "I want you to look at what you reflected on and noticed from these two pieces and think about those questions to help you relate to your writing identity."

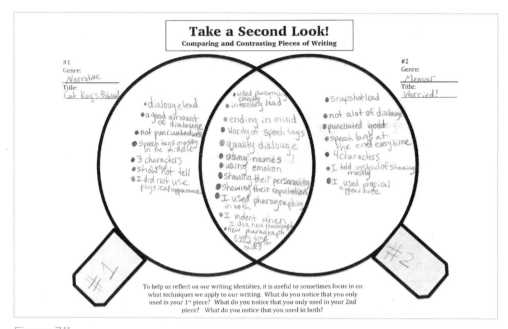

Figure 7.11

Comparing and contrasting writing

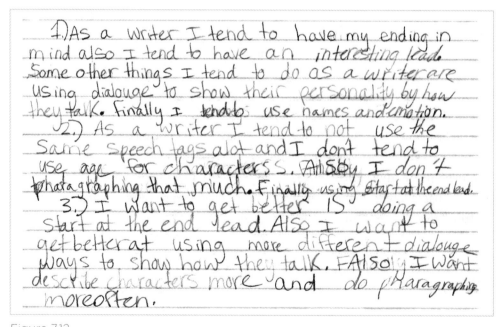

Figure 7.12

Comparing and contrasting writing

Reflecting on Patterns

The popularity of books and shows with a *do this, not that!* theme is entertaining but also informative. They raise our awareness about the choices we make and behaviors in which we engage. Frequently, we use examples *and* nonexamples in our classrooms to teach concepts and skills and to frame our expectations for students. In writing, we often teach examples of strong, effective writing to help our students envision the possibilities. Students' awareness of these helpful patterns was raised, but their awareness of the less effective patterns in their own writing was unexamined. Were we missing an opportunity to frame our expectations more precisely for some of our students?

In her book *Seven Strategies of Assessment for Learning*, Jan Chappuis suggests providing examples and models to students of strong *and* weak work. She reasons, "Carefully chosen examples of the range of quality can create and refine students' understanding of the learning goal by helping students answer the questions, *What defines quality work?* and *What are some problems to avoid?*" (Chappuis 2009, 12). Our mentor texts and exemplars typically present the high end of the range, which is not always synchronized with the quality of work our students produce. How can they begin to appreciate a range when we only address one end of the spectrum?

Rather than only addressing these patterns *after* they appear in student writing, I want to spotlight some common pitfalls that writers often encounter to help them self-monitor, self-revise, and self-regulate their writing. I don't want to just talk at them about it; I want them to have fun and play around with it. It's my hope that by immersing them in the composition of these moves we can increase their familiarity with them and this in turn can foster greater awareness of avoiding or self-monitoring these instances. They can more clearly envision a range for writing that meets expectations.

PEEK INSIDE A CLASSROOM: COMMON WRITING PATTERNS

Amber Davis and I have had many conversations about her fourth graders' writing. As I worked in classrooms throughout the district and looked closely at student writing, several unhelpful patterns were frequently prevalent. Amber and I are noticing many of these patterns in her students' writing. We want to see whether raising their awareness about these pitfalls in a fun way might help students to avoid or revise them. I put together a chart to label these patterns and descriptions to reveal the characteristics (Figure 7.13). I then write my own brief exemplars to highlight these patterns. I find catchy labels can help activate schema pretty quickly for our students.

PATTERN	FICTION	NONFICTION
ALL ABOUTS	In FICTION they tend to be listy, almost a schedule or agenda of an event. "Watermelon" ideas instead of "seed" ideas. *NO Problem/Resolution, mostly description*	In NONFICTION topics are very broad and not deeply explored. Often literally titled "All About…" They tend to list some facts but sentences may not connect or expand Ideas.
FIZZLERS	In FICTION These pieces may start out with an engaging lead or a strong start and literally fizzle. May have a beginning and middle but ends abruptly.	In NONFICTION piece starts strong but looks like writer lost interest or stamina.
SHIFTERS	In FICTION These pieces may change setting or transition in time abruptly. It can leave the reader wondering what happened in between 'scenes'. The pieces may contain a lot of *thens* or *ands* for transition words or may contain no transition words or phrases. Do NOT write with the end in mind & cannot explain the heart of their story.	In NONFICTION pieces the elements do not connect to one another. They need ways to connect ideas and topics more smoothly. They often lack a nonfiction organizational structure. and/or transition and signal words. Main Idea may be hard to find. Often very similar to ALL ABOUTS style.
GENERICS	In FICTION these pieces have characters w little detail or description, no backstory, no reaction to events. The setting is often not mentioned or not described well. We cannot envision the intended 'world' of the writer. No evidence of engaging lead (hook), "exploded moments" or voice.	In NONFICTION they do not use domain specific vocabulary and speak in generalities about their subject. May contain "dry" and somewhat uninteresting facts. They may be true, but they do not engage the reader. (closely related to ALL ABOUTS)
TALKERS	In FICTION these pieces are almost exclusive or overbearing with dialogue. It is almost a transcript of a conversation.	In NONFICTION pieces the author 'talks' about their opinions rather than facts. They may write sentences that could easily have the words "I think…" inserted at the beginning. (ex. *Penguins are the coolest bird.*)
HUSHERS	In FICTION these pieces contain no dialogue or no 'thoughtshots' (a look at what a character is thinking or feeling). Reaction to events is usually tell, not show (*He was scared*, rather than "What was that?" he screamed)	In NONFICTION they may not contain any quotes from experts or from texts that they cite.
SLANGERS	The writer uses slang or non-standard grammar/vocabulary. They may not notice how 'non-standard' it sounds to others because it represents the way they speak.	The writer uses slang or non-standard grammar/vocabulary. They may not notice how 'non-standard' it sounds to others because it represents the way they speak.

Figure 7.13

Common patterns of writing considered nonexamples

"We are going to have some fun today! I call this my Best Worst Writing Lesson! We are going to learn about some common writing patterns that many writers often use when drafting that aren't particularly helpful. Sometimes it makes the reading difficult, confusing, or uninteresting for other readers. I call them common writing patterns, or CWPs for short. We often show you examples of helpful writing. Today, we're going to look at some nonexamples." One by one I go through the characteristics and share my own CWP examples. Then, the students find evidence of the pattern in my work. There are lots of chuckles as I show them my hyperbolic examples of *shifter, generic, talker,* or *fizzler.* We talk briefly about what I can do differently if I notice this pattern emerging in my writing. They all have great recommendations for revision.

The students are then randomly assigned a CWP and invited to create their own non-examples (Figure 7.14). Amber and I circulate around the room, helping students to write their own versions of these patterns that often exist in drafts. It seems counterintuitive, but purposefulness in using one of these patterns may trigger a greater awareness if they begin seeing it in their own drafts. As a bonus, the students are having a blast trying to be "bad" writers.

After about fifteen minutes we regroup. The students share their CWPs, and to add to the fun, we comment on their "bad" writing with calls of "Terrible! Terrible!" or "Awful, simply atrocious! Bravo!" Each writer takes a bow and beams with pride. This approach may not work with all students. You need to know their sensitivities and personalities pretty well, but for these kids, humor was the key to their engagement and awareness. To this day, I have students make comments like, "Mrs. Bourque, this was generic, but I added more details!"

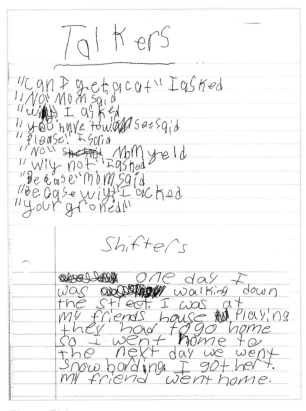

Figure 7.14

Students play with nonexamples to raise their awareness of common writing patterns.

Reflecting on Our Writing Identity: Exploring a Body of Work

The end of the year is often a prime time to stop and reflect on our accomplishments. We encourage students to look closely with a variety of lenses to focus their reflection, as well as give them time to read and remember their writing lives during the past year. It helps us to see the growth we have made, the patterns and tendencies of our choices, and the range of our writing over time on a body of work. It can broaden our understanding of who we are as writers and shape our aspirations for where we want to go. Classrooms that keep portfolios or samples of student writing throughout the year provide students with a history of their learning on this journey.

Sometimes the end of the year is incredibly hectic. The beginning of the year may be a better time for you to pull out the previous year's portfolios and reflect on a body of work

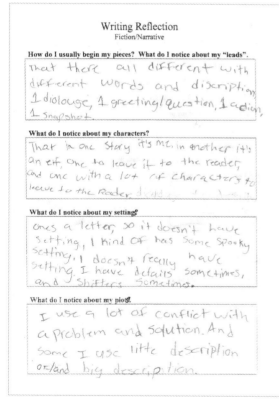

Figure 7.15

Fourth-grade reflection

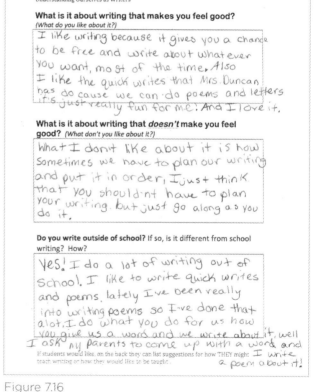

Figure 7.16

Fifth-grade reflection

so students can set goals for the upcoming year and anticipate how much growth they can potentially achieve as writers. Midyear may be a more opportune time to plan for some analysis and reflection. This encourages students to examine their accomplishments, reflect on their choices, and set a course for the rest of the year. Consider your purpose for reflecting what you want students to understand about themselves and their work, and let that drive your questions and your timing.

Figures 7.15–7.17 are some examples of the types of writing reflections we have done with our students.

Considerations for English Language Learners

Encouraging our English language learner (ELL) students to continually reread their work and reflect on their writing as they go will give them increased practice with reading as well. The words are all within their speaking and writing vocabularies, so they can exercise their reading skills, as long as the spellings are reasonably accurate. If they cannot reread their work because the spelling does not support their word recognition, it will be difficult for the writer to reflect on their ideas, so teachers may wish to give additional support in that area for some students.

Varying the focus for reflection can help our ELL students get a bigger picture of the writing process. Often they feel less proficient than their English-speaking peers in many things. The ability to focus in on a specific aspect of writing can give them a chance to build proficiency and not worry about getting everything right.

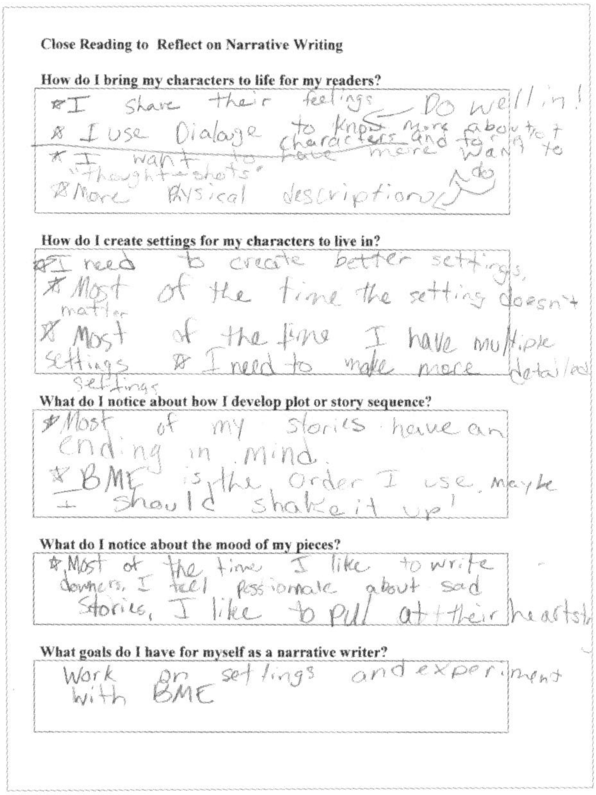

Figure 7.17

Sixth-grade reflection

The Gist of the Story

Before students can revise, they must be aware of what they have written and what they need. Rereading and reflecting are important steps on the road to revision. We can support mindful close writing and help students develop habits for noticing as they reread and reflect by

- developing habits for rereading our work consistently;

- shifting from wide lenses (step back and look) to close lenses (step in and look) to gain perspective on our writing;

- asking questions of ourselves and others (as authors) that encourage close reading;

- raising awareness of patterns that might help or hinder our writing; and

- reflecting on our writing identity.

Drafting Your Story

Take some time to contemplate your students' strategies for rereading and reflecting on their writing. On your own, or with colleagues, think about the following:

- How self-regulated is your students' practice of closely reading or rereading their writing?

- How often do your students reflect on a piece of their writing, a collection of writing, or their writing identity?

- Are there any CWPs that you or your students notice that are prevalent in their drafts?

- What questions would you pose to your students to encourage reflection on their writing identities?

- What would you like to try after reading this chapter?

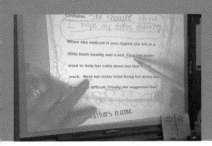

CHAPTER 8

Revising: Revisiting and Revisioning

Revision is where stories start to sing. Where lumpy writing gets smoothed out and where good writing turns into great writing. It's the part where the real magic happens. —Kate Messner

hen I asked several classrooms of fourth- and fifth-grade students, What does revision mean to you? it was clear that not all students had the same understanding (see Figures 8.1 and 8.2).

We need to be sure that our students know what we mean when we are talking about revision and what our expectations are. There are so many amazing books on revision. Some of my go-to titles include Georgia Heard's *Revision Toolbox* (2014), Donald Murray's *The Craft of Revision,* (2012), Barry Lane's *After the End* (1993), and Kate Messner's *Real Revision* (2011). My story isn't a compilation of revision strategies or techniques. My goal is to help teachers and students recognize how being in touch with their writing can make these revision approaches more obvious, accessible, and successful.

The moral of this story: Close writers understand that revision is where possibilities become realities for authors.

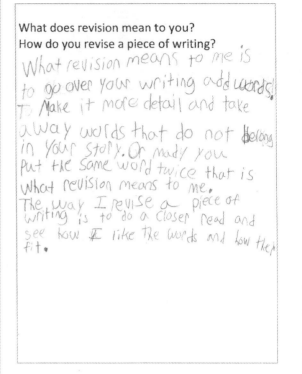

What does revision mean to you?
How do you revise a piece of writing?

I Oont think I shood Do reviseing Because h ow wants to Chans thair work thay just spent a long time on. and revision sands werd Cinduv Sands like Duvison

Figure 8.1
One fourth grader's thoughts on revision

What does revision mean to you?
How do you revise a piece of writing?

What revision means to me is to go over your writing add words! To Make it more detail and take away words that do not belong in Your story. Or mady you Put the same word twice that is what revision means to me. The way I revise a piece of writing is to do a closer read and see how I like the words and how they fit.

Figure 8.2
Another fourth grader's thoughts on revision

Overcoming Resistance

Before our students can grow as writers, they must overcome their resistance to revision. It's an understandable position. As Donald Murray says, "Writing is always an act of self-exposure. When we finish a draft, all writers feel vulnerable. Writing strips away our intellectual clothes and shows the world what we know and what we don't know; it reveals what we think and feel, it documents how well we write" (Murray 2012, 2). Teachers who write understand this and can empathize with the writers in their classrooms. We know they are handing over a little piece of themselves and want us to love it just the way it is.

But we also know the joy and sense of accomplishment that comes from taking an idea and developing it into a satisfying story or compelling argument. When we go back into a piece and discover new ideas about a topic or insights about ourselves, it is incredibly rewarding. I want *that* for our students, too. I want them to have that fulfilling experience, knowing that once they do, they may never want to write without revising again.

We can make sure they have these experiences by setting them up for success. We define that success as growth, with a focus on the process, not a perfect product. Studies suggest that the adage "success breeds success" is indeed true because of performance-enhancing effects of psychological momentum (Iso-Ahola and Dotson 2014). We foster close writing strategies that encourage mindful rereading and reflecting, so that students begin to notice and celebrate their thriving writing skills. They experience success. There needs to be a payoff for the effort of revising, and close writing (and a little fun) helps them to recognize and appreciate that payoff.

Recognizing the Need for Revision

Revising requires writers to recognize when the ideas in their mind (intended) begin to differ from the words that represent them on the paper (actual) and to make adjustments to align them. Sometimes our stories are so familiar to us that it is difficult to determine areas of that divide. Sometimes ideas are so complete in our minds that our brain fills in the gaps when we read the words on the page. We have explored a few considerations that have helped our writers understand the necessity or advantages to revising by helping them notice their writing more effectively.

- See it differently

- Narrow the scope

- Develop some distance

Seeing It Differently

Many of the rereading and reflection approaches I shared in the previous chapter were designed as ways to help our students see their writing in a slightly different way. When we take pieces out of context, hear our words read by someone else, or compare our work side by side with another piece, we are pushing ourselves to approach our writing from a different angle. This fresh perspective is often enough to help us envision possibilities and try out new techniques.

Having a variety of ways to reframe our approach to our writing engages students. We put a premium on having fun as we work through a piece of writing. No one likes the idea that our work was wrong or bad, so we don't like to think about fixing it. Avoiding the value judgments often associated with reflection or revision, and simply focusing on what we notice or observe, can help our students see their work differently.

Narrowing the Scope

Writing can be completely overwhelming for some students. The number of items in their work that require focus varies with the proficiency of the writer. Our most proficient writers have acquired automaticity with many aspects of the writing process and can shift their focus more easily. Sadly, the least proficient writers often have the most issues to think about, and this slows down their writing process.

If they lack automaticity with encoding or conventional spelling, they need more time to stop and think about how to spell the words they want to use. If they have limited vocabularies, they need time to think of the words that best convey their ideas. You can see where this is going. If getting the ideas down on paper is a Herculean task, it is no wonder students have an aversion to going back and "redoing" what they have worked on so hard in the first place.

By narrowing the scope of reflection and revision, we do not hold students accountable for every possible option that might improve their writing. Focusing in on what we have previously taught makes it more feasible for students to try out new choices. Limiting the amount of expected revisions makes the amount of work reasonable for our young writers. Encourage students with a few powerful possibilities. Don't overwhelm them with the magnitude of writing techniques and approaches. Students are always encouraged to reflect and revise beyond that scope, but our assessment and grading can be guided by reasonable parameters.

Developing Some Distance

Sarah Albee, best-selling author of more than 100 books, including *Bugged: How Insects Changed History* and *Why'd They Wear That?*, gave me some advice for writers. "If you possibly can, write a draft and then shove it into a drawer for a day, two days, however long you can. When you come back and read something with fresh eyes, you'll see things you didn't see when you were in the thick of things."

Author Ammi Joan Paquette (author of *Rules for Ghosting* and *Princess Juniper of the Hourglass* among others) echoes that same strategy. When I interviewed her about writing, she said, "Giving your work time to rest is a very important part of the writing process. Setting aside a piece of writing—whether it's for a day or a week or even more—is a way of starting fresh. When that piece of writing comes back out, you will be reading it with new eyes, and will have a better gauge of its weaknesses—and its strengths!" Maybe we don't have that luxury in many of our classrooms, but we could look at how we might try out this approach with some of our writing.

Delaying revision on some drafts might make revision easier for our students by removing some of the familiarity and immediacy of the work that can get in the way of noticing. Some thoughts we have discussed around this concept include the following:

- When the ideas are fresh in the writer's mind, the brain often overlooks gaps and mismatches that it encounters on the page. Filling in the gaps might be less likely when the work seems less familiar.

- When students have put a lot of effort into their work, they are reluctant to change it. Time away from the work may lessen some of the emotions connected with the intense effort and make it easier to approach it again.

- With passing time, a writer acquires new skills, ideas, and knowledge they may have lacked when originally working on a piece. Bringing those strengths back to a previous piece may make it much easier to revise.

Close writing does not require a constant closeness to each piece of writing. It includes an awareness of when distance might better serve the writing. However, students still need to work within the parameters of our classroom and curriculum. They don't often have the option of saying, "I think I'll put this piece away and work on it next month." But as teachers, we can think about how we could offer some opportunities for distancing the writer and the writing. For those whose students have writer's notebooks filled with writing, it can be an option to go back and pull out an older piece to revise. Perhaps a unit of study could incorporate an intentional break for a week or two to pursue other writing and then come back to revise with fresh eyes.

Close Writing Revision Approaches

Remember: when people tell you something's wrong or doesn't work for them, they are almost always right. When they tell you exactly what they think is wrong and how to fix it, they are almost always wrong. —Neil Gaiman

When we read our students' writing, it is often quite obvious to us what revisions are necessary or what the writers' next steps should be. But close revision should reflect the writer's intention and purpose, not ours. We decided to observe our students during revision to see what it is that they are noticing. We wanted to make that invisible thinking more visible.

PEEK INSIDE A CLASSROOM: REVISION STRIPS

Becky Foster's fifth graders have already reflected on their midyear writing prompts with a Notice and Next Steps lesson. Today, they are going to take those next steps and revise their pieces. Becky and I hand out writing paper cut in half lengthwise to each student. We tape these to the edges of their writing.

"These sheets are your *revision strips*. This is where you will make your revisions. Sometimes when writers revise, they erase their previous work, and we lose that history of their thinking and decision making. This activity helps you to keep your original writing intact and allows you to make additions or changes in this big margin. Then, Mrs. Foster and I can see some of the choices you made for revision, but more importantly, you can see more clearly how your thinking has changed and what choices you are making as a writer."

"Take a look at the Notice and Next Steps sheet you took notes on last week (Figure 8.3). On the Next Steps side, you wrote down some things that you want to remember to do as a writer. Today, you are going to try some of those things with this piece of writing. Look for places in your piece where you can revise and then draw a line from that place to the revision strip, where you will write the revisions. Then label what it was you were doing. If you added more dialogue, next to your revision write *dialogue*. I find that when we give something a name it is like using a container to hold our thinking. It makes it a lot easier to think about something, remember it, and then repeat it."

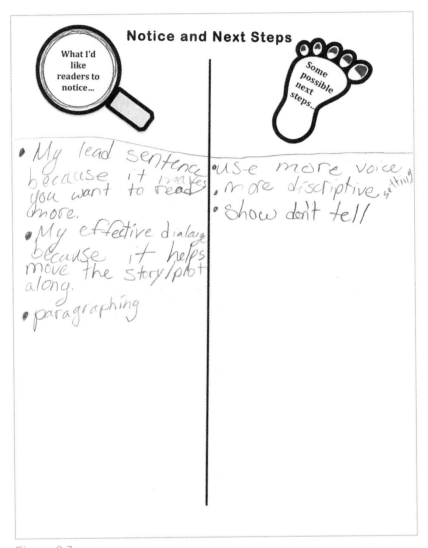

Notice and Next Steps

What I'd like readers to notice...

Some possible next steps..

• My lead sentence use more voice,
because it makes, more discriptive, thing
you want to read, more.
more.
• My effective dialaug • Show don't tell
because it helps
move the story/plot
along.
• paragraphing

Figure 8.3
Students reflect on what they did well and possible revisions.

Becky and I walk about as the students start rereading their work and finding places for their Next Steps revision ideas. Some students need more support than others, but within fifteen minutes, most students have a least one revision idea, if not several. We allow writers time at the end of the lesson to share some of their revisions and discuss their thinking. Students can not only hear about one another's revision ideas, they can also see them laid on the pages as they are shared.

REVISION STRIPS

MAKING REVISION MOVES VISIBLE

Often students do not want to "mess up" their writing with revisions, or they may erase their earlier drafts when revising, so we can't see the moves they are making in their writing. One way to help make those moves more visible and more legible is to add revision strips to the original piece (see Figure 8.4).

- Take a sheet of paper the same size as the students' original and cut it in half lengthwise so that you have two strips.

- Tape these strips to either side of the students' original writing to resemble a trifold board.

- This is where students can try out the revision ideas they would like to make to their drafts. They can draw lines from the work on the strips to the point in the story they would like to see it.

- Teachers may ask students to label the revision move ("character description," "word choice," "show, don't tell," etc.) on the strip next to the revision.

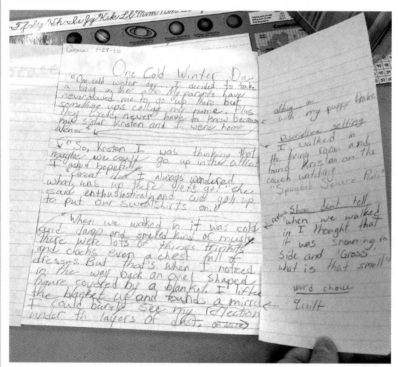

Figure 8.4

Using revision strips makes thinking visible.

Figure 8.5
Katie Dutil observes Rainbow Revision.

PEEK INSIDE A CLASSROOM: RAINBOW REVISION

Katie Dutil's third graders are about to do some close reading of the drafts they had been working on. She wants them to reflect on their use of the craft techniques that were a target of previous mini-lessons and are now posted on the classroom anchor chart. She doesn't want her students to skim through their pieces and declare all is well! She wants them to look for specific evidence that demonstrates the use of these techniques.

"Before we begin, let's go over our Rainbow Revision. We are going to use our checklist to help us." Katie goes through the Rainbow Revision chart with her students. They'll color-code spicy describing words in yellow, sequences and transitions in green, thoughts and feelings in blue, dialogue in pink, strong setting in orange, thoughts and feelings in blue, and so on.

She then passes out some sticky notes, "While you are reading and highlighting, you might be going through your piece and realize you don't have any pink, and you think, *That would be a perfect place for some dialogue.* You can write it on the sticky note, and then, stick it where you want it in the story." As the students pull out their highlighters and begin reading through their pieces, Katie and I circulate through the room to watch the process and check in with a few writers (Figure 8.5).

Katie has established a routine with her students that makes reflection and revision tangible. These writers enjoy closely reading and marking their writing to find evidence of taught traits and strong technique. They can easily see whether they are lacking in any area by the absence of color. Not every piece goes through this process, but this is a scaffold that has helped raise their awareness in all writing.

RAINBOW REVISION

CLOSE READING TO REFLECT AND REVISE

When students read closely to look for evidence in the text, it helps them to focus in on writing expectations. Highlighting that evidence helps to make it much more concrete/obvious for writers. Once a color-coding system has been established, students can begin to take on this approach on their own (see Figure 8.6).

- Assign a color to represent specific techniques or traits that students have been taught and encouraged to apply to their writing.

- Invite students to closely read through their pieces and highlight evidence that reflects use of that technique or trait.

  - A more structured approach would be to ask students to look for one technique at a time. A less-structured approach would let students decide how they want to closely read and look for evidence.

- Once students have finished highlighting, ask them to jot down revision ideas on a sticky note or Next Steps note.

- Encourage some discussion on what students noticed and their ideas for revision. The more opportunities students have to learn from the observation and experiences of others, the more they can envision possibilities in their own writing.

Figure 8.6

Student highlights and revises where he perceives a need.

PEEK INSIDE A CLASSROOM: EVALUATING "SPICY" WORD CHOICE

Katie has carried this strategy to other classes and lessons. Encouraging students to read closely and look for evidence of writing skills and techniques is an expectation she has for all of her writers. Today, they are looking at word choice. They have been referring to precise and interesting words as *spicy*.

"To help us notice them, you are going to highlight the words that you think are spicy. So take some time to carefully read through your writing, highlight those words you think are spicy, or if you see a place where a spicy word would work, you can use a caret to write it in."

Katie and I walk around observing. Almost immediately students begin questioning, "Is this a spicy word?" I take this as a good sign. Students are becoming mindful of word choice and trying to discern the quality. Many don't yet feel confident in their ability to evaluate, while others are madly marking their papers with yellow ink. Katie and I respond to the questioners with comments that try to turn the responsibility back over to the student.

"Well, what do *you* think? You are the writer; do *you* think that is a strong way to describe that? Do *you* know any other words that might mean the same thing but are a little spicier?" Students usually generate several alternatives before choosing one they are satisfied with. It is evident that their noticing abilities vary, and the lexicon of adjectives and verbs are wide ranging. What might be spicy to one student is blasé to another student.

The goal of the lesson is that students begin to reflect on and evaluate their own writing, to look for possibilities and to grow as writers. The goal isn't to fix a word or just this piece. Katie and I want to improve the skills of the writer so that every piece of writing can be stronger. However, some students still want us to evaluate their word choice.

I address the group. "I notice a lot of you wondering and asking, *Is this a spicy word?* When I think about spices, I know that some are very hot, and some are kind of mild. So I want you to think about your spicy words. There are probably some that you know right away are very spicy, like a *hot spice*." I wave my hand in front of my mouth in a cooling motion. "Then there are some that you are not quite sure about. You tried to be spicy, but you aren't sure if they are strong words. Maybe these are a *mild spice*." I rub my tummy as if what I've eaten was yummy and satisfying. "We want *you* to think about how spicy your words are. Someone might think *huge* is a hot spice word; someone else might think it is a mild spice word. That's OK. You can both be right. The important thing is that you are thinking about your choices to make your writing better. So go back into your piece and analyze those spicy words. Maybe you want to take a mild spice [rub tummy] and replace it with a hot spice [mouth fanning]."

Katie adds, "Those of you who need to finish writing your piece can be thinking about opportunities to include some spicy words as you are writing, too." She wants them to realize this is not only a revision strategy but also a composing strategy. She is planting the seed for possibilities and teaching for transfer.

PEEK INSIDE TWO CLASSROOMS: TALK IT OUT—"INVISIBLE INK" REVISION

Alice Drummond's fifth graders have been working on opinion pieces. She is concerned that her students are not developing their opinions or ideas with enough details. We look at the students' drafts and decide we will focus on one paragraph at a time to help them explore their ideas more fully. We aren't concerned with fixing up this particular piece of writing so much as we want them to develop some strategies for incorporating more details to strengthen all of their writing.

I bring my own writer's notebook into class to model our Talk It Out strategy. "Boys and girls, today I want to show you a strategy that could help you revise your writing to help your readers get a clearer picture of what you are trying to say by adding more details and information. This strategy is going to let you think about lots of different possibilities for doing that and let you play around with those possibilities before you put them down on paper. It's called Talk It Out. I'm going to go back into my paper, reread a bit, and then talk it out with a partner. I'll think about any ideas, details, or examples I could use to help my readers get a better picture in their heads of what I am talking about. My partner is going to listen and then maybe ask me some questions if something isn't clear."

I choose Meliana to be my partner. "Meliana and I are going to take turns reading and talking. I will read a sentence or two and then talk out a few more ideas. I'm not going to talk *about* my story; I'm going to talk as if I am writing these words down. I'm going to use a book-talk kind of language. Let me show you what that looks and sounds like."

I read the first sentence of one of my paragraphs. "*Winter is a season filled with festive events, especially at the beginning.* Hmm . . . I've got some ideas but instead of talking about my ideas I'm going to talk as if I am writing them down. *Winter is an incredible season, filled with my favorite festive events, especially at the beginning. It begins unofficially just after Thanksgiving, but for me that is the start of it all. Soon the celebrations include Christmas and Hanukkah, all time to enjoy the company of family and friends. Not only is it beautiful outside, but the people are filled with a caring spirit and generous nature. It's a time to think of others and do kind things for others. Even though it is cold outside, I feel warm inside.* Now I do not have to write all of those words down right now. I am just exploring the ideas more and playing around with the possibilities. Meliana, is there anything as a reader you are wondering about that I might think about including?"

"What about a Christmas tree?" she asks.

"Oh yeah! I totally forgot about that; it's one of my very favorite parts of the season. I probably wouldn't have thought of it if she hadn't asked me that. Let's see . . ." I continue talking it out. *The adventure of selecting our family Christmas tree is always one of my favorite events. Our whole family visits the local tree farm in search of the perfect tree. One year Bailey gets to choose. The next year it's Casey's turn. They never seem to agree, but I always think they are perfect.*

I nod and smile, looking pretty satisfied with myself. I want to impress upon them that I am not writing all of this down at the moment. I am simply talking out the possibilities to explore my topic. "Now it will be Meliana's turn. She will read her first few sentences to me and do the same thing. I will ask her any questions that would help me get a better picture in my head. You are going to work with your partners and do the same."

The students pair off and begin reading their pieces to one another. Mrs. Drummond and I circulate, listening in and scaffolding their conversations. We remind students not to *talk about* their piece but to *talk it out.* The students catch on pretty quickly.

After about ten minutes of talk, I ask the students, "How many of you have more ideas for your writing now?" Hands shoot up. "How many of you can think of some good details to add to your paragraph that would help the reader get a better picture in their head?" Again, the hands fly up. "OK, I want you to revise just that one paragraph now that you have all of these ideas floating in your head. You can reflect on what you have already written and decide what you want to add, change, or move around. I'm going to give you about ten minutes to do this." The students grab their pencils and begin (Figure 8.7).

Jessica Walling's fourth graders had been writing some narratives recently, and she noticed that many of her students were not including details that would help the reader get a better picture of the people and events the students were writing about. They hadn't done any formal revision lessons yet this year, so we decided we would start with the Talk It Out strategy. We discussed how talking out their stories helps to open up the range of possibilities they can write down when drafting or revising. She wanted us to try this strategy for revising some of their earlier drafts.

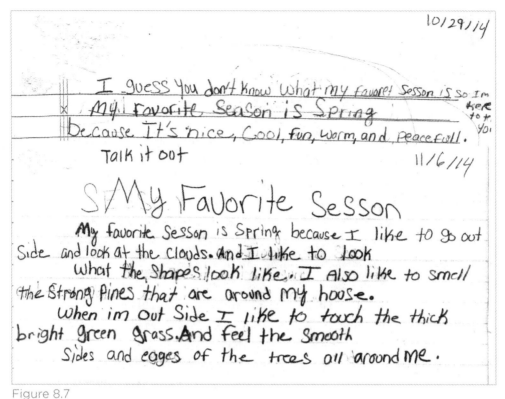

10/29/14

I guess You dont know What my favoret Sesson iS so Im here to you

× My favorite Season is Spring
Because It's nice, Cool, Fun, warm, and Peacefull.

Talk it out

11/6/14

s/My Favorite Sesson
My favorite Sesson is Spring because I like to go out
Side and look at the clouds. And I like to look
What the Shapes look like. I Also like to smell
the Strong Pines that are around my house.
When im Out Side I like to touch the thick
bright green grass. And feel the smooth
Sides and edges of the trees all around me.

Figure 8.7
Before (top) and after (bottom) talking it out and revising

I start the lesson by sharing one of my own drafts with the students under the document camera. I read the first few paragraphs and then ask, "Do you think I could have said anything else here, or is this all the possible ideas I could have included?" Most of the students respond with variations of "There's more." So I continue, "I'm going to show you a strategy today to help you think about lots of other possibilities for ideas you can choose from to revise your writing. You aren't going to have to write down all of the ideas or possibilities, but you are going to get a chance to talk out many of those ideas."

I model the Talk It Out strategy for the students. I am not writing anything down at first, only immersing the students in the possibilities.

"So, now that I've talked out more ideas with this paragraph, I am going to go back and revise it. With all the possibilities I just rehearsed, it should be pretty easy to add more details." I take a second piece of paper and model my process. I keep some of the sentences, tweak a few, and add some others. It's not a totally different story, but it is altered by the talk and the reflection.

We partner the students to talk out one of their paragraphs (see Figure 8.8). We want to focus on a short amount of text at first to practice the strategy. We notice several students talking about their story or ideas but not talking it out. I model for these students how I sometimes remind myself to use book talk by writing in the air with invisible ink. The kids take to it right away, and the motion completely shifts their stance from talking about their ideas to telling the story. After about ten minutes, we invite them to revise the paragraph and encourage them to use many of the ideas, words, or sentences they talked out and "wrote" with their invisible ink.

We ask them to compare the two versions of writing and to highlight any changes they made to their revised piece (see Figure 8.9). We want those revisions to be obvious to the students. They are eager to share what they have done and to talk about the moves they have made as writers.

Figure 8.8
Student orally rehearses possible revisions with Talk It Out.

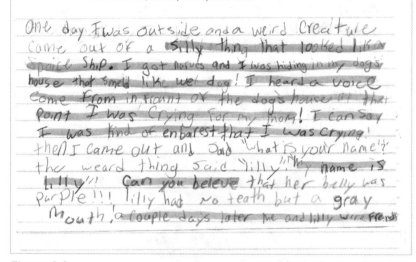

What I Saw In My Backyard

One day I went in my   back yard and I saw that there was a weird animal. I got so scared but then I saw that it was nice. So then I asked her what her name was and she said, "My name is Lilly." Can you believe that Lilly's belly was purple and baby blue? Her face was light purple , her eyes were gray and blue and Lilly had 3 legs and they were all blue! She also had blue antennaes! Lilly had no teeth but a gray mouth, how weird is that? She also had a very fat belly and a yellow nose!

One day I was outside and a weird creature came out of a silly thing that looked like a space ship. I got nerves and I was hiding in my dog's house that smeld like wet dog! I heard a voice come from in fromt of the dog's house at that point I was crying for my mom! I can say I was kind of embarest that I was crying! then I came out and said "what is your name?" the weard thing said "lilly" "My name is lilly"! Can you beleve that her belly was purple!!! lilly had no teeth but a gray mouth. a couple days later me and lilly were friends

Figure 8.9
Highlights show revisions inspired by Talk It Out.

Mrs. Walling has quite a few English language learners (ELLs) in her classroom. We have had several conversations about the importance of opportunities to talk and orally rehearse during writing workshop. We are interested to see whether this would make an impact on their writing. Though sometimes repetitive, the volume of writing increased for Ahmed dramatically after talking out his ideas with a partner. In fact, he does not want to stop writing at the end of the workshop.

We end the lesson by reflecting on the strategy. "Boys and girls, you can use the Talk It Out strategy anytime you go back to your piece to revise. You could use this strategy before you even begin your draft. Talking out lots of possibilities helps writers to think about what they want to say, and using that invisible ink helps writers to think about how they want to say it."

TALK IT OUT—"INVISIBLE INK"

ORAL REHEARSAL FOR REVISING

Similar to the oral rehearsal techniques for brainstorming and drafting (see Chapter 3), students can play around with the possibilities of revision ideas before committing them to paper.

- Pair up students, with each bringing a draft to revise. The students may choose a portion of the text they want to revise or the entire piece if it is short.

- The first partner (author) reads a sentence or two or perhaps an entire paragraph and then orally rehearses possible revisions.

- The second partner (listener) may ask them clarifying questions, "Where were you when this happened?" "Can you tell me what your character looks like?"

- Then the author rehearses possible revisions out loud. The listener should remind the author to say it the way it would be written (maybe encouraging him or her to write it out with invisible ink).

- The students can switch roles or continue with the same roles for another section of the first partner's piece.

- Once both students have had a turn, the students can then go back into their pieces and make desired revisions.

Stepping Back
Writing is never done, only due.—Author unknown

Sometimes we must remove our scaffolds and see how solid the writing structure has become for our writers. We explain, teach, model, and reinforce to help our students become close writers, but we must be careful we aren't creating dependent writers. I am not proposing we stop teaching at some arbitrary point in the year and allow our students to sink or swim. We are never done teaching, and they are never done learning. Part of that process is to reevaluate the zone of proximal development to see what students can do themselves and where they might need assistance.

We need to encourage students to choose a piece of their own writing and apply all the skills they know about drafting, revising, and editing independently (see Figure 8.10). This can allow us to see where they still need support, and where they no longer need explicit instruction. We know our students are not equally skilled writers and that differentiating instruction is important. Giving them opportunities to show us what they need and what they know will help us be more effective teachers of writing.

Considerations for English Language Learners

Learning to write in a second language is hard work. Knowing that there will be opportunities to revisit, reflect, and revise their work can relieve the pressure of getting it right the first time. It can free students from the perception that their writing needs to be perfect and help them focus on a few areas at a time that need work. Taking them step-by-step through the expected revisions will provide them with the needed support to be successful.

The modeling that we do in these lessons will make the expectations explicit for all students but may be even more supportive for ELL students. The academic language that accompanies the modeling and think-alouds is important vocabulary for our students to be immersed in. Naming or labeling techniques and moves helps to frame that thinking effectively for students and can give ELL students a concrete link to attach those concepts. Making the invisible visible can be accomplished through mindful modeling, supportive anchor charts, and clear exemplars of student work.

Figure 8.10
Observing students' independent revision process is valuable information for a teacher.

Although it is controversial in some schools, ELL students should have opportunities to write in their first languages. The writing process is not language dependent. Conceptualizing ideas and capturing them on paper is not unique to the English language. If students can successfully do this in their native language, they have developed a system for writing on which we can layer the vocabulary, spelling, and conventions of English. These will need to be conversations and decisions that schools and teachers make. Understanding the benefits of this approach will be an important consideration for that determination.

The Gist of the Story

Many students are reluctant to revise. To some, it seems like a lot of work that they don't think they need. To encourage strategic revision, we must help students to see the need and easily envision the possibilities. We can do this in the following ways:

- Narrowing the scope of revisions to more feasible expectations.

- Reflecting and revising at varying points in the writing process so that students do not get the misconception that revising means to fix up your work when you are done.

- Sharing our process with our students to make the task visible and achievable.

- Keeping it fun. Students sometimes perceive revision as punishment for bad first drafts. Looking for ways to counter that perception will be key.

- Focusing on the writer and not fixing up the writing. Encouraging students to make choices, even if they aren't the ones we teachers would choose, are keys to self-regulated behavior.

Drafting Your Story

Take a moment to think about revision in your classroom. It might be helpful to discuss the following questions with colleagues:

- How do your students perceive and approach revision? What does it mean to them?

- How do you teach and support revision in your writing workshop?

- Who decides what revisions will be made and when the piece of writing is "done"?

- What are some things you might try after reading this chapter?

CHAPTER 9

Eyes and Ears of an Editor

Proofread carefully to see if you any words out.
—Author unknown

O ur stories are like music, punctuation the notes to our lyrics. A songwriter wants her song to be sung the way she hears it, and so she gives directions in her composition by laying musical notes over the lyrics. If a writer wants her piece to be read the way she hears it, she also needs to give direction to the reader. Punctuation is her sharps, flats, and rests. Every composition is open to artistic interpretation, but the reader can easily decipher the intent of the artist when the direction is clear.

A close writer understands that transaction between the composer and the "singer." We have a responsibility to be clear in our composition if we want the meaning to be construed consistently by our readers. In Chapter 3, I discussed the importance of the writer reading, making sure the story sounds the way we want it to and fostering a closer connection with our writing as we bring it to life. That's the Authorial Reading I that Rosenblatt speaks of (see Chapter 2). When we edit carefully, we practice Authorial Reading II, considering the needs of our readers to clearly interpret our meaning.

The moral of this story: Close writers vary the way they look at and listen to their writing so they can effectively edit with consideration for their readers.

Using Our Ears

Always write with the ear, not the eye. You should hear every sentence you write as if it was being read aloud or spoken. If it does not sound nice, try again. —C. S. Lewis

Many authors I spoke with talked about listening to the rhythm, cadence, and flow of the words they were writing. Using oral rehearsal techniques helps a writer play around with the words and the sounds of their ideas before committing them to paper. We encourage our writers to listen for the pauses, the exclamations, or the rising of their voices with questions to know where the commas, exclamation marks, and question marks should be placed (see Figure 9.1). Punctuation will help other readers read it the same way.

After composing, we prompt our writers to reread their writing the way a teacher might perform a read-aloud or an author might create an audiobook. We have taught them the writer reading approach to read with prosody and bring life to their words (see Chapter

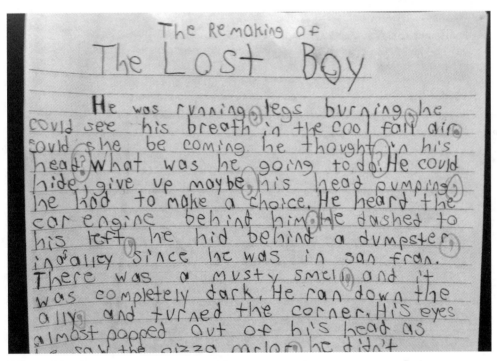

Figure 9.1

A story punctuated by ear

3). This approach has helped students tune into *how* the words should be read and not just *what* words are being read. We ask others to read our work to see whether our punctuation led them to read it the same way. If not, we can revisit and edit our work as needed.

When we engage in a genre study in our classroom, we can examine the punctuation and conventions that are a part of these texts. Students need to develop an ear for the genres they read. We can provide opportunities for children to listen and follow along with nonfiction and notice how the author signals important facts or ideas with dashes, colons, or parenthesis, inviting the reader to pause and contemplate. They could listen to Poetry Out Loud and follow the poem to observe how the punctuation or spacing cued the reader. Our students may notice more genre-specific punctuation if they are given time to explore and discover. They can then begin to notice their own use of punctuation when writing in those genres.

PUNCTUATION DICTATION

LISTENING FOR PUNCTUATION

For students who need scaffolding to hear and practice punctuation in writing, try Janet Angelillo's (2002) approach:

- Choose one to two sentences from books children know well and that contain easily spellable words (so that students can focus on punctuation).
- Read the sentences with prosody but not exaggeration, and invite the students to write the sentences with accurate punctuation on cards.
- Compare their cards with others and discuss their choices before checking with the published text.
- Focus not on being right or wrong but on the decisions behind their choices.
- Collect the cards as a formative assessment to determine who may need some additional support.

Using Our Eyes
Reading is like listening with your eyes. —Author unknown

Unless we are visually impaired, our eyes are the portals for reading. The squiggles, symbols, and dots on a page must pass through our eyes to our brains to be converted to meaningful ideas and images. Looking and seeing are not exactly the same thing. Looking is to gaze at something and acknowledge its presence, whereas seeing is the more active and perceptive attention we give to something in order to understand it. When we want our students to notice something in their writing, we need to teach them how to look in order to see. We often refer to this as *noticing*.

THE IMPORTANCE OF NOTICING

Students can't fix what they don't notice. How many times have we asked students to read through a piece of writing to look for any spelling, punctuation, or capitalization errors and they perform what I sometimes refer to as the *skim and grin*? They read through the piece with a cursory skim and then look up with a satisfied grin, "Yup, all set." We watch them read right through missing punctuation, mumble through mangled spellings, and treat every *i* as a not-so-personal pronoun. They are merely looking over their writing and not seeing what needs to be noticed.

One reason this happens with many of our writers is because they still don't think of punctuation or capitalization as integral to their writing. Students focus so much energy and consideration on ideas, organization, and word choice as they draft and revise. That is where their attention lies. When I think back on my mini-lessons or the mentor texts I have shared, that has probably been my focus as well. I haven't explicitly shown them the role punctuation plays in telling stories or in sharing information when writing. I haven't impressed on them Lynne Truss's suggestion that "proper punctuation is both the sign and the cause of clear thinking" (Truss 2004, 202).

One way we can help students notice is to approach our writing by focusing on the clarity of our message. We don't want students to work diligently at creating stories or researching information only to have the reader confused or distracted by the way it was presented. Ensuring that they understand the important role editing has in shaping and conveying their ideas will help them see purpose in this work.

WHY IT'S HARD TO SPOT OUR MISMATCHES

How many times have you read something you've written or typed to check for spelling or typos and felt confident that it was accurate, only to have the next person who reads it immediately spot an error? At that moment the error is obvious, but why not before?

Tom Stafford, a psychologist at the University of Sheffield in England, studies typos. In an interview with *Wired* magazine, he contends that what we are doing isn't careless; it is actually very smart. He says, "When you're writing, you're trying to convey meaning. It's a very high-level task. We don't catch every detail; we're not like computers or NSA databases. Rather, we take in sensory information and combine it with what we expect, and we extract meaning" (Stockton 2014).

We know what we are trying to say, and we don't expect our message to have missing parts or mismatches. We are so focused and familiar with our ideas that our brains fill in the gaps. The version we see on the paper competes with the version we have in our heads and our expected version often wins out. It is easier to pick up on the errors of others because we do not have a familiar or anticipated meaning competing with the information we are taking in as we read. Stafford suggests that we try to make our work as unfamiliar as possible. He offers, "Once you've learned something in a particular way, it's hard to see the details without changing the visual form" (Stockton 2014).

Becoming a close writer means understanding our writing process more deeply. Learning a bit about how our brain works and how it affects our ability to detect errors can help students approach editing more openly. Some kids will protest, "It's fine. There are no mistakes." They are sometimes defensive about editing. No one wants to feel like his or her hard work is wrong. When they can comprehend that those errors or inability to easily detect them do not indicate that they are "bad" writers but rather that their brains are working hard at making meaning, they may embrace some editing strategies as part of the process.

TEACHING EDITING OUT OF CONTEXT

Over the years, I have seen students practice proofreading skills with worksheets or Daily Oral Language (DOL) packets. These are badly written pieces of writing by others that students need to proofread and correct. As Stafford's research has shown, it is much easier to spot the errors in others' work. Students who seemed to do well with these worksheets did not necessarily show a greater ability to detect similar errors in their own writing. There seemed to be little transfer of their skills at detecting errors from DOL to drafting or editing their own writing with greater precision.

Whenever I contemplate an approach, I ask myself, "What is my purpose?" So I pondered the purpose of editing. I have been telling my students that we edit our writing so our message is clear and credible. We want the reader to easily understand what we are trying to say and to have confidence that we know what we are saying. I realized the DOL practice had an entirely different purpose. Students needed to spot mistakes. The work was not their own, so there was no personal attachment to it. Finding those mistakes in their own writing was more difficult, perhaps because it was so familiar or reflected their thinking so personally. When they read through their writing later, it seemed as whole and clear on paper as it was in their mind when they wrote it.

There is also a different anticipatory set for each activity. Students expect and look for errors in the DOL. They are not thinking about creating meaningful and authentic writing. When students edit their own work they may focus on the meaning of their stories, reliving the memories, visualizing the information, or experiencing the feelings associated with their writing. DOL might prepare students for peer editing, but it doesn't necessarily lead to greater editing skills in their own writing.

Close-Up Editing

One way to see our work in an unfamiliar way, as Stafford suggests, is to get really close to it when we edit and proofread. If you have ever seen images of a butterfly's wing under a microscope, you can appreciate its incredible beauty in an entirely different way than when it's fluttering about your garden. It is no longer familiar but still fascinating. Finding ways to look more closely at our writing can give us a different (and perhaps fascinating) perspective by removing some of the familiarity.

When teaching and reviewing rules for punctuation, capitalization, and spelling, teachers can invite students to reflect on their skill with each area. "How many of you find this to be a bit tricky when you edit your writing? Let's look at how we can make that easier. So when you are editing, remember that this is one of the areas you might need to look a little more closely." This encourages students to be mindful of their strengths and vulnerabilities.

You can also share examples of student work that demonstrate competency with the skill (student mentor texts) for editing, or invite students who are strong in an area to be a mentor author. "Madison has been really focusing on editing for spelling. Can you share with us some tips that have been helpful?" Making those connections personal can enhance a writer's identity and sense of agency.

Close Editing Approaches

There are a variety of ways we can encourage mindfulness as students are asked to edit their work. Remembering that the purpose is not necessarily to fix any one piece of writing, but to strengthen the awareness and skill of the writer, will help us determine the best approaches.

CLASSROOM STYLE GUIDE

One way we encouraged our writers to reflect on their editing was to simply ask them. Haley Duncan invited her fourth graders to quick-write a response to the following prompt: *How can I get better at editing my writing?* (See Figure 9.2.) Haley and I decided to put the collection of these thoughtful tips together into a class book. The students could read and reflect on the variety or similarity of approaches of their classmates and feel a sense of authority on their ability as editors.

We can always add chapters on tips for specific editing areas in the future and perhaps include student examples. The options vary, but the aim is to share our thinking, to support one another, and to build expertise in our editing. We told the students that we would use this book with next year's fourth graders to help them learn more about editing. They are now mentors for others, another positive aspect to their writer identities.

PEEK INSIDE A CLASSROOM: DRY-ERASE EDITING

I'm working with two writers from Haley's fourth grade. I want to increase their awareness of their editing skills and make that a part of their close writing identity. We are looking through their writer's notebooks filled with unedited quick-writes. The girls each select a piece, and I place it inside a transparent plastic sleeve that I write on with dry-erase markers. I do not want to alter their original work with my edits.

I want to know what they typically edit for when they write so I ask, "What would you like me to look for when I edit your quick-write?"

"Capital letters and punctuation," says Ayla.

"Yeah, and spelling," adds Gina.

"What kind of punctuation do you look for?" I ask.

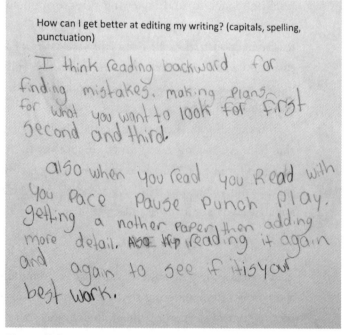

How can I get better at editing my writing? (capitals, spelling, punctuation)

I think reading backward for finding mistakes. making plans for what you want to look for first second and third.

also when you read you Read with you Pace Pause Punch Play. getting a nother paper then adding more detail. Also Kep reading it again and again to see if itisyour best work.

Figure 9.2

Students share their strategies for editing in an in-class style guide.

Figure 9.3
Dry-erase editing

"Just periods and commas and stuff," Ayla's comments give me some insight into what she considers punctuation. With my dry-erase marker, I edit their stories for these areas on the plastic sleeve. I remove their stories from the sleeve and ask them to also edit it for spelling, capital letters, and punctuation. They cannot see the marks that I made on the sleeve.

I notice both girls read through several times (see Figure 9.3). After a few minutes, they finish. I take Ayla's paper and put it back in the sleeve, careful to align it with the original editing marks.

"Let's see if you found some things I missed or if I found some things you missed." Ayla scans the paper.

"Oh, I forgot to make that a capital letter. Oh yeah, I put *where* instead of *were*." She finds several of the same errors that I did, but many others go unnoticed.

We repeat the same activity for Gina. She notices she has left out commas in her dialogue. She successfully finds about half of the mismatches I did. She expresses several "aha" moments when she recognizes some of them.

I want the girls to think about what was easy for them to recognize and what was more difficult. I can point things out to them, but it is their awareness that is important if they are going to become more independent with this skill.

Gina goes first, "The spelling. First I went through and just did the spelling."

Ayla concurs, "Yeah, me too. Spelling was pretty easy to find."

"But then I read it again and I was looking for capital letters and punctuation. Just mostly periods," adds Gina.

I want them to reflect on the repeated readings. "You both read it several times, were you looking for something different each time or were you checking for everything a few times? Both girls talk about how they look for one thing at a time and then go back and reread for something else.

Figure 9.4
Fourth grader's editing reflection

I want them to reflect on what they were able to notice. "One way we can get better at editing is when we recognize that something is kind of tricky for us, so we can take more time to look carefully. What was something that was tricky for you to find? Maybe something I found, but you didn't."

Gina quickly answers, "Commas. I don't know where to put commas," Ayla agrees. Gina did leave out commas in her dialogue; we talk a bit about where the commas go to separate speech tags from dialogue. I am confident next time Gina and Ayla write dialogue they will be thinking about the commas. They missed other mismatches as well, but getting them to recognize one area to focus on for now will increase the likelihood for success with that aspect of editing (see Figure 9.4).

EDIT WITH A SINGLE FOCUS

Once students have a solid understanding of the rules and expectations for editing, as well as some awareness of their own editing skills, we can look for ways to make editing more successful. One way is to make the writing less familiar to the writer, as Stafford suggests. Another is to narrow the focus to make it easier to look. Editing with a single focus can help strip away the "distractions" of meaning and story.

HIGHLIGHTING

Many of our teachers have found that editing is more successful when students highlight one targeted feature at a time. Nicole Clark encourages her sixth-grade students to do this. They highlight all end punctuation in yellow. They can then more easily notice whether there are large areas with no yellow, a possible indicator that some end punctuation is missing. Once that is complete, an easy next step is to highlight the first letter they see after that end punctuation in orange to make sure it is capitalized appropriately. They continue editing their piece, noticing and highlighting one focus area at a time (see Figure 9.5).

Figure 9.5
Sixth grader using rainbow editing

Figure 9.6
Nicole Clark's rainbow editing

When only one area is being examined, it frees up the students' attention and allows them to focus more carefully. Teachers can do a refresher lesson on the rules or reasons for one feature at a time. Keeping a list of focused edits can be helpful for students to reflect on when they are working independently. These are areas for which they can be held accountable. This can become a self-check list for independent editing of future pieces (see Figure 9.6).

READING BACKWARD

Some edits require understanding the meaning of the text; however, spelling typically doesn't. (An exception might include homophones in which the reader would need to recognize the intended meaning in order to choose the correct spelling: *their, there, they're.*) As we've read, meaning might actually get in the way of noticing spelling when the writer knows what he wants it to say, and he reads it the way it was intended, rather than how it is actually presented. We can remove that familiarity to focus in on the spelling patterns by reading the text out of sequence. Reading backward has helped many writers spot words that don't look right. When they can't anticipate the word, their brain is less efficient at filling in the blanks.

You can also read backward at the sentence level, rather than word by word. Read the last sentence of your paper and listen for grammar, sentence fragments, left-out words, or repetition. Then, read the prior sentence following the same technique. While maintaining the meaning of the sentence, you read each out of context and remove a layer of familiarity. Students won't be reading to understand the content; they'll be focusing more on the sentence construction.

HAVE A GO

Once students have highlighted or targeted words they suspect are misspelled, there are a variety of approaches they can take to check and correct the spellings. Certainly, looking up words in a dictionary is a skill that can lead to correct spellings. However, it does consume a lot of time and can be difficult if the misspelled word is too far off from the correct spelling to locate it.

One strategy we have tried with our students is Have a Go (adapted from Parry and Hornsby 1988). Students take a word they've identified as misspelled and write it on a separate sheet of paper or sticky note. This takes the word out of context and removes a layer of familiarity so the student can focus only on the spelling patterns of the word. They then try writing the word a few different ways (see Figure 9.7). Usually, by the second or third try, students recognize the correct spelling. Even if they don't, their approximations often become much stronger as they focus on the word and reflect on what they know about spelling.

LIMITING THE READING FIELD

Have you ever wondered why racehorses wear blinders? Their eyes are on the sides of their heads, so they have peripheral vision and can easily end up running off course unless they are made to focus straight ahead. The blinder ensures the horse stays focused on the racetrack and is not distracted by the horses or jockeys around him. Limiting their vision keeps them focused and efficient with their given task. This same strategy can work well with editing. Students don't necessarily strap on blinders, but we can use simple tools to help focus in on a smaller area of text at a time.

A plain piece of paper can be used to cover all but a line or two of writing. As the student reads, the paper can be pulled down to expose the next line of text. I created an

Figure 9.7
Have-a-Go strategy

edit slider to use as a tool for this task (see Figure 9.8). I made a frame by cutting a 1-inch by 7-inch space out of a piece of tagboard that can be placed over the writing. This space allows two lines of text to show at a time, and can be pulled down or pushed up the page as the writer reads. Students can make edits right inside the frame before moving on.

As clichéd as it might seem, a magnifying glass can help students detect editing errors more easily. Distorting and limiting the text that is seen is another way to remove some of the familiarity of the content, as well as the familiar reading habit. Sometimes editing is a chore that students dislike. Inserting an element of fun into a task can keep the students engaged. It's equally important for students to understand that the purpose of these tools is to help them improve their editing skills and that if there is little improvement, use of the tool will need to be reevaluated. The idea isn't to replace editing practice with fun activities; it is to encourage focused and purposeful editing skills as part of the writing process. The tools and approaches should serve this goal. The more students enjoy what they are doing, the more likely they will remain engaged and learning.

Figure 9.8
Using an edit slider to narrow our field of noticing

CHANGING THE VISUAL FORM

Sometimes, to *see* our writing differently, we need to *present* our writing differently. For students who write using a computer, changing the font, enlarging the size of the text, or changing the color of the text could accomplish this. Sometimes printing out a paper copy, rather than editing on the screen can help the writer look at the piece differently. You don't want to see it the way you wrote it; you want your brain to read it as though it is a different piece of work.

CAUTION: PROCEED SLOWLY

When you are driving along and encounter a road sign that urges you to use caution or slow down, you adjust your driving and heighten your awareness of your surroundings. There are some challenging editing areas that might require some similar attention. We can use students' writing to track the most common errors, and we can encourage students to reflect on those errors they find most tricky to notice. From this, we can create some *caution* anchor charts to warn students about potential pitfalls or hazards in writing (see Figure 9.9).

Encouraging students to be aware of their own caution spots, the way Gina and Ayla did with our dry-erase editing, can help them to slow down and then proceed with caution when they are writing or editing. We won't expect perfection, but we will anticipate a stronger process for our writers as they continually reflect on what they do as writers. Reminding them of these caution spots before they edit, and even encouraging a focused reading for one of these areas at a time, can help them to be more mindful writers.

Editing with Some Distance

Sometimes these strategies will work even better when the story or the writing is not so fresh in the writer's mind. As I mentioned with revision, many authors talk about the need to distance themselves from their writing to get some objectivity. We can think about ways to increase distance from the writing in order to edit more effectively. Showing students how that distance could be helpful supports close writing strategies.

Occasionally, editing outside of the writing workshop could create some distance in time as well as the writer's mind. Instead of a DOL packet, students could edit a piece of their own writing or a peer's writing as an entry task in the morning. Working on editing in a different environment than where the piece was written may also help the writer to see it in a slightly different way. Once they understand how it could benefit them as writers, it would be great to have them engage in the planning process.

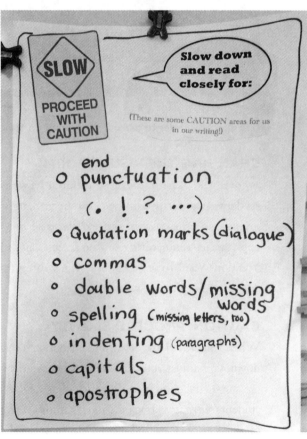

Figure 9.9

Raising awareness for the tricky parts of editing

PEER EDITING

Peer editing often doesn't go as planned. We must consider many variables (privacy concerns, classroom chemistry, and skill levels) when students review other students' work. These sometimes lead to unintended outcomes that discourage teachers from trying this approach. If done well, we can begin to use a valuable resource (one another) to encourage and explore writing as a community.

There are many ways to approach peer editing, but my biggest piece of advice has been to narrow the scope of responsibility and feedback. Rather than soliciting evaluative feedback, peers can be a writer's objective eyes and ears. They can often notice mismatches more easily than the writer because they aren't focusing on the content and they aren't emotionally tied to the message. When we ask peers to look for one thing at a time and then share that with the writer in a nonjudgmental way, we are increasing writing support. It is very time-consuming for the teacher to be the only other set of eyes for a student's writing. We should take advantage of the numerous eyes and ears in our classrooms to increase our editing expertise.

Peer editing does not need to be a whole-class event. Some students may be ready for it or benefit from it and others may not. Only after students demonstrate skill at performing these editing tasks on their own writing would I begin to encourage peer editing. If students continually get off task or are inappropriate, the approach will be considered ineffective and suspended. Students shouldn't see this as buddy time to get together and share writing. It should be tied to expected outcomes or learning targets.

PEER EDOTS

GRADUAL RELEASE FOR CLOSE EDITING

To help students edit with a more focused lens, peers can point out where to look, without necessarily showing them what they should see. Students should have a certain amount of skill with a convention or spelling before become Edoting Partners:

- Focus on one editing area a time.

- If an editing error is found, the partner places a dot to the left of the text on the line in which it occurs. If there is more than one error, the partner places more than one dot for each error. (See Figure 9.10.)

- Writers then have a more focused "lens" for close reading and correcting.

VARIATIONS

- For greater release of control, teachers can ask peers to place dots at the bottom of the page, rather than on the line in which it occurs. Students would then know the number of editing corrections they will be expected to make but would need to locate them with a less-focused lens.

- Peers can read through a second or third time for additional editing areas; a different colored dot or symbol could signify the various edits necessary.

Figure 9.10

Peer editors dot the lines that need the writer's attention.

Punctuation Mentor Texts

If we immerse our students in the study of how authors effectively use punctuation, we will heighten their awareness and appreciation for punctuation. When they can recognize how punctuation shapes the message, they can begin to see why they should pay attention to it. There are some wonderful books that would be useful resources for teachers to share as mentor texts for conventions and punctuation. Some books are about punctuation and use humor to demonstrate the importance of correct usage. Then, there are books in which author's clever or interesting use of punctuation is integral to the story. Here are some of my favorites. You may want your students to search for helpful mentor texts as well.

MENTOR TEXTS ABOUT PUNCTUATION AND CONVENTIONS

Barretta, Gene. 2010. *Dear Deer: A Book of Homophones.* New York: Square Fish.

Blaisdell, Molly, and Sara Gray. 2009. *If You Were Quotation Marks.* Mankato, MN: Picture Window Books.

Bruno, Elsa Knight. 2012. *Punctuation Celebration.* New York: Henry Holt.

Carr, Jan. 2009. *Greedy Apostrophe: A Cautionary Tale.* New York: Holiday House.

Cleary, Brian P. 2012. *I'm and Won't, They're and Don't: What's a Contraction?* Minneapolis, MN: Milbrook Press.

Pulver, Robin, and Lynn Rowe Reed. 2004. *Punctuation Takes a Vacation.* New York: Holiday House.

Truss, Lynne, and Bonnie Timmons. 2006. *Eats, Shoots & Leaves: Why, Commas Really Do Make a Difference!* New York: G. P. Putnam's Sons.

———. 2007. *The Girl's Like Spaghetti: Why, You Can't Manage Without Apostrophes!* New York: G. P. Putnam's Sons.

———. 2008. *Twenty-Odd Ducks: Why, Every Punctuation Mark Counts!* New York: G. P. Putnam's Sons.

MENTOR TEXTS WITH INTERESTING/EFFECTIVE PUNCTUATION

Cronin, Doreen. 2011. *Click, Clack, Moo: Cows That Type.* New York: Simon and Schuster Books for Young Readers.

Jenkins, Steve, and Robin Page. 2012. *Sisters and Brothers: Sibling Relationships in the Animal World.* Boston: HMH Books for Young Readers.

Raschka, Chris. 2007. *Yo! Yes?* New York: Scholastic.

Shannon, David. 1998. *No, David!* New York: Blue Sky Press.

Willems, Mo. 2012. *Don't Let the Pigeon Drive the Bus!* New York: Hyperion Books for Children.

Sharing mentor texts with students helps to raise their awareness about certain aspects in writing. We want them to use that awareness to seek out their own examples in what they are reading and apply their knowledge in their own writing. Let's look at some activities we can try with our students to encourage them to continually look and see!

PUNCTUATION MENTOR SENTENCES

LOOKING BEYOND THE WORDS IN PRINT

Once students have some understanding and interest in how punctuation is used to craft a piece of writing, we can encourage them to find it in their reading. These can then be used as exemplars to support their writing.

- Invite students to collect examples of interesting or effective punctuation in the books they are reading. They can copy it onto sticky notes or cards and add them to a bulletin board or graffiti board.

- Teachers could copy pages from texts in which students found strong examples of punctuation use. These could be bound and kept in an anthology.

- The binder could be separated by type of punctuation so that students categorize their examples.

- Students can find examples of punctuation in their environment. They may even find examples where it is misused!

- Take some time to analyze the choices the author made and why.

DO THIS, NOT THAT

EXAMPLES AND NONEXAMPLES OF CLEAR WRITING

If students engage in a scavenger hunt for punctuation examples, they could be used for this activity as well.

- Make a list of areas that we would like our students to pay more careful attention in their writing (spelling, commas, quotation marks, etc.).

- Challenge students to find examples in their reading where authors successfully did this. Copy the example exactly as it is found in the book and cite the author's name.

- Now ask the student to strip away the punctuation, alter the spelling, or modify the grammar of a sentence. Choose one aspect to vary.

- Create a two-column chart labeled *Do This, Not That*. Place the correct examples in the Do This column and the incorrect examples in the Not That column. (See Figure 9.11.)

- Invite students to discuss how the altered examples would affect a reader's ability to appreciate the writer's work.

- Encourage students that editing is a way of reminding ourselves how we want our work to be seen and received. Editing prompts us to *do this, not that*.

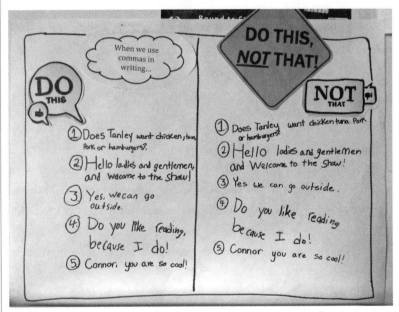

Figure 9.11

Create anchor charts that make editing a more enjoyable process.

When Teachers Edit: The Gradual Release of Responsibility

Sometimes students' work needs a teacher's editing. Somewhere between doing it for them and expecting complete independence is a range of options for supporting our students' growth in editing. Most of us fall somewhere within that span, but what if that range varied for groups of students within our classroom? What if our level of support looked different for different students?

Consider these approaches. Sandy gets her paper from the teacher. She scans the piece looking for any marks. She sees several words that have three lines under the first letter. She quickly changes those letters to capitals. She sees small circles drawn at the end of a few sentences and pops periods into the center of them. She notices a ¶ symbol before one of her words, so she erases the word and squishes it over to the right to indent. Done. She grabs a fresh piece of paper and begins her final copy.

Andy gets his paper back from the teacher. He reads the comments at the bottom.

You have put together a convincing argument with solid evidence. Some areas I'd like you to consider and edit are

- *How to begin and end complete sentences*
- *When to begin a new paragraph*

By noticing the marks his teacher made, Andy knows there are four places the teacher would like him to find and edit for capital letters at the beginnings of sentences and punctuation at the end and two areas where he should begin new paragraphs. Andy goes back into his writing and closely reads for these things. He does not want errors to detract from his message.

Which student was more engaged with his or her writing? Which learned more about editing? Which approach encourages close writing?

If we want our students to become better at editing, we need to look for ways to gradually turn over that responsibility. Some students go from "Sandy to solo" with few scaffolds in between. Teaching them how to closely read their work as editors can be done by supporting where or how to look but not telling them what to see or do.

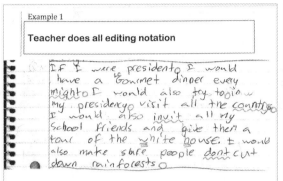

Figure 9.12
Gradual release for editing

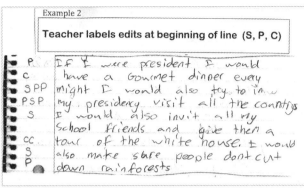

Figure 9.13
Gradual release for editing

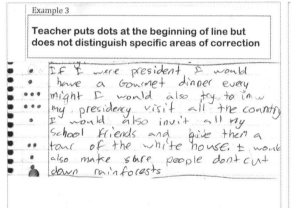

Figure 9.14
Gradual release for editing

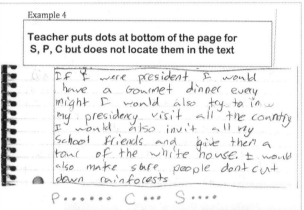

Figure 9.15
Gradual release for editing

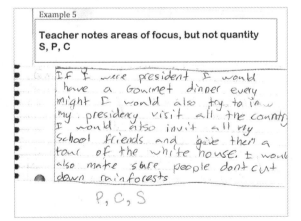

Figure 9.16
Gradual release for editing

Figures 9.12–9.16 show some approaches for gradually releasing responsibility for editing to the writer. These are based on Jan Chappuis's work on effective formative feedback (2012). As students demonstrate greater skill, we can gradually remove our scaffolds and encourage greater independence.

Don't Save Editing for the End

When we save editing for the end, careful attention takes a back seat to eager completion. When a student has been focusing on crafting an idea into a story, she feels like her work ends when the story ends. By the time a piece is "finished" and ready for editing, it is frequently quite long, and there are many conventions that need scrutiny. Also, editing immediately after finishing allows for no distance. Students may be too close emotionally or consciously to the content to notice the nuts and bolts.

I started questioning the tradition of editing at the end of the writing process. Some classrooms were only editing pieces that were going to be "published," and I was worried that this cut into opportunities for practice. I also thought it undermined the importance of editing as a means of ensuring clarity in our message. When we are "done," we don't revisit the piece to appreciate how the editing has shaped or clarified our writing.

I wondered how it would affect the entire writing process if we periodically incorporated editing into various parts of our writing. If we stopped to do a little editing during the drafting, would it help to focus the writer's awareness of that skill or use of punctuation moving forward? Would students be more likely to pick up on mismatches when there is less text to read through? I also wanted to make it easy to incorporate into writing time and not take away from the composing. I wanted to try "flash editing."

PEEK INSIDE A CLASSROOM: FLASH EDITING

Liz Chadwick wants her fifth graders to develop stronger editing skills. She looks through some of their recent pieces and notices that students still lack a lot of punctuation. We decide to do a flash edit lesson to listen for end punctuation. Students pull out their writer's notebooks and find an older piece of writing. (This provides some distance from the piece.)

I begin by asking the students, "When do you typically edit your writing?"

"When you are all done."

"When you are ready to publish," they respond.

I agree with them, "Yeah, usually students wait until they are nearly done before they edit their writing. But this can make editing harder for some kids for two reasons. First, if you wait until the end to edit, there is a lot more writing to look through. Second, when we have been working on something for quite awhile, and we feel like we are done, we are ready to be *done*! We might be eager to publish. We are tired of working on it, or we are just ready to move on to something else, so we don't give our writing our best attention.

"Today we are going to practice a strategy I call *flash editing*. We might do a flash edit after a few paragraphs, or pages, or every few days. The big ideas are that we don't save editing for the end, and we focus on looking for just one thing at a time. It's quite difficult to catch all the spelling, capitals, punctuation, spacing, and indentations at the same time. So, today, we are going to flash edit for just one thing—end punctuation. "To make that easier, we are going to do two things. The first is to slow down. If you read with a fast pace, you will have difficulty hearing the pauses." I demonstrate on a student's piece of writing, slowing my pace so it is much easier to hear where I stop or pause. "The other way is to read it out loud. I know most of you have switched over to reading silently, so this will be a little stretch for you, but I have noticed when students read to themselves they tend to fill in the blanks or not notice mismatches so much."

I then invite the students to try a flash edit for the next several minutes, focusing on end punctuation (see Figure 9.17). I circulate the room listening in on students' oral reading, reminding a few to slow their pace and a few others to try reading aloud. After about three or four minutes, most of the students have finished.

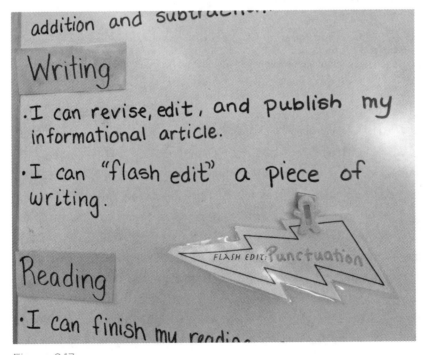

Figure 9.17
Select a focus for editing during the writing process.

"Who was able to find a place where they needed end punctuation and added it?" Eleven students raise their hands and share their editing successes. I want to celebrate their awareness and editing process, so I don't focus any attention on students who thought their papers were "perfect" already. We want to encourage a growth mindset when it comes to editing.

FLASH EDIT

For many reasons, editing only at the end of a piece can be problematic for some writers. To encourage more frequent and focused editing, try encouraging flash editing periodically during a project.

- To introduce this approach, the teacher models a flash edit, choosing only one editing skill.

- She projects her writing for all to see and reads with appropriate pace and pause to help students listen and look for the focused skill.

- She makes corrections as she reads and can even invite students to help her. The goal is to keep it quick and focused (flash!) so that the writer can then return to drafting or revising and not think of the paper as done.

- Invite students to closely read their own pieces with the specific flash focus and make corrections.

To gradually release the responsibility, students select their own focused skill and closely read/edit for that choice. They can fill out a flash edit note (available online at www.stenhouse.com/closewritingbook) and mark it on their text when they feel "finished."

Considerations for English Language Learners

Even with all of these ideas and approaches for helping students hear and see their writing as editors, it can still be particularly difficult for our English language learner (ELL) students to recognize the mismatches. Their writing errors may not necessarily be attributed to a lack of noticing; they may be more closely related to their limited understanding of standard English grammar and punctuation. The expectations we have for our ELL students with regard to editing should be in line with their English proficiency.

We have many students whose native language follows grammatical or conventional structures that greatly differ from English. We see writing that does not contain plurals, articles, or past tense verbs. The directionality and phonetic symbols may be confusing. One of the first things we can do as teachers is to observe and notice what our students already control in their writing and what is beyond their understanding. We can ask ourselves, *What would be easiest for this student to notice and monitor? What does this student almost control in his or her writing?* We can then narrow our focus for instruction and accountability.

Sometimes the writing of older ELL students resembles many of our emergent students' writing. The foundations for ELL students' language acquisition follow a similar path as those of early literacy acquisition for native speakers. Our primary teachers can be an excellent resource to determine a good scope and sequence for these students' writing. When we watch them teach emergent students, we will notice lots of immersion in talk, clear modeling, and targeted feedback to lift the students' literacy levels.

The Gist of the Story

Editing our work can be difficult for a number of reasons. Research suggests that our brains often override the mismatches as the information on the paper competes with the intended message of the author. Our work is often too familiar, or we are too emotionally tied to effort and ideas for us to objectively notice errors that others might easily see. There are many facets to editing, such as spelling, punctuation, capitalization, and grammar. There may be too many areas competing for our attention and sometimes students are unaware of the rules that govern each area. They do not know what they do not know. We can support our students' editing efforts and encourage more purposeful attention (close writing) when we do the following:

- We show them how punctuation affects the sound of the reading, especially as it is used in each genre.

- We encourage them to listen for punctuation as they compose and edit.

- We help them understand that our brains often fill in the gaps and make it more difficult to spot mismatches when the work is so familiar and compensate for this by varying how we look at our writing.

- We focus on one aspect at a time to edit, repeating the process with a variety of lenses.

- We raise students' awareness of what is tricky to notice, so they can learn to adjust their attention more effectively.

- We gradually release our level of support for noticing in response to students' increasing skill and awareness.

- We review and reteach the rules for grammar and punctuation in response to student need.

- We use mentor texts to analyze and appreciate how writers use punctuation to make their message clear and credible.

- We don't always save editing for the end. Flash editing at various points in the writing process invites success and engagement before students decide they are *done*.

Drafting Your Story

Take a moment to think about editing in your classroom. On your own, or with colleagues, think about the following:

- How do your students perceive and approach editing? What does it mean to them (purpose)?

- How do you teach and encourage your students to edit?

- What are some of the challenges and successes you have experienced when teaching your students about editing?

- What are some things you might try after reading this chapter?

CHAPTER 10

Assessment and Feedback for Close Writing

Criticism, like rain, should be gentle enough to nourish a man's growth without destroying his roots.—Frank A. Clark

When I was in school, my writing was assessed in one way: a grade when I was finished. I can remember seeing an A or B at the top of my paper, a few vague comments such as "Yes!" or "Nice!" in the margins, and occasionally a few editing marks to point out punctuation errors. I can remember wondering, *What did she think of this? What was she saying "yes" to?* If I got a B, I would be left wondering why it wasn't an A. If I got an A, I stopped reflecting altogether. The grade signaled the end of my learning, not a continuation.

Today, this type of assessment still has a role in evaluating student performance, but it doesn't invite close writing. This summative assessment comes at the end of a learning event, when the writer has no reason to reconnect with the work. However, the use of formative assessments is a supportive tool for fostering close writing. They are being used to support learning, not just report learning.

> **The moral of this story:**
> Close writers use learning targets, formative assessments, and feedback to help them reflect on their learning and plan next steps in their writing.

Summative Assessments

When the cook tastes the soup, that's formative; when the guests taste the soup, that's summative. —Robert Stake

The grade my teacher gave me at the end of my writing assignment is an example of a summative assessment. Its purpose is to evaluate the student's performance or understanding at the end of a unit of study in relation to some standard or benchmark. It sums up the teaching and learning experience. Typically, no more learning (other than incidental) takes place or is expected from the student. It tends to be more product-oriented.

Formative Assessments

The purpose of a formative assessment is to provide information during the unit of study that guides next steps for teaching and learning. It focuses on student outcomes or learning targets and provides feedback to the learners on where their work lies in relation to that target, so that they can take action in moving closer toward it. The assessment is not always teacher directed; student self-assessments are powerful methods of formative assessments.

SUMMATIVE ASSESSMENT	FORMATIVE ASSESSMENT
Reports out learning at the end of unit of study	Reflects on learning during unit of study
Final feedback	Ongoing feedback
Sums up attainment of targets or standards	Informs learner about proximity to targets or standards
Product oriented	Process oriented
Evaluative feedback	Objective, actionable feedback
Teacher directed	Teacher, peer, or self-directed

Both types of assessments have a role in our classrooms; one is not superior to the other. But our story focuses on the use of formative assessments to encourage close writing. The information we get and the ways we use it help us to promote a closer relationship between the writer and the writing.

Creating a Feedback Loop

My son, Casey, has a little free time, so he pulls out his phone and plays a modern version of a classic arcade game. His goal is to help the chicken cross the road, but a variety of obstacles make it challenging. Depending on the moves he makes, his chicken may be run over, fall into a river, get carried away by an eagle, or experience a variety of trauma. However, if he can anticipate these obstacles and navigate skillfully, his chicken can cross the road successfully.

Video games provide a familiar analogy for a feedback loop. Casey understands what the target is and performs an action to achieve that target. Almost immediately, he receives feedback as he sees the result of his action. Based on that feedback, he learns to adjust to improve his performance. The game also receives information about Casey's performance and adjusts the level of difficulty. Both Casey and the game modify their actions in response to the feedback. This is a learning model for engagement and success.

Our classrooms that use formative assessments effectively are creating a similar structure (Figure 10.1). The feedback cycle is actually two loops in a close writing classroom, both the teacher and the students respond to the information they receive. The bottom loop demonstrates the teacher's role in the feedback cycle. The top loop represents the role of the student. The middle area can be teacher or student (close writer) directed. With this close writing model, students take a more active role in assessing their work in relation to the learning targets, making adjustments in response. They do not necessarily wait for the teacher to determine next steps and revisions. The teacher strives to offer feedback and support that allows the students to determine next steps; they encourage more awareness and self-regulation.

STUDENT FEEDBACK LOOP

The student is presented with new learning from the teacher and then writes to demonstrate the intended learning (learning target) in his work. He will closely read and reflect on his writing in relation to the learning target. Based on that reflection, the student can assess his work. He might also receive feedback from the teacher or a peer. The student must then decide on an appropriate response, which may include revising, editing, or additional writing.

TEACHER FEEDBACK LOOP

The teacher determines the new learning for the students, based on standards, curriculum, and previous work. She shares the learning target and models the intended learning. She may also model the internal dialogue to help students monitor their work against the

Formative Feedback Loop for Close Writing

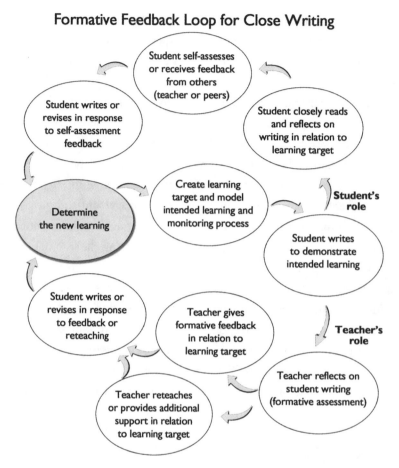

Figure 10.1
Formative feedback loop for teachers and students

expected learning. The teacher reads, reflects on, or evaluates the student's writing as a mode of formative assessment. If the student work is not a direct hit on the learning target, the teacher has a few choices. If the student's work is way off the mark, reteaching or stronger models may be necessary. If the student's work is close to the intended learning target, she can provide formative feedback to move the student closer to the target. She provides information on where he is in relation to the target and hints or ideas to help close the gap. The teacher can then determine the new learning that would be appropriate. Eventually, close writers can begin to determine new learning as they become more self-regulated. Let's take a look at how this has unfolded in many of our classrooms.

DETERMINING THE LEARNING: START WITH THE END IN MIND

To begin with the end in mind means to start with a clear understanding of your destination. It means to know where you're going so that you better understand where you are now so that the steps you take are always in the right direction. —Stephen R. Covey

When we begin with the end in mind, we identify the intended learning using standards and curriculum, but we also consider what our students are bringing to the process. We continually consider student work to select the next appropriate steps for learning. We then identify the success criteria, *I'll know I can do this when I* _____. There should be specific observable or measurable evidence that can help the learner self-assess. Then, we can determine the sequence of lessons that will help the students achieve the desired learning.

CLEAR EXPECTATIONS

When my son was in kindergarten, he wrote page after page of stories (see Figure 10.2). It was such a joy to read the work of my little author.

At some point in first grade, we noticed the amount of writing decreased dramatically. The writing he did at home was still prolific, but his work at school was incredibly brief. We asked him about this when he brought home his monthly writing journal. He responded, "My teacher said we needed to write two sentences each day."

I followed up, "Casey, I don't think she meant to write *just* two sentences. You can write more than that if you want."

"No, Mom. She said two sentences." There was a strong degree of certainty in his voice. It was important for him to do what his teacher expected, and he wasn't going to change without her consent or direction. Luckily, he had a wonderful first-grade teacher, so when my husband and I met with her, we shared our son's interpretation of her directions. She was disturbed to learn that Casey mistook her instructions to write *at least* two sentences each day as write *only* two sentences each day. Her intention to encourage more writing had the opposite effect. Needless to say, she revised her directions the next day.

That example stuck with me over the years. It made me more aware that sometimes the expectations we share with our students may not be as clear as we assume. We may

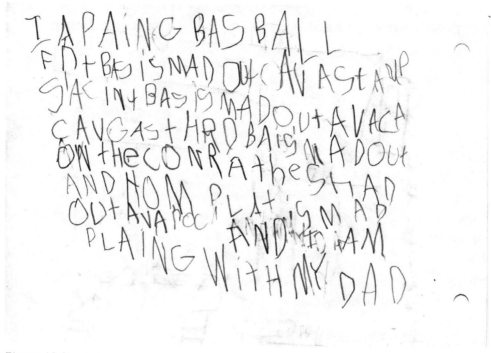

Figure 10.2
Casey's kindergarten writing

unintentionally constrain or shape the work we are asking of them in ways that were never intended. If she had provided some modeling or exemplars of her expectations, it would have become apparent to Casey that two sentences were a minimum expectation, not a maximum.

The purpose in writing this is not to make anyone feel guilty or to discourage us from setting expectations or assessing student work. It is simply to remind myself of the importance of seeing things through the eyes of my students; their perception is their reality. Creating student-friendly learning targets and assessing student work in relation to those expectations has become a focus of my work with teachers and students.

Learning Targets

Learning targets focus on what the students are learning. When we shift our language from *Students will be able to...*, which conveys the teachers' expectations toward *I can...*, which declares the learner's expectations, we begin to shift responsibility from the teacher to the learner. Learning targets are designed for the students and are instrumental in developing self-regulated learners or close writers.

Several years ago our district began focusing in on creating and using learning targets in our classrooms. With the adoption of the Common Core State Standards (CCSS), we found it an opportune time to unpack each of the standards that we were addressing in our lessons and tease out what we wanted our students to know and to do. We realized how incredibly dense some standards were and how ambiguous others seemed to be. Our work on creating learning targets with one another generated some meaningful conversations about teaching and learning.

CREATING LEARNING TARGETS

We decided to write the targets in the form of "I can" statements. Using the word *can* implies that this learning is not only attainable but expected. We want our students to know that we believe they can but, more importantly, that they believe it themselves. We can make it easier for students to visualize and reflect on a target if we follow *I can* _____ with . . . *when I* _____ to include success criteria. (See examples in Figures 10.3–10.5.)

Next, we talk about using kid-friendly language. This was surprisingly tricky at first. Trying to strip a standard of jargon and rephrase it in accessible language to our students took practice. If we simply post, "Use precise language and domain-specific vocabulary to inform about or explain the topic" (CCSS.ELA-Literacy.W.5.2.d), many of our students will be at a loss for what to do. So we draft targets such as "I can write like an expert when I use strong words and specific vocabulary about my topic" or "I can write like a scientist when I use science vocabulary to teach about my topic."

STEPS FOR WRITING LEARNING TARGETS

- Decide on a lesson-sized amount of learning based on standards and curriculum.
- Frame the expectation in kid-friendly language (*I can* _____)
- Ensure the expectation is easily observable, evaluable, or measurable by the student (*When I* _____).
- Discuss and model the expected learning or behavior.
- Post the target and reference it before, during, and after the lesson.

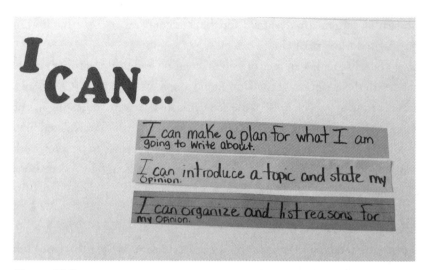

Figure 10.3
I Can 1

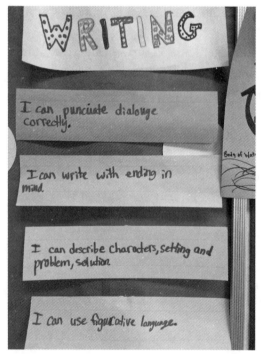

Figure 10.4
I Can 2

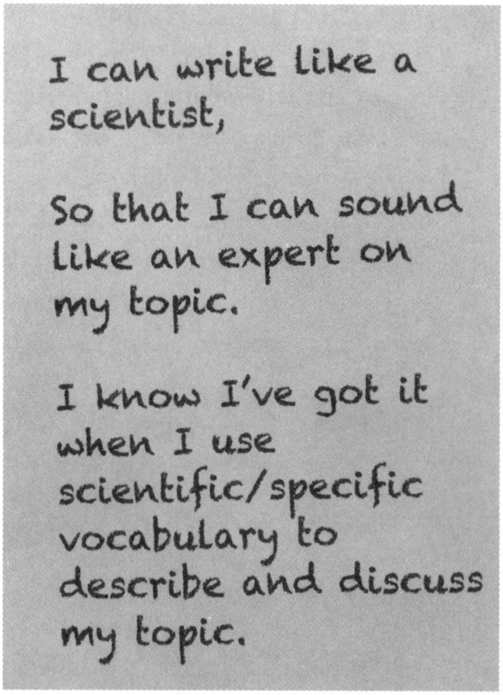

I can write like a scientist,

So that I can sound like an expert on my topic.

I know I've got it when I use scientific/specific vocabulary to describe and discuss my topic.

Figure 10.5
I Can 3

USING LEARNING TARGETS

We introduce the target as a part of our mini-lessons to ensure students understand the language being used. For example: *I can use scientific vocabulary to write like an expert on my topic.* We model what the behavior or writing should look like, using clear exemplars and explicit demonstrations to make the target even more visible and comprehensible for the students.

Language such as, "Today we are going to write like scientists. We want to sound like experts on our topic, and to do that, we need to use the words a scientist would use. We might use words like *habitat* instead of *home*, or *nocturnal* instead of *awake at night*. As you are researching and writing today, I want you to look out for science vocabulary that you will use in your informational pieces to teach readers about your topic."

Then, students are expected to reflect on the learning target to self-assess, "How am I doing?" This is when the ability to closely read one's writing becomes an important skill. Students can narrow their lens and focus on a specific aspect of writing; making reflection more manageable. If we have given them some internal dialogue to frame their thinking they can self-evaluate more effectively: *I'm writing like a scientist when I'm using scientific words.*

USING LEARNING TARGETS

Before the lesson
- To determine the lesson-sized amount of learning
- To consider criteria that would demonstrate success

During the lesson
- To share and model the intended learning during a mini-lesson
- To help the students self-reflect on their work in relation to the target
- To help teachers give formative feedback to guide students' work

After the lesson
- For students to self-assess their learning and consider next steps
- For teachers to assess student work to determine next step and needs

During a unit of study
- Use collections of learning targets to create an assessment rubric (either formative or summative in nature)
- Use collections to serve as a learning history for students (encourage growth mindset)
- Posted targets can serve as a bridge between units of study (teach for transfer)

LEARNING TARGETS AND FORMATIVE ASSESSMENTS

Along with the use of learning targets in our classrooms, our district has been digging into the use of formative assessments to refine our instruction and support student achievement. The more immediate the feedback, the more likely students will use it to adjust their thinking and writing. But with so many writers, we often felt like we couldn't get to everyone in a timely manner. By using some quick, formative assessments many of us were able to prioritize and differentiate our students' needs more efficiently. Following are some examples:

SWIFT SORT

One of the simplest methods of formative assessment is a swift sort (see Figure 10.6). It gives the teacher a cursory indication of how students performed in relation to the day's expectations or a specific learning target.

- Collect the student work (open notebooks to the day's work) at the end of a lesson

- Pull out the day's learning target (expectation/focus of mini-lesson)

- Create three piles of student work

    1. No understanding or application of learning target

    2. Some understanding or application of learning target

    3. Strong understanding or application of learning target

- Students in the number 1 pile will need reteaching and supportive examples

- Students in the number 2 pile may need some targeted feedback or closer observing

- Students in the number 3 pile are good to go

This sort will not diagnose students' specific issues, but it allows the teacher to prioritize time and energy where it is most needed.

Figure 10.6

Luanne Phair and I sort student writing by level of proficiency.

TARGET TALLY

ANALYZING SUCCESS WITH LEARNING TARGETS

Another approach to rapidly identifying student strengths and needs would be to look for evidence of learning targets in student writing. (See Figure 10.7.)

- Create a simple table with learning targets in the left-hand column.

- To the right are three columns as follows: 1 = Does not meet (or "No Go"), 2 = Partially meets (or "So-So"), 3 = Meets (or "Good Go").

- As you read through each child's piece, mark a tally using names or initials that relate to the level of proficiency concerning each standard (Figure 10.8).

You can begin to look for patterns that guide instruction and the level of support students will need to be successful.

Figure 10.7

Andrea Bryant analyzes and tallies student proficiency with each target.

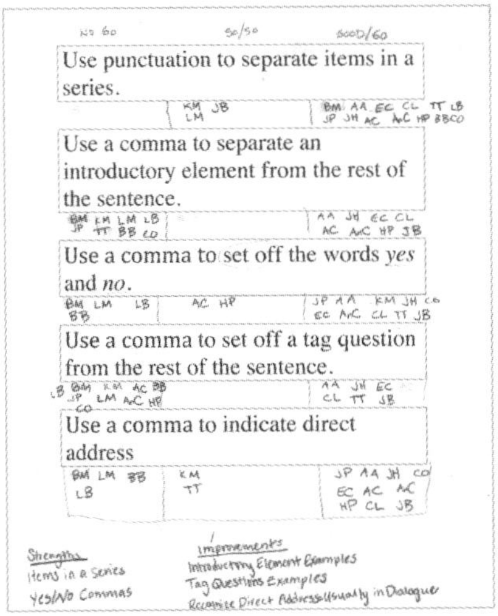

Figure 10.8

Andrea can quickly determine levels of support for each student and target.

SELF-RATE

REFLECTING ON PROXIMITY TO LEARNING TARGETS

One way to help students become more aware of the expectations and to evaluate how close their work comes to hitting the target is to invite them to self-assess. This could be done one target at a time or similar to the target tally table. (Templates can be found online at www.stenhouse.com/closewritingbook.)

Exit Slip

- Write the day's learning target on an exit slip. Ask the students to rate their perceived level of mastery or required support (see Figures 10.9 and 10.10).

1 = Not close	2 = Getting closer	3 = Hit the bull's-eye (target)
1 = Need Help	2 = Need Practice	3 = I could teach it

- Ask the students for a brief explanation of why they chose the rating.
- Compare the students' perception with the teacher's observation/assessment.

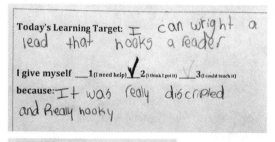

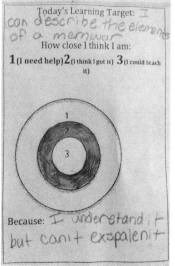

Figure 10.9

Students evaluate their understanding of the learning target.

Figure 10.10

Students contemplate how close they are to hitting the learning target.

CHECKLISTS AND RUBRICS

TARGETED SKILLS FOR ASSESSMENT

Learning targets are critical for precise teaching and self-directed learning, but they are also used for formative or summative assessments with checklists and rubrics.

- Create a list of learning targets for the unit of study that the students will be accountable for demonstrating in their work.

- These can be turned into simple checklists that can be used to closely read and look for evidence. (See Figures 10.11 and 10.12.)

- They can also be used for rubrics that evaluate the learning on a scale of proficiency (does not yet meet, partially meets, meets, or exceeds expectations).

Students will not be surprised or confused about our expectations when we are clear and forthcoming. These tools help them to take ownership for their work as self-directed learners.

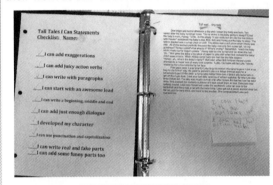

Figure 10.11

Fifth grader self-assesses with learning targets.

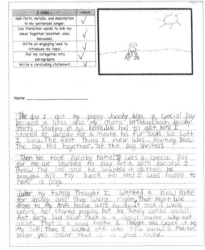

Figure 10.12

Third-grade *I can* self-assessment

SELF-ASSESSMENT

Teachers and peers can assess and give feedback to guide writers, but an essential element of close writing is to evaluate our own work honestly and purposefully. The reflections we discuss in Chapter 8 can be thought of as formative self-assessments, and many of the formative assessments teachers do can also be done by students to become more aware of strengths, needs, and next steps. The more opportunities students have for self-assessment, the more accurate their perceptions and more self-directed their actions can become.

TEACHERS USE FORMATIVE ASSESSMENTS TO:

- Preassess student understanding and skill to determine focus of new learning.

- Foster a growth mindset in their classroom: "There will be things you can't do *yet*, but as we work through this unit you will learn to do it."

- Continually evaluate student learning in relation to learning targets. How close is a student's work to meeting the expectations?

- Differentiate instruction: reteaching, small-group instruction, more examples, targeted feedback?

- Regularly evaluate scaffolds. Can I remove some supports? Do I increase or decrease that level of support more gradually? Is it time for a new scaffold?

- Create new learning targets. Based on what they show me they can do, what are the next steps? Do I need to break down a target more carefully or move on to another?

- Look for patterns in student work that reflect common understandings or misconceptions.

- Involve the students in their learning. Assessing is not a teacher-only domain. How can I create opportunities and provide support so students can self-assess their work more effectively?

This might seem like a lot of work, but Grant Wiggins suggests, "By teaching less and providing more feedback, we can produce greater learning" (Wiggins 2012, 12). The more we look at student writing in relation to our expectations, the more seamless the teaching–learning feedback loop. When teachers have a clear idea of what we expect (learning target) and we allow ourselves to prioritize our focus (observe), we can more easily evaluate how close a student's work comes to meeting that expectation (assess). So anytime a teacher observes student work with the intention to evaluate it against an expected learning target, it is, in essence, an assessment.

FORMATIVE FEEDBACK

When I refer to formative feedback, I am not talking about evaluation, praise, or advice, which do not invite close writing. Those encourage dependence on others to answer questions such as, "Is this good?" or "What do I need to do next?" To help us frame our understanding of formative feedback, let's look at some examples of what formative feedback is and isn't in relation to the learning target: I can use dialogue to develop my characters.

FORMATIVE FEEDBACK ISN'T:	FORMATIVE FEEDBACK IS:
Praise *Nice job! Great dialogue.*	**Describing what students can already do or partially do** *You've used dialogue right at the beginning, but after this first paragraph I'm not seeing any more.*
Evaluation *B+ This would have been an A with more dialogue. This is not your best work.*	**Reflecting on the learning target** *What did we say some of the purposes of dialogue could be?*
Advice *Next time try to use more dialogue.*	**Reflecting on the work** *How could we learn more about your characters through what they say, how they say it, or to whom they are talking?*
Directions *Write some dialogue in that second paragraph when she is meeting Marie. She could invite Marie to the party.*	**Inviting action** *When you reread your work, look for some places where your characters are interacting and think about how some dialogue might help us get to know them better.*

Peter Johnston is my go-to for considering how language shapes learning in the classroom. His book *Choice Words* is one of the few books I consider a must-read for all teachers. He demonstrates how the things we say (or don't say) affect the level of self-regulation our students achieve and shares language that supports and encourages strategic thinkers. In an article on formative feedback in *Educational Leadership*, Johnston advises, "When a teacher draws a student's attention to the compositional choices he or she made (to construct a convincing argument), the teacher invites that student to construct a self-narrative that says, I did x (added a detail to my illustration of a key point), the consequence of which was y (I got my meaning across better). This kind of feedback positions students as people who can accomplish things by acting strategically" (Johnston 2012, 65–66). Close writing encourages strategic thinking, not compliant behavior. Formative feedback is a powerful tool for supporting this.

PEER FEEDBACK

Peer feedback is not always easy or helpful. When we consider how difficult it can be for us, as experienced teachers, to offer insights or support to some of our students, we can begin to appreciate the challenges our novice writers face. The feedback is often only weak praise: "I like your story. You made great illustrations." This may be nice to hear, but it doesn't encourage closer writing.

If we want our students to offer feedback to one another, we need to be specific, focusing on the learning target to guide the interaction. We can model the conversation, "Today's learning target was _____, can you show me where you were able to do this?" If there are specific things we want peers to look for and comment on, we need to model this.

One successful peer feedback approach is a quick-draw. Similar to a quick-write, students draw (rather than write) in response to a peer's piece of writing. The writer is then given visual feedback on what resonated or seemed important to the listener (potential reader).

Figure 10.13

Tommy reads while his peers quick-draw.

PEEK INSIDE A CLASSROOM: QUICK-DRAW

Haley Duncan's fourth graders are finishing drafts for historical fiction stories. We want to give them an opportunity to get feedback from potential readers before they decide they are finished.

"Boys and girls, today we are going to try an activity that will help us better understand the pictures that readers will get in their heads when they hear our writing. It's called a quick-draw. One of you will share a part of your story, and the rest of us are going to listen carefully and see what pictures we get in our heads. We'll think about the details you use to help us create clear pictures and then we'll have about ten minutes to draw the big ideas, or big pictures, that emerge in our minds. We aren't going to do our own version of the story. We want to really think about the words the writer used and let them help create the pictures. This will give feedback to the writer about what the readers will think is important."

Haley chooses Tommy, who reads a few paragraphs aloud while the class listens (Figure 10.13). Once Tommy finishes the first reading, students begin sketching their pictures. Tommy reads it again so the class can listen for additional key details.

After ten minutes, we collect all the drawings, and without commenting or discussing, I place each under the document camera for students to see (see an example in Figure 10.14). I ask the class what they are noticing about the pictures.

"There are a lot of pictures of the waterfall."

"So this must have been an important picture in a lot of your minds. Tommy, do any of these pictures look like the picture you had in your mind as you were writing the story?" I ask.

Figure 10.14

Classmates quick-draw feedback for Tommy's story.

"Some. But some weren't right. I picture it more of a river with the waterfall."

"So is there more about that waterfall that you could add that might help them think of it more as a river?" Tommy talks about some additional details that would help create a stronger image.

We partner the students to try a quick-draw with a part from their story they think is important for the reader to envision. The students complete another quick-draw and talk to their "illustrators" about their images. When the pictures differ, I encourage the writer to think about why that might be. After about ten minutes, we pull the group back together and reflect on how this activity could help us with our writing:

- If the reader has a different vision, we can add more details to help them have the same vision.

- We can stretch out the important moments with more details. If they didn't draw an important part maybe, we didn't write enough about it.

- We want the reader to understand what we are trying to say; it helps us see if they understand.

- The details from the drawings might inspire more ideas. They might have details in their picture we could add with words.

I invite them to try out this activity with a buddy sometime. They often read their story to a partner and talk about it, but the comments tend to provide little insight or valuable feedback. The pictures provide a catalyst for discussion around intent, importance, and precision that their conversations often lack.

QUICK-DRAW

VISUALIZING FOR FEEDBACK

Similar to a quick-write, students draw (rather than write) in response to a peer's piece of writing.

- Ask a student to share a part of their writing (it could be a story, informational, persuasive) that they feel like they have tried to paint a clear picture.
- Ask partner or class to listen to the portion first for meaning and then for details to draw a picture of images the story created in their minds.
- Share the pictures and discuss any differences. How did the writer's choice of words or use of detail influence the drawings? What could the writers learn from the drawings that would help them revise their writing?

Our use of formative assessment and feedback is still in its infancy. It looks very different in each classroom. We strive to incorporate the fundamental elements of clear learning intentions, ongoing formative assessments, timely feedback, and responsive next steps. From grade to grade, school to school, and classroom to classroom, I see a variety of styles and methods employed. A common goal is that we are constantly asking ourselves, What is it we should be learning, and how are we doing? For classrooms encouraging close writing, we want to make sure our students ask themselves the same questions. Formative assessments and feedback provide us a structure for answering those questions.

A DISTRICT APPROACH TO WRITING ASSESSMENT: COLLABORATIVELY LOOKING AT WRITING

Several years ago I helped my district design a writing continuum as an assessment tool to help us hone our observations of student writing. We knew it was important that we were consistent with our expectations so we used anchor papers that reflected the characteristics of writing for each level of the continuum. With close reading and thoughtful discussions, our observations are becoming keener, and our scoring is more calibrated with our writing continuum. We have had time together to observe, to discuss, and to evaluate student writing that has raised our awareness and refined our expectations. We all approach a piece of writing through our own prism of experience and understanding, but through our work together, we have been able to strengthen our observational skills and begin to appreciate student work more effectively.

Seldom does a student's paper fall neatly into one of our categories. We highlight characteristics across a range of levels. We are careful to look beyond the number and focus on the observable behaviors and characteristics to plan for instruction and offer specific feedback. The writer is not characterized as a level, but the writing done on a given day receives a score, giving us a point of reference. (See Figures 10.15 and 10.16.)

We constantly tweak the scoring and the continuum as we have learned more about the process of writing and the expectations we have for our writers. We have layered Common Core Standards into our levels, pulled in more anchor papers with analytical comments, incorporated more user-friendly language into the descriptors, and given a great deal of thought to the prompts that would be used. The process has encouraged us to look closely at our student writing in a more collaborative and systematic way.

Through this process, I have realized that there is no perfect tool; ours certainly isn't. No rubric or continuum can capture the infinite possibilities for writing, nor should it

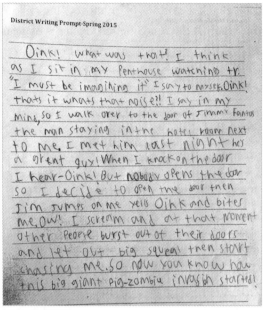

District Writing Prompt-Spring 2015

Oink! what was that! I think
as I sit in my penthouse watching tv.
"I must be imagining it" I say to myself. Oink!
thats it whats that noise?!! I say in my
mind, so I walk over to the door of Jimmy Fantos
the man staying in the hotel room next
to me. I met him last night hes
a great guy! When I knock on the door
I hear-Oink! But nobody opens the door
so I decide to open the door then
Jim jumps on me yells Oink and bites
me. Ow! I scream and at that moment
other people burst out of their doors
and let out big squeal then start
chasing me. So now you know how
this big giant pig-zombie invasion started!

Figure 10.15

Fourth-grade writing prompt

	Pablo, , Al, Mr. Franklin,	The Escape, Crack!, Monroe Children, Marcie! Same Couch as Me	Mittens, is The C
	Planning 10	**Elaborating** 11	
	• Leads introduce characters, setting or situations. • The event sequence unfolds naturally, but may have gaps, sometimes long and rambling • May use dialogue and/or detailed description of characters' actions, thoughts and feelings. • Use transition or temporal words and phrases to signal event sequences or changes • Beginning, middle and end (endings may not be satisfying) • Evidence of voice, humor or connection to reader • Varies word choice (adjectives, proper nouns, precise words) • Varies sentence beginnings, structures or types	• Strong lead, introduces characters, setting or plot to orient the reader • Events unfold thoughtfully (though may lack mature logic) with a variety of temporal words and phrases. • Effectively uses dialogue or 'thoughtshots' to develop characters or show reaction to events • Sense of paragraphing emerging • Use specific, concrete, or sensory words and phrases to describe and convey events/experiences precisely. • Characters/settings often have names • Use of conventions does not detract from the writing	• Stron reade • Well- (probl • Narra pacing exter • Crea the p • Write • Well- phra • temp • Write appr • Cons conv
ns, The rm	The New Landscape, Old Man Dwight, The Frenchman, PUSH		Next time..., U Capt

Handwritten annotations: 10.5, onomatopoeia, 1st person, burst, squeal! invasion, paragraph/ punctuate dialogue to be stronger

Figure 10.16

Fourth-grade scored continuum

be the only lens through which we view our writers and their writing, but we needed to start somewhere. The process of carefully looking and conversing about student writing is what we find most important. Our continuum just helps us to use some common language and fine-tune our expectations. (Continuum can be found online at www.stenhouse.com/closewritingbook.)

STUDENTS UNDERSTANDING THE ASSESSMENT

Many teachers share the writing continuum with their students by posting the benchmarks along with correlating student writing samples. This has given students greater insight into the expectations. They can see that many of our learning targets are lifted directly from the continuum, which reflects CCSS writing standards. Though there is a degree of subjectivity, the students can sometimes use this tool for self-assessment. Involving them in the process has empowered many to set goals and reflect on their writing more mindfully. (See Figure 10.17.)

Assessment Empathy

Because a big part of close writing is helping writers develop a closer relationship with their writing, we can better help them when we understand their experiences. Occasionally, walking in the shoes of our learners can create a greater understanding of what is required to complete the assignments, take the tests, and hear the feedback through the lens of a child. We realized we have given our district writing prompt many times without trying it out for ourselves, so we decide it's time that we do.

It's a Tuesday afternoon, and the last bus has been called. Teachers Dan

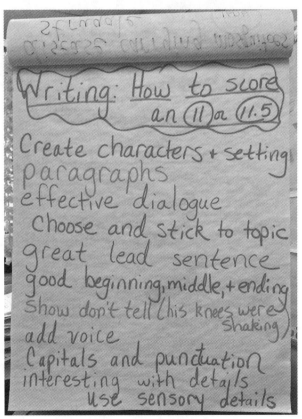

Figure 10.17

Fifth graders generate writing expectations.

Figure 10.18

We give ourselves the same writing assessment we give our students.

Johnston, Guy Meader, Kelley Capen, Andrea Bryant, Haley Duncan, and I gather in a classroom for a writing assessment (Figure 10.18). We want to become more familiar with our district writing prompt by seeing it from a fresh perspective: that of our students. We know we can't emulate it exactly, but we try to incorporate some of the key features: unknown, on-demand prompt, fixed time limit, and independent/quiet work time.

We use the website http://writingexercises.co.uk/index.php to generate a random prompt. We click on *random picture* from the children's writing exercises. The first image is indecipherable, so we click again. A car buried under the rubble of a garage pops up. We are ready to write. We set a twenty-minute time limit, and we are off!

It's hard for us to keep from talking or joking with a colleague. Hmmm, we can all recall those students in our classrooms. After a while, someone asks, "When did we start? How much time do I have?" We all start thinking about how we are going to pull a cohesive story together. We know a lot of students who can't.

When the time is up, we all immediately begin talking, letting off some bottled-up energy perhaps. I think about the students in our classrooms working alone on a piece for up to forty minutes. If they connect to the topic or enjoy writing, the time must sail by. If they are stumped for ideas, can't connect, or struggle with writing, the time must really drag. We all agree that our time went by much quicker than we thought it would.

Our students often have to wait for days before we can score papers with the careful attention they deserve, so we decide we should wait, too. I ask them to write out a quick exit slip that expresses what they were thinking, wondering, or concerned about as they took the assessment. I could see some common thoughts emerging:

> "I was anxious to find out what the prompt would be and wondering if I would be able to write to it."

> "I was hoping I'd get something that inspires me. I loved it! I instantly got an idea and ran with it. I was messy and would have liked to edit and revise more."

> "I was hoping I could come up with a story and that I wouldn't freeze up. The first prompt I had no clue what the picture was even about . . . I wonder if kids ever experience that."

> "I was a little nervous whether I would be able to connect to the prompt. I know I started thinking, *This better be good* if my peers are going to read this. I wonder if kids worry about being judged by their teacher. Will she think less of me?"

> "I was a little stressed! I want to do well and not have a 'stupid' idea. I needed to do more preplanning. I only made it halfway through my story at the end of twenty minutes!"

> "I felt kind of rushed and worried I wouldn't finish. I can better understand some of their anxiety."

WALKING THE PROVERBIAL MILE

It's a few days later, and we are gathered for lunch. There is a lot of joking as we hand back the scored papers to our colleagues. Humor seems to ease the tension we are feeling about "judging" our peers' writing. I ask the teachers to talk a little bit about the experience and how it has helped them think about the assessment process for our students.

Haley shared, "I have to say I was a little nervous to score a colleague's prompt as well as having mine scored. I know that many of my students get very nervous about the prompts we give them, knowing I'm going to score it. It helped that I was working with colleagues I am comfortable with. I can only hope that my students are comfortable enough with me that it takes some of the stress off of the scoring part. I think it's important to put us in our students' shoes to experience what we have them do. Sometimes, it's easy to tell students what to do; it's informative to see their side of it. It reminds me of how antsy I get at long meetings or workshop days, which is why I like to incorporate brain breaks!"

Guy adds, "I think the thing that I take away from this is how hard it is to develop a solid piece in a short period. While ours was shorter than the actual writing prompt, I can sympathize with the students, especially those who struggle with writing, when trying to write something that shows their best skills and fighting the clock. While we are not necessarily looking for them to hit the marks of a final piece, coming up with something new and developing it on the spot is quite hard!"

GIVING IT OUR PROMPT ATTENTION

WALKING THE TALK FOR ASSESSMENTS

Teachers who write understand writers. To explore this more intentionally, we will walk the talk of the on-demand writing prompt.

- Gather a group of teachers together and present them with an on-demand writing prompt, similar to a recent student assignment/assessment.

- Try to re-create the student conditions as much as possible.

- Discuss your experience and any insights/wonderings you might have.

- Decide who will score the papers. Use the same criteria/rubrics by which the student papers are assessed.

- Jot down a quick "exit slip." "What have I discovered, confirmed, or wondered as a result of this activity?"

Considerations for English Language Learners

All students need to have an explicit understanding of the expectations for their learning and their work. The more clearly they perceive the target, the more likely they will hit it. Sometimes assumptions are made about expectations that many of our English language learner (ELL) students do not pick up on or misinterpret. The use of learning targets in the classroom along with demonstration and exemplars can help minimize those misunderstandings. They are also learning the academic language more easily when it is phrased in more kid-friendly language. Teachers need to be cautious, however, in reflecting on whether there are words or terms that may be outside the vocabulary of their ELL students.

Once the ELL students have a solid understanding of the work expected of them, they can monitor their own efforts in relation to clear exemplars or targets. For those in earlier stages of language acquisition, the demonstration and the examples will be a major scaffold. As they become more proficient, they can begin to use the written learning targets as a way to self-assess their progress in relation to the goal. This will allow for greater independence and increased confidence.

The empathy exercise my teachers and I conducted (Giving It Our Prompt Attention), could be broadened to incorporate the perspective of our ELL students. If we attempted to walk in the shoes of our ELL students with some of our lessons in a foreign language, what would we notice? What kind of feedback would we want? How would we respond to assessments and grades? How frustrating would it be to have our cognitive ability limited by our language proficiency? A week I recently spent in Spain and France provided me with some of that empathy, as I came to know firsthand how important communication is to learning and how language affects experience.

The Gist of the Story

Assessment for close writing is focused around providing information that will continually guide the teaching and learning in our classrooms. Formative assessment creates a continuous feedback loop for both teachers and students as they reflect on their work and modify their "next steps." It differs from summative assessments, which are useful for evaluating the effectiveness of our curriculum or instruction but less effective in supporting close writing strategies. Formative assessment and feedback can effectively promote close writing when:

TEACHERS . . .

- Start with the end in mind and determine the intended learning and the success criteria.

- Share those expectations as kid-friendly learning targets that are written as *I can* statements. This expresses our faith that the learning is indeed achievable.

- Demonstrate or model the expected learning and share exemplars of model work.

- Use formative assessments to help us differentiate our instruction and refine our conversations based on student need.

- Provide formative feedback to guide students toward success with the intended learning.

- Consistently discuss and convey expectations among all educators within our school so that students can build trust and understanding of the continuum of intended learning.

STUDENTS . . .

- Have opportunities to cocreate the learning targets and exemplars of work and express them as *I can* statements that encourage a self-fulfilling prophecy and build skills toward self-regulation.

- Continually self-assess their own work and make modifications (as needed) based on that assessment.

- Reflect on (and appreciate) success with the intended learning. Opportunities to celebrate and contemplate transfer are as important as time to "fix up" our writing.

- Give and receive feedback to peers on their work in relation to the learning targets.

Drafting Your Story

Take a moment to reflect on how you currently assess student writing in your classroom and district. Do your thoughts differ from those of your colleagues or students?

- How do you assess student writing? How does it promote close writing strategies and thinking?

- How do you convey intended learning to your students? Do you use learning targets?

- How do your students know whether they are successful with their writing?

- How does your school or district develop and/or assess common expectations for writing throughout the K–6 span?

- What are some things you might try after reading this chapter?

CHAPTER 11

Publishing and Performing: The Process and the Product

[A book] is not complete until somebody reads it. It takes the reader to complete it. You can write and write and write, but it's only half the thing. You have to throw your heart over the fence. … It's scary, and the fear never goes away.—Kate DiCamillo

My daughter, Bailey, strides onto the stage and takes her position. The music begins and all of the work she has put into dance these past few months comes pouring forth in her solo. She loves to dance just for herself, but there is a different energy when she is in front of an audience. Although the spectators watch the dance intently, we may see it differently as her mom, or her teacher, or a judge. This performance is not the end product of her dancing but an opportunity to share the culmination of toil, sweat, and tears with others. She will receive feedback that she can use to grow as a dancer, as well as to celebrate her accomplishments. We often approach writing the same way.

> **The moral of this story:** Close writers understand that the way they publish or present their writing can highlight the purposeful work that created it.

Not every piece of work our students complete is taken through the writing process to the publishing stage, nor should it be. We write for a number of reasons, some of which do not involve an audience. We do quick-writes to help us explore ideas and encourage writing fluency. We write poems or journals that are intensely private and for our eyes only. We engage in writing to reflect or to construct thinking that is shared with teachers only. But if we never have opportunities to write for a genuine audience, we are missing an important component of close writing.

When we tell students that writing is a transaction between writer and reader, but we provide limited transactions, we aren't walking the talk. We want our students to anticipate the potential of the words they laid down on paper to be lifted off the page by others. We want them to experience the various interpretations or reflections of others in response to those words. Publishing and/or performing bring the writer and the readers together in powerful ways.

Involve the Students

Part of being a close writer is fostering that relationship between the writer and the writing through all phases of the writing process; the publishing stage should be no different. If we want students to become more self-regulated in their learning and more independent with their work, they should frequently have a say in what the final product could be.

I have been working with a group of students over the past several years on a variety of writing projects. As sixth graders, they have had a range of publishing and presenting experiences. I want to discuss this part of the writing process and get their thoughts. I record their conversation (transcribed below) in class. I do not identify the students by name. Some comment several times, and I have more than a few "aha" moments as I listen to them talk.

I ask the kids, "Is it important for students to have an opportunity to publish or present their writing?" I am met with an immediate chorus of "Yes!" So I ask them to tell me why they think that is so.

"If you have a really good piece of writing you would want to have other people see it. Other people might get inspiration from your writing."

"If you are writing a story about something, people can see you are respectful of what's going on. If you are a victim of bullying, you can put down what happened. It could inform people about what happened and maybe others could learn from that and do something about it."

"I think it is important because if students don't have an audience there is going to be no motivation, they have no real reason to try."

"The books we read are written by adults, and obviously every adult was a kid at some point, but it is important to see things from other perspectives, and kids need to see things from the perspective of other kids, not just grown-ups remembering to be kids. Adults are not the only perspective we should read."

"Freedom for kids! Freedom for kids!"

"When all we read are things written by adults, we could get that mindset that it's a world where a kid can't have a chance to actually get his or her writing out there, and they might get a mindset that it can only be adults that are allowed to do this."

"Kids need a chance to express their ideas without needing to be adults."

"Some kids have vivid imaginations, and it can help some people. A child who has a very good image in their mind of something they want to happen, if they were to write about it, they could change the world, if they were to be able to publish it. They could impact the world, like adults, and they actually help the world, and not make it worse."

"Basically, everybody has a voice."

"I think kids have a really powerful imagination and they can write, too. It doesn't just need to be adults. I think kids should start turning the table. Kids should all get a chance to make something and publish it to a really big audience."

"BASICALLY, EVERYBODY HAS A VOICE."

I was prepared for answers that touched on the motivation and fun that publishing or performing a piece of writing brought to students. I wasn't anticipating the responses that expressed writing as a way to empower kids. They want their voices to be heard. They see writing as a way to share the human experience, solve problems, and create empathy and understanding. They want to hear the voices of other kids in what they read as well, not just adults. I am touched by the impromptu chanting, "Freedom for kids!" in which several classmates join in. They value the potential power that writing can offer. I am inspired!

I continue the discussion by asking, "What are some ways we could help you to publish or present your work?" Many students mention the Internet; they know the potential audience on sites like YouTube. Several mention making books that they can share with others and put into the library. Others talk about recording themselves reading their work, perhaps using an app to make an audiobook or podcast.

I didn't start our conversation with, "What would be fun ways to publish your work?" I started with "Is it important to share your work?" for a reason. I want them to understand the principle *form follows function*. How we choose to publish or perform our writing should be designed to reach our intended audience. Close writers think about their audience long before this point in the process, so perhaps they can begin to think about the best ways to reach their audience.

We can foster close writing when we begin to involve students in the design of some of our writing projects and the decisions about whether or how to publish. I realize we don't always have unlimited time and options but allowing choice doesn't mean offering infinite possibilities. We can certainly narrow the options to those with which we can easily complete. We can also be selective in what we choose to publish and make sure students are aware of those decisions early in the process.

I'm careful that the publishing project doesn't trump the writing and learning. I have seen far too many dazzling PowerPoints with amazing transitions and animation but very little thinking or writing. When we keep the intended learning clear and consistent during the writing process, it will remain the focus of our writing. The publishing will be a way to share that, not upstage it!

REFLECT WITH TEACHERS

I asked the teachers in my district why they thought publishing student writing was important. How does this final step in the writing process improve student writing? How can publishing promote close writing?

WHY PUBLISH?

- Motivates the writers to do their very best. There is someone other than the teacher who will evaluate his or her writing, and they want to impress him or her.

- Builds confidence in writers. It validates the students' work. It says, "This is important. You are important."

- Adds dimension and purpose to revision. Anticipating the needs of future readers invites alternate possibilities, greater clarification, and more precision than if it was simply to satisfy our needs. The writing often makes sense to us because it is our story, but how does it sound to others?

- Makes editing relevant. When they know they have to be considerate of other readers, they have a genuine purpose for editing carefully.

- Makes the reading–writing connection more visible and obvious. Kids get to see that their writing is meant to be read.
- Builds a sense of identity as a writer. Kids know authors publish and when *they* do, they become a part of that circle of real authors.
- Creates a writing community. When we work on writing together and help each other, we can all take some pride in the work that gets published.
- Fosters an understanding of audience. Rather than imagining how an audience might receive their work, they can reflect on the actual experience.
- Gives practice purpose. When a student is going to perform his or her writing for an audience, he or she must engage with it repeatedly and purposefully.

Look-Fors

Teachers are always being encouraged to focus on the writer, not the writing. When it comes to publishing, however, we can inadvertently give off mixed messages about our focus when so much emphasis is on the product. A while back we had a superintendent who did not want writing posted in the hallways that contained spelling errors. She felt this did not project the high standards we should have for our students. This was a tough one for many of us. We understood the desire to put our students' best work forward to the public, but if we fixed all the student errors, whose work was it? If only error-free student work went up, we'd have some pretty bare hallways. If we pushed the need for perfection over process and risk taking, we'd no longer have interesting or creative pieces in abundance to share.

This caused me to ponder, what *do* parents, administrators, teachers, and students see when they look at work that has been published to the hallways? It became obvious that we see through our individual lens of understanding and purpose. If someone thought the purpose of published writing in the hall was to display only our best and most polished work, he or she may have very different expectations for what should be seen than others might. So, why do we post student work? And does the audience understand that purpose?

Rather than hoping someone notices all the work that went into the writing we have published, we can define the experience, we can shape the narrative, and we can be proactive! I have been encouraging teachers to create and post look-fors next to the published writing in hallways or the classroom. These are intended to inform the audience of the process the writer went through to create this piece. They help direct the readers to notice the effort and intention the writers gave to their writing.

It's a bit like having a docent in a museum that helps us look at the works of art more deeply. We can view a painting and understand it on one level, but when someone points out aspects that we might not have noticed, we can appreciate it on an entirely different level. These look-fors act as a proxy docent for our student work. They help to make the invisible process that went into creating the writing more visible to the audience. They put the focus back on the learning and not on the activity or the product. There are several ways teachers in my district direct the audience's attention to the learning that is represented by the work:

- Post standards that align to the work

- Post teacher-created look-fors

- Post student-created look-fors

When teachers post the standards used in creating and implementing the writing lesson, it informs the audience that our work is intentional (see Figure 11.1). It reframes the standard from some vague state-mandated initiative into real classroom goals and

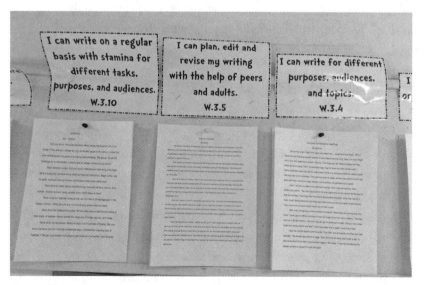

Figure 11.1
User-friendly third-grade Common Core State Standards

application. Seeing student work represented by the standard helps the audience become more familiar with the expectations, perhaps demystifying these criteria. For some, it may provide reassurance that our students are appropriately learning what is expected of them.

I find that the standards do not always adequately describe the amount of teaching and learning that goes into the writing product the audience sees. They lay out what is supposed to be taught, but do not describe the success criteria for what is learned. I have been encouraging teachers to share the learning targets or mini-lessons that went into the creation of that writing artifact in a set of look-fors (see one example in Figure 11.2). These direct the audience's attention to specific aspects of instruction and can be observed in the writing.

To foster a greater sense of awareness and ownership in the work that is being shared, some teachers invite their students to create the look-fors as well. They ask the students, "What is it you want others to notice and appreciate about your writing or the work you put into it?" These can become a single document for the group of work, or each child can create an individual look-for to post with his or her work. Some teachers have also used an approach called "pride tags" in which the student posts a small tag that describes something about the writing piece of which they feel particularly proud and want the readers to notice.

PEEK INSIDE SOME CLASSROOMS: LOOK-FORS: ASKING STUDENTS TO HELP US NOTICE

Jessica Walling's fourth graders have just completed their informational booklets on Maine branches of government. She wants to display their published work in the hallway as a means to share the

---

Our Writing LOOK-FORS

Your children did a lot of learning about the writing process and themselves as writers during this project on famous people with Maine ties. As a class, we would like you to notice how we:

• **Plan and organize our writing into paragraphs**

• **Arrange events in chronological order**

• **Obtain and paraphrase information from a variety of sources**

• **Identify key ideas from reading material**

Figure 11.2

Jess Walling's fourth-grade look-fors

information with readers and celebrate the efforts of her writers. I ask her, "What do you want others to notice and appreciate about this project?"

"Probably how they organized their information and used text features as part of that structure." We glance through several examples.

"So what do you think the students want others to notice? If we ask them to post look-fors on their pieces, we can encourage them to reflect on what they felt they did well and highlight that for their audience. It gives them a chance to evaluate and celebrate their efforts on this piece of writing and gives the people who walk by in the hallway a greater appreciation for the learning."

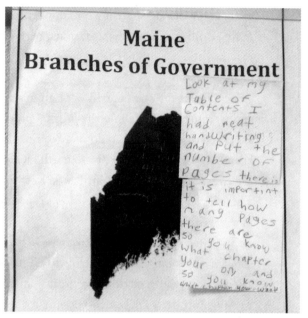

Figure 11.3
Students post look-fors on their reports.

Jessica is eager to have her students try this. "When we hang your reports out in the hallway, we want the people who read them to notice your work. We want you to closely read through your report and think about something you did well that you want other people to look for and notice. We'll call these our *look-fors*. On a sticky note, write down what you want someone to look for in your report and why it would be a good thing for them to notice."

The students point out various text features or definitions they want the readers to notice and place a sticky note on the cover of their reports (Figure 11.3). These are then displayed in the hallway, celebrating the process, as well as the product of their writing.

Publishing and Presenting Options

There are numerous ways to publish student work. Creating a menu of options with your class or colleagues can help you consider ways to bring your students' work to a wider audience. We must consider the intended audience and the purpose of the writing (as well as time and resources) to help us make those decisions. Looking at authentic forms of writing in the world around us can help us consider choices, and encouraging creativity fosters individuality and innovation. In the end, the *product* should highlight the learning that was achieved during the *process*.

STUDENT BOOKS

Simple folded, stapled, or glued books remain a favorite way for many K–6 students to publish. When students publish in book form, we are given some valuable insight into their understanding of how books work and how the structure supports the reader. Some teachers offer scaffolds for page layouts and encourage students to organize their work more systematically. Others offer a blank page for the writer to create the layout and structure independently. Knowing your writers, and knowing the intended audience of the book, can guide the level of scaffolding necessary.

There are commercial publishing companies that will turn student work into hardbound books, and sometimes parent volunteers will desktop publish student writing so that it seems more professional (see Figure 11.4). These alternatives can often require a larger time commitment than student-created books, but kids truly consider themselves published authors when they hold them in their hands. Think about the publishing issues you have had in the past, create a list of those concerns, and share it with your students. Invite their input and advice for dealing with them effectively. This gives them a sense of ownership and responsibility, both desirable characteristics of close writers.

Figure 11.4
Commercially published student book

ANTHOLOGIES

Creating class books or anthologies (Figure 11.5) is not a new idea, but it tends to be left behind as students get older. Lots of primary classrooms staple together collections of student stories, which are

Figure 11.5

Haley Duncan shares her students' historical fiction anthology.

typically short, to create a book. As student writing gets longer, it tends to be published as stand-alone texts. Creating collections of student writing on a similar topic or genre is powerful for several reasons.

STUDENT ANTHOLOGIES

- Foster a community of writers. Students recognize this collection represents all of us. Each of us contributed to making this book possible.

- Invite reflection. We can see quite easily how different writers approached related topics and examine similarities and differences in style, format, tone, etc.

- Create a learning history. These pieces represent the work we have done in class and the learning we have achieved.

- Foster writing identity. We can review one another's work more easily and can begin to recognize and appreciate the strengths of one another. We can recognize the mentors and experts that exist within the walls of our own classrooms.

PLAYWRITING

Marcia Hughes's writing club pens all forms of written works. Last year they collaborated on a script and then turned it into a play. They created costumes, made props, and after rehearsing their lines, invited classes in first through fourth grade to come to the gymnasium for their performance. These authors had a true audience for their writing and received immediate feedback on their work.

Not every child may want to write play scripts or screenplays, but without too much effort, stories can be turned into reader's theater scripts or a round-robin reading event. They can divide up sections of the text and assign portions to various readers to rehearse and then perform as a read-aloud. There is something very satisfying for many writers to hear their words spoken or performed by others.

TECH PUBLISHING/PRESENTING

Some of our teachers have found innovative ways to help students share their work. They are encouraged by the Common Core State Standards (CCSS) to "use technology, including the Internet, to produce and publish writing and to interact and collaborate with others" (CCSS.W.6). They know that many of their students are motivated by technology and are often quite tech savvy. Some teachers consider listening and speaking standards, such as "add audio recordings and visual displays to presentations when appropriate to enhance the development of main ideas or themes" (CCSS.SL.4.5) or "include multimedia components (e.g., graphics, images, music, sound) and visual displays in presentations to clarify information" (CCSS.SL.6.5) to help plan methods that enhance and clarify their writing to a listening audience. It seems as if there are new possibilities available almost daily.

WEBSITE PUBLISHING

There are various websites that will post/publish student writing. One of our favorites is 30/30 Poetry Kids (http://3030poetrykids.com). Every April, during National Poetry month, they send out a word or phrase prompt each day, and our students create poems inspired by it. Our teachers submit the poems via e-mail, and the webmaster posts them each evening. Our students can't wait to see their published poems. They share the web link with parents and family, and they feel like true authors whose work can be read by a wide audience.

BLOGS, WIKISPACES, AND SOCIAL MEDIA

Many people think of blogs as public web spaces, but there are many private blogging platforms for classrooms that can be a great site for publishing. Caroline Eldridge's second-grade class posted informational articles on vernal pools and extinct animals to their classroom blog where they could read and respond to one another's posts. Now her students are publishing poetry to the blog and are motivated to give and receive comments from their peers on their published poems.

Similar to blogs, some teachers use educational websites, such as Wikispaces, Edmodo, Moodle, or Google Sites, to increase student engagement and to create a collaborative platform for sharing writing. These sites allow students to work together or to share writing beyond the classroom walls. Teachers control the privacy settings and content, but students feel like they have access to a wider audience for their work.

VOICETHREAD

Another innovative technology application is VoiceThread (www.voicethread.com). On this platform, teachers can upload writing work as an image, and students can add comments or voice recordings to accompany those images. Caroline Eldridge's second graders are writing informational reports on the life cycle of a plant. We have been doing some lessons on rereading nonfiction with writer reading (see Chapter 3) to help others think about our ideas more clearly.

We tell them, "We want our listeners to hear what we think is important and that we sound like experts on our topic. When someone clicks on your report, they can hear you reading it to them. Try using your *pace*, *pause*, *punch*, and *play* to help your audience get a good picture in their heads!" I set up a VoiceThread that allows us to post a copy of the students' work to a page and record the students reading their pieces with their expert voices. We can share the link with parents or just play it in class for peers. Caroline posts the student writing in the hallway as well. This activity adds another dimension to the students' work that encourages them to think carefully about what they have written and how they want it to be read.

PODCASTS

A similar approach to presenting audio versions of student work is the creation of a podcast. Several teachers have used apps like GarageBand to lay down the tracks of students reading as well as music and sounds to present stories, research, and poems in unique

Figure 11.6
Janet Frake's fifth graders create poetry podcasts.

ways. Students can record and re-record sections until it sounds the way they want—encouraging careful listening and reading. Hearing their voices, and their individual reading styles, can be quite informative for many writers.

Janet Frake's fifth graders have been writing poetry for several weeks. We want to give them a chance to publish and present some of their poems. We submit them to *30/30 Kids Poetry*, and they are published on the website. We also create podcasts of students reading one of their favorite poems so they can also appreciate the sound of one another's poetry. They practice the pace and tone that will reflect their intended mood, and some layer music or sounds into the recording. (See Figure 11.6.)

Kelley Capen's fifth graders create podcasts of their horror and suspense stories during a narrative writing unit of study. They record their voice tracks, trying to create suspense with their pace or their character voices (Figure 11.7). To add some postproduction enhancements, they choose music and sound effects that will support the presentation of their work for a Halloween share.

Figure 11.7
Kelley Capen's fifth graders create horror story podcasts.

Guy Meader's sixth graders create a series of science podcasts on the topic of deposition and erosion. They present the facts and concepts they have been learning quite creatively. There are fairy tales, celebrity radio interviews, and breaking news reports that all inform the listener about these geologic concepts in innovative ways.

As students write for and prepare these presentations, they learn a great deal about the format for audiobooks, interviews, and breaking news. They also understand the content they have been researching on a deep and personal level in order for them to incorporate facts, vocabulary, and theories into their presentational style accurately. Later, as the students listen to the podcasts from one another, they hear these facts and theories about erosion and deposition in multiple ways, building a greater schema for these concepts.

PODCAST PUBLISHING

AUDIO PRESENTATIONS

Bringing student writing to life is fun and relatively easy with podcasts. You'll need a little time and some technology, but they make a great format for sharing student work.

- Choose software or an app available to you (perhaps GarageBand for Mac or Audacity for PC). You could also try a simpler format such as VoiceThread or even a quick video. If you are unfamiliar with how to use any of these formats, just remember there is a YouTube instructional video for *everything!*

- If students know they will be recording their work, they may consider their audience when contemplating the writing for the podcast and think about how they will engage them.

- Writers should reread and rehearse their writing before the recording session; this will minimize the number of retakes.

- Students can layer music or sound effects to create a mood or emphasize an aspect of their writing.

- Save the podcasts as digital files that can be shared and retrieved by students (flash drives, shared servers, etc.).

- Host a podcast party (similar to an author's tea) to showcase the students' work and accompanied writing.

VIDEOS

A live audience can give writers some immediate feedback on how their work is coming across and being received, but it's not always possible to make time for everyone. One approach to encourage students to read their work aloud and present it to an authentic audience is to record it for future viewing. This supports the idea that writing is a transaction between the writer and future readers; the video is a transaction between the writer and future viewers.

Teachers have used tablets and computers with simple recording capabilities, such as Photo Booth, to create these videos. Computers, recorders, or smartphone video cameras can be set up in a corner of the room for students to self-record their reading. These can be saved as video files for peers or younger students to select and listen, or they can be part of a student's digital portfolio for writing.

AUTHOR SHARES

As fun and exciting as technology may be, opportunities to share our work with an appreciative audience will always remain a favorite. Teachers host author teas and invite family and friends to come in to listen to student writing. They partner with classroom buddies to share their work and mentor other students. They often have an author's chair, as a place of prominence and importance for reading and sharing. They host writing clubs where students can bring their creative work to share with colleagues (Figure 11.8). These live interactions allow the author to interpret the writing for the audience and get immediate feedback on its reception. The sense of pride and importance the writers feel when they are the center of attention is often greater than if they are digitally recorded for broadcast at a later date!

PEEK INSIDE A CLASSROOM: THE ROLE OF AN OBSERVANT AUDIENCE

Scheduling issues during a testing week made it hard for two teachers to bring their students together the way they wanted. So Haley Duncan's fourth-grade students have sent their historical fiction picture books to Andrea Bryant's fifth-grade class, along with a list of look-fors they are hoping the readers will notice. Andrea and I ask the students to read through the stories and give the young authors some encouraging feedback on

Figure 11.8
Writing Club shares their work with one another.

those areas where the students focused their writing efforts. They each write some comments on a sticky note to give feedback to the writers (Figure 11.9). Andrea and I help to guide some of the most critical reviewers!

We know these comments will be helpful to many of the fourth graders, but I want to know whether this experience is helpful for the fifth graders as well. I ask them, "How could reading and reflecting on another student's writing help you as a writer?"

Katrina responds, "We could look at some of the same things in our own writing that we need to work on."

"By noticing what they did, good and bad, and trying to put that in your own writing," adds Keefer.

Eli suggests, "You could find things that you find interesting, like techniques that they used, and see if you can borrow that and make your writing better."

We decide that other students' writing

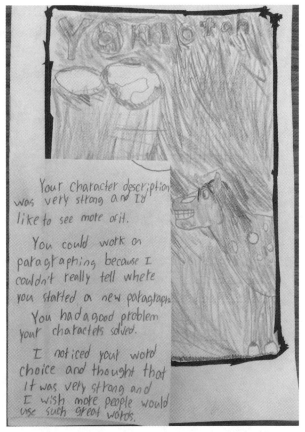

Figure 11.9

Fifth graders give feedback to fourth graders on their historical fiction stories.

can serve as a mentor text for us if we read it with some focused lenses. We don't need to criticize; we need to notice. We conclude that being the audience for others' writing can also help us with our own writing.

WRITERS' IMPROV

When students put their ideas down on paper, they usually seem so complete to the writer. When we ask, "Does it say everything you want it to say?" They often respond, "Yes!" As they read through it, their minds create vivid and detailed images, everything is there (to them), but not necessarily reflected in their words! I want them to see how important the words they put to paper, and those they leave out, are to the reader or listener in re-creating the intended image or message.

PEEK INSIDE A CLASSROOM: DRAMATIC INTERPRETATIONS

Samantha Simmons's fourth graders have written historical fiction stories. They have talked about the importance of rising action, climax, and falling action in creating an interesting plot. I ask the students to find the place in their story where they previously identified the rising action. We choose a reader and some actors (Figure 11.10). "Boys and girls, the author is going to read one paragraph at a time, and we are going to think about what is happening. Our actors are going to turn those words into actions by acting out the story—the way it is written. They are not going to add anything that isn't included with words."

Aria begins reading her story while Lily and Pat act it out. Lily tries to re-create the dialogue from the piece, but we see pretty quickly that there isn't much action. Aria has written some detailed descriptions of character and setting, but her plot is not as developed. When she gets to the climax of the story, the action happens quite swiftly. Everyone seems to enjoy the performance, even Aria. I want to know what she thinks of it.

"Did our actors interpret your story the way you would have?"

Figure 11.10
Students improvise historical fiction stories.

"Well, they got some."

We discuss the importance of details that help the reader envision the characters, the actions, the reactions, and the dialogue. Aria shares a few ideas she thinks she could have included that would have helped the actors.

Then, all of the students get a chance to work with partners; one reads and the other acts. They switch places and repeat the process. We come back together as a group. I want them to think about how sharing their work in this way could help them as a writer. Some of their comments included:

"It helps you picture your characters better."

"If the actor isn't doing much acting, that means you need more action."

"Yeah, we are supposed to have rising action, so we need to make sure there's actually action!"

"I thought about dialogue, too, and if the acting doesn't make any sense, then maybe you can make it better by making your story more clear."

These students are thinking about the needs of their readers to create explicit pictures so that they interpret the stories accurately. They are seeing that the ideas in their minds are not always relayed as clearly as they intended.

Presenting the Process

Some classes publish the finished products of a unit of study, but they also present each step of the process for that unit to demonstrate the learning that occurred. They sometimes attach prewriting organizers, a discovery draft, revision strips, and editing markups to a typed or polished final product (Figure 11.11). This helps the audience to see the writing and learning steps the author took on the journey to publishing. Sometimes their transformation from rough draft to final copy is a powerful testimony to the learning that occurred.

LIVE ACTION PROCESS

Some teachers and I have just started playing around with creating student videos to explain the process of a writing activity as part of a final presentation. A student can talk us through the steps of the project to help us appreciate the depth of thinking and learning that went into the piece. These videos could be set up in the hallways to accompany the students' published writing for author nights or parent conferences. They could be sent home as part of a digital newsletter that shares the week's or month's work in the classroom. These videos could not only accompany the published work but also be archived

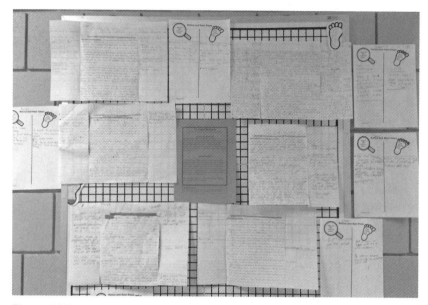

Figure 11.11

Becky Foster displays her students' revision process with look-fors.

and used as mentor clips for future classes of students or other colleagues' classes. The idea is to emphasize that we value the process as much as—or even more than—the product of our writing.

"WE"TUBE

STUDENT-CREATED CHRONOLOGY OF WRITING

Many schools have iPads, iPods, or video cameras that students could use to create a video chronology of their writing process. (Many have smartphones of their own that can do this.)

- Most students are aware of stages of the writing process. They are often posted and visible in many rooms. They move in and out of stages daily, as needed.

- Invite them to produce a video that demonstrates how they use the writing process to create a piece of writing.

- Ask them to think about how they would explain the process so that it accurately reflects the thinking and work that they do at each phase in their writing.

- Challenge them to make their video three minutes or less, so that they have to condense it into the essential learning.

- Share videos alongside the completed or published piece so that the audience can appreciate the process and the product of that student's writing.

Postpublishing Pondering

In whatever format we decide to publish or present student work, I always want us to ask ourselves, "How does this support the writer?" If we are vigilant in reminding ourselves that the publishing should continue to *invite* learning and not just *reflect* learning, we will create a community of close writers. That is especially true when the students share that same awareness.

One of the quickest ways to find out how publishing influenced or continues to influence student work and learning is to ask. A quick conversation around a few of these questions might provide us with some important insights and encourage our students to connect continually with their writing process.

- How did publishing (presenting) this writing help you to be a better writer?

- Is there another way we could have published/shared this work that would highlight your writing efforts?

- How did publishing this piece of writing help you think about how you will approach your next piece of writing?

When we offer time for discussion or reflection at the end of a unit of study, with a feed-forward focus (future learning), we are encouraging mindfulness. Close writers take what they learned from the process and the published piece into their future pieces of writing. The first time we have conversations like this, the reflections are not usually very deep, but when we consistently offer opportunity for reflection, students can anticipate these questions for themselves and not only answer them but also act on them.

Don't Forget "About the Author"

The books that "real" authors publish almost always contain some blurb about that author on the dust jacket. These give us biographical information as well as some insights into how they see themselves and express their identity. When we encourage our students to tell us about themselves (as authors), we are helping them to shape their writing identities by reinforcing the concept that they *are* authors and that we value who they are.

This example (Figure 11.12) is from one of the most reluctant writers I worked with this year. He had so many wonderful ideas and stories in his head, but he struggled to get them down on paper. In a recent project with his nurturing teacher, something clicked,

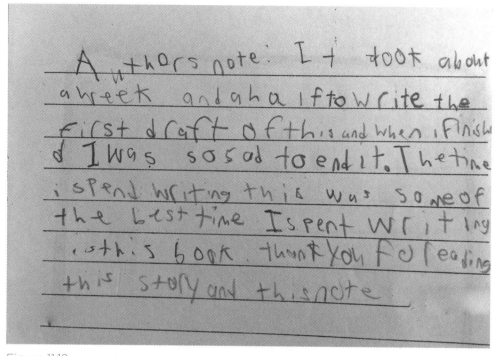

Figure 11.12

About the Author can reveal a lot about a student's writing identity.

and he wrote a five-page story. His author's note brought tears to my eyes when I realized he truly enjoyed writing for one of the first times in his life. He sees himself as an author. How do other writers see themselves? Perhaps we can find out from their authors' notes.

Considerations for English Language Learners

It is important for all students to have opportunities to publish their writing. Our English language learner (ELL) students are no exception. The supports we offer to help polish the finished pieces should depend on the purpose for sharing and the needs of the student. Celebrating the diversity of writing rather than expecting cookie-cutter products will make publishing and presenting work easier for all students.

There have been occasions when our ELL students were only able to write a few sentences in the time it took other students to draft an entire story. ELL students wrote what they could, and then when students were publishing, they shared the pen with the teacher or dictated a more detailed story. This did not take away from the work of the student but allowed them to have similarly published works like their peers.

I would certainly encourage look-fors when publishing or sharing the work of ELL students. Pointing out the amazing work they have accomplished, and the language and literacy they have acquired during the project or unit of study, would impress most audiences, who often have no idea of the obstacles students must overcome. We don't want audiences to focus on what they cannot yet do but celebrate what they *can* do.

The Gist of the Story

Publishing is frequently considered the last step of the writing process, but it doesn't have to signal the end of the learning. *How* we choose to publish or present our writing can be a consideration during the process that shapes our work. *When* we publish or present our work, we are given an opportunity to see how an audience receives it, potentially shaping future work. Publishing can support close writing in the following ways:

- We reflect on and acknowledge why publishing is an important part of the writing process.

- We create look-fors to make the process as visible as the product to our audiences, to share the techniques, elements, and skills we want them to notice.

- We take the time to recognize and celebrate what we were able to accomplish and think about how we can better appreciate the work of others.

- We consider creative options to share our writing so that we can think flexibly about the process in a variety of ways.

- We contemplate how technology can broaden our audience and what implications that may have for us as writers.

- We take the time to reflect on how others received our work and how we would like it to be received to help us plan for future writing.

- We connect with and celebrate our writing identities. Publishing and presenting give us opportunities to reflect on ourselves as writers in mindful ways.

Drafting Your Story

Take a moment to think about the publishing or presenting that you and your students do in your classroom. On your own, or with colleagues, think about the following:

- How do you decide when and how your students will publish or present their writing? What role do students have in that decision?

- What are some of the ways you publish? What are some ways you and your students would like to try?

- How does publishing or presenting writing improve your students' writing?

- Think about a recent writing project that you published in your classroom. What look-fors would you post to showcase the learning? What look-fors would your students come up with?

- What is something you are thinking about or might try after reading this chapter?

Close Writing with Authors

Getting Close to Writers to *Be* Close Writers

"How do they do that?" Whenever I finish reading a really good book, I find myself filled with wonder. I'm fascinated by how those marks on the paper caused me to cry, cringe, or chuckle. When I think about close writing, I want our students to appreciate that process on a personal level. When we write, we should always be our own first reader but hopefully not our last. To share the story in our heads effectively through writing, we need to be clear, coherent, and captivating. We can learn best from those whose writing we love to read.

In the past year, I sought out authors whose work has moved me and asked them to talk to me a bit about their writing process. I want our students to see that books don't just magically happen but that there is a hard-working writer who nurtured these stories into being. I also want our kids to see that these writers are like them in so many ways. They are curious about the world, write about things they love, get frustrated from time to time, and, most of all, reread and revise their work. The writing process is, in essence, the same for all writers. What differs is how we choose to engage with it.

I had so many questions. They had so many ideas, but in the interest of space, I have included two interview questions from each. You can see some of the other responses online at www.stenhouse.com/closewritingbook. At the end of this section, I offer some fun activities to help our students engage with the authors' responses—to help them get close to these amazing writers.

Megan Frazer Blakemore

Megan's books include *The Water Castle*, *The Spy Catchers of Maple Hill*, and *The Friendship Riddle*. Find her at http://www.meganfrazer.com/.

It is obvious from the details in your books that you do some research. How can doing research help young authors with their stories?

Whenever possible, visit the place you are writing about. Remember that history happens everywhere, even in your own backyard. You can visit your local library or historical society, and they can point you toward interesting historical places in your own town. If you can't visit your location, or speak with people who were alive then, try to find pictures or other primary source documents that can give you information about what life was like then. A lot of museums have parts of their collection online. Spend a lot of time examining these objects and pull out interesting details to add to your story.

Can you talk about your process for rereading your writing? What are you looking or listening for that helps you reflect or revise?

I reread my writing over and over again. Early on in the writing process, I am looking for big problems. Is this character consistent? Do their actions make sense? As I go through drafts I get more and more specific. I start looking for tone and imagery. By the end, I start looking for what I consider my "crutch words." For me, those are things like *kind of*, *very*, *really*. I also have an addiction to characters shrugging. So I go through and weed out all those words that I overuse.

A big problem I have is making sure I do all these rereadings and rewritings. I just want to be done. Sometimes it helps to take a break and then come back to it with fresh eyes. That makes it easier for me to admit that it's not quite ready yet.

Rob Buyea

Rob's award-winning books include *Because of Mr. Terupt*, *Mr. Terupt Falls Again*, and *Saving Mr. Terupt*. Visit him at www.robbuyea.com.

In your Mr. Terupt books, you write from a number of different perspectives. What are some tips you could offer for writing from multiple perspectives?

One thing is the better you know your character, the better you are going to be at creating voice and perspective. For me, I didn't necessarily know everything about these characters [in *Mr. Terupt*] when I got started. I ask my character the questions, *Why are you doing this, feeling this, saying this? Why? Why? Why?* And as you uncover answers to those questions, you get to know more and more about your character. Then you can think more about perspective and voice, vocabulary and language, and how your character might react to different situations. Knowing that I don't have it all figured out the first time I do it is important. There is a lot of going back and redoing it over and over and over. Revision is most of the work—by far!

When you are working on a project and go back to reread your writing, what are you looking or listening for?

One of the things I might do is read it aloud to myself (or to my dogs) so that I can hear how it flows. I am listening to make sure I haven't been redundant with different words and phrases, especially with seven different storytellers. I want to make sure I haven't used the same phrasing from one kid to the next. By reading aloud, I catch some of those areas.

I'll also read it aloud and listen for transitions, moving from one scene to the next, one paragraph to the next, or from one character to the next. If it is a funny scene, I'll read it to see if I have done everything I can to make it funny. If it is suspenseful, I listen to see if I've built suspense by slowing it down enough. I'll reread it thinking about my reader.

Selene Castrovilla

Selene is the award-winning author of *Revolutionary Friends*, *By the Sword*, *Upon Secrecy*, *MELT*, *The Girl Next Door*, and *Saved by the Music*. Visit her at www.SeleneCastrovilla.com.

When you reread your work, what are you listening for or looking for? Is it different for different genres?

When I reread, I look for different things each time. I check to make sure I've used as many sensory details as possible—in fact, I make a "sensory detail" list for each scene: potential things that could be included. I also do a word check, making sure the perfect words are employed. I use a superpowered thesaurus called *The Writer's Digest Flip Dictionary* to look for word possibilities. I always read my work out loud. That's how I really get a sense of its balance and rhythm.

What is a tip or technique or exercise you could share with young writers to help them with their own writing process?

- Interview your character. Find out what he or she really *wants*. Once you know this, you must convey it to the reader. This is what makes the reader care.

- Reread books you love and study them to learn what makes you love them.

- Try writing in different perspectives—maybe a different narrator or more than one. Try writing in first, third, or even second person. Each has a different feel, and you need to find the one that suits you.

- Know your setting! You must use enough well-placed detail to make us feel *there*. Furthermore, we need to see the setting through the characters' eyes.

- Listen to all advice, but don't feel obliged to take it unless it sits right with you. However, if several people offer the same comment, that might indicate you're not getting your intended message across. You have to keep going until you do, or take it out. Pick your battles!

- Ideas are everywhere. You just have to be willing to see them and let them in. What makes a story unique is your perspective.

Erin Dionne

Erin's books are *Models Don't Eat Chocolate Cookies*, *The Total Tragedy of a Girl Named Hamlet*, *Notes from an Accidental Band Geek*, and *Moxie and the Art of Rule Breaking: A 14-Day Mystery*. Visit her at http://erindionne.com.

Can you talk a little bit about your habits or routines that help you to be a close writer?

First, I make a list of what I want to accomplish for the day, writing-wise. This helps me get focused. If I'm in drafting mode, I've recently added a fifteen-minute freewrite about my current project in a journal. This gets any anxiety out of my head, helps me work out a plot problem, and gets me warmed up. Then, I dive into the manuscript. If I am revising, I stick to the list but skip the freewrite and, instead, reread the last five pages of my manuscript and review notes.

I think drawing a scene from a story is a great way to help students become close writers. Then they can make a list of details they included in their drawing—the color of the chair, the number of people in the room, the weather, and so forth—and then see if those details are present in their writing. If not, they can add them in to make their scene more real for the reader.

How do you approach closely reading your own writing?

I feel like I'm constantly close reading my work. I read sections out loud when I'm drafting and revising. I talk myself through a lot of scenes too, *She would never do that! Why did you write that?* Or, *What does it look like when you make __ hand gesture?* and then I act it out. I also print out my manuscripts and edit by hand, which allows me to see my words in a different way than I do on screen. I watch for repeated words. I watch for lazy writing (skimping on a description, summarizing or telling, instead of showing), and words that sound like ones *I* would use, not my character. My goal is always authenticity.

Jennifer Jacobson

Among Jennifer's books are the Andy Shane early chapter books, *Small as an Elephant*, *Paper Things*, and her resource for teachers, *No More "I'm Done!" Fostering Independence in the Primary Grades*. Visit her at http://jenniferjacobson.com/.

Can you talk about your process for reading your own work?

While writing, I reread my work (both silently and aloud) over and over and over again. I'm reading for meaning, to determine the presence (or lack) of voice, to make sure the sentences delight. I'm checking the pacing (does the story have to speed up or slow down?) and I'm fixing conventional errors. Rereading gives my brain a chance to slow down and think about my reader—to consider what the reader might be longing for at any given point. It's an essential part of the process.

In your book No More "I'm Done!" *you offered lessons for teachers to foster more independence in writing for primary writers. What are some habits or routines you have found that help support close writing for our middle grade writers?*

Here are the things that I believe support independence in all writers:

- Daily writing (even if it's only for ten minutes).

- Choice of topic (even though everyone may be writing in the same genre). When students choose their own topics, they write with more engagement and voice. They have time to think when away from the writing, and they never utter, "I'm Done!" in class, because they know that if one piece is finished, they simply start another.

- Time to think (staring into space is a *positive* writer-like behavior). I recommend beginning writing workshop with Quiet 5, in which the teacher plays soothing music and everyone in the room writes, without talk or movement—even the teacher.

- Time to share. Sharing our work builds a sense of audience and helps us develop a better understanding of the reader's needs.

Lester Laminack

Lester's books include *Saturdays and Tea Cakes*, *Jake's 100th Day of School*, *Snow Day!*, and *Three Hens and a Peacock*. His newest book, *Writers ARE Readers: Flipping Reading Instruction into Writing Opportunities*, is now available. Follow him at http://www.lesterlaminack.com.

What are some writing routines you have established that help you to do so much writing and how do you approach reading aloud your own writing?

I keep a notebook with me almost all the time. I carry a messenger bag with a notebook, a pen, a camera, my phone, and my wallet when I leave my house. Somehow having that notebook near is a comfort. I collect snatches of conversation, observed behaviors, random connections to song lyrics, or some comment on the news. The notebook habit keeps ideas sprouting. There is something about jotting them down that keeps them present in my thinking.

When I am reading aloud a work in progress, I come to it with insight about the tone and pacing I intend as I write. I listen for the "sound" of it. I listen for rhythm and flow and the poetry of phrases. I listen to the voices of characters with attention to who they are and whether I have captured the language they would actually speak. I read aloud with attention to the feel of the language in my mouth. That is, I notice where I trip over words, break the rhythm in the language, or say things that aren't on the page. Those are clear invitations to revision.

What are some questions students could ask themselves that could help them reflect more closely on their own writing?

Take a good look at your topic and ask, Does this really matter to me? Why do I care? Do I want others to care? What am I doing to show others that this matters? Before you reread your draft, stop and ask yourself, What would I like the reader to remember after he finishes this story? Does this sound like the people I am thinking of as I write? Am I focused? Can the reader stay with me from the first line to the last word and not get lost?

Ideas come from questions like what next? Why not? What if? Curiosity is a spark that lights the flame of idea.

Cynthia Lord

Author of *Rules*, *Touch Blue*, *Half a Chance*, *A Handful of Stars*, *Hot Rod Hamster*, and the Shelter Pet Squad series. You can visit her at www.cynthialord.com.

So many of your books seem inspired by the people, places, and animals around you. What advice do you have for young writers?

Places, people, and things we've known and experienced may seem little to us, but they hold honest emotion and real truth. It's that honest emotion we relate to in each other, more than the big, showy moments in our lives.

When you add details you know or write based on things you have experienced, you are able to step past what *everyone* could imagine or research. You go beyond the "tourist" view to the real heart and complicated truth of something. Everything has contrasts.

Can you talk a little about your revision process? What are you looking for or listening for when you reread and reflect on your writing?

All of my books are revised many, many times. In the early revisions, I'm looking at big things. Does the character solve her own problem? Does the conflict increase in the story because of something the main character is doing? It will be more compelling if the story happens *because of* the main character, instead of it happening *to* her. Is there character development? Does the main character make a choice at the end of the book that she couldn't have made in Chapter 1?

Then, in the middle revisions, I'm looking at chapters and paragraphs. What changes for the main character in this chapter? Are there scenes that don't move the story ahead? Have I described this too much or not enough?

Finally, it's about editing. I look at sentences and words. Can I cut this "she said"? Does that chapter end with a compelling hook? Are the details consistent (the house is yellow in Chapter 3 and brown in Chapter 9)? I often use tools at this point: maps, charts, calendars, etc., to make sure all my details are consistent.

The truth is that nobody's first draft is good! Revision is where you'll *make* it good. First drafts are just to create something to start with.

Kate Messner

Kate Messner is the author of *All the Answers*, *Over and Under the Snow*, *Up in the Garden and Down in the Dirt*, and the popular Ranger in Time series, as well as *Real Revision* and *59 Reasons to Write*, both from Stenhouse. Follow Kate on Twitter @KateMessner or at www. katemessner.com.

On your website you talk about carrying a notebook so you can scribble down ideas before you forget. What are some other writing routines or habits that support your writing?

One huge benefit of a writer's notebook is that it trains us to think like writers. When we're carrying a notebook, we look at the world differently—more closely, for starters, but also through the lens of a writer, and we begin to see stories everywhere.

Aside from carrying a notebook, I think the best habit for a writer to have is a reading habit. I've always been a voracious reader, but I've found that the more I write, the more I read like a writer, too—noticing the craft of writing as I read. How did that author build suspense? How did this one create a character who was so flawed but so likable? Reading to answer questions like those is also a skill that kids can develop. Everything we read makes us better writers.

When you go back to reread your work, what are you typically looking or listening for that can help you reflect or revise?

While I'm writing a first draft, I don't stop to revise, but I do keep a list of "known issues," which is my way of saying, *These are the things that I already know can be improved.* A recent list of these issues included directives, such as "Rewrite beginning to add scene with Mom," "Make Danny more rounded—what are his hobbies/friends?" and "Add more goats!"

Once I tackle that list, I always read my manuscript aloud. This takes time, but it's amazing how many things we notice when we read aloud. Our ears catch awkward sentences that our eyes would skim right past. And, of course, another step in my writing/revision process is having a critique partner read my work as well, offering suggestions on what works and asking questions about what might not be effective or clear.

Lynn Plourde

The author of thirty children's books, including *Pigs in the Mud in the Middle of the Rud*, *Wild Child*, *Dino Pets*, and *You're Wearing THAT to School?!* Visit her at www.lynnplourde.com.

You have written so many fun books. What habits or routines do you have as a writer that have helped you?

I can't be a writer without first and always being a *reader*. I have to fill myself up with good words before I have any hope of writing good words. When I read words that speak to me, I pause and reread the words and ask myself, "How did that author *do* that?"

I've recently started keeping a reading journal, and it's simply filled with words I read in others' books that I love. I write down dialogue a character says in a story, a descriptive phrase an author uses, or wise words about a life lesson. I want to save these words. They are treasures.

I also keep an idea notebook. Whenever I get an idea, I write it down so that I don't have to worry about forgetting it. I have hundreds of ideas. They shouldn't all grow into stories, and they won't. It's OK to have too many ideas. It's like having money in the bank—I'm glad they're there even if I never "spend" them.

I really love reading your stories. They are truly meant to be shared out loud. How do you closely read (reread) your work?

I am the Queen of Rereading. I write one sentence and read it aloud. I add a second sentence and read them both aloud. I add a third sentence and read all three aloud. And so on. By rereading my writing aloud, it lets me listen for meaning (Do the words say what I mean to say?), for rhythm (Do the words flow?), for drama (Do I use words that surprise the reader?), and so on.

After I read my pieces of writing aloud sentence by sentence to myself, then I pass my writing to my husband to have him read it aloud to me. I want to see how it sounds when someone else reads it, when I can just concentrate on listening, when I can pretend someone else wrote those words and be more objective. Often I find places that are off when he reads aloud to me. So then I go back and revise. I read my writing aloud again with the revisions, then have him read aloud to me again, and so on, until the words make my ears happy.

Liesl Shurtliff

Liesl Shurtliff is the author of *Rump: The True Story of Rumpelstiltskin*, *Jack: The True Story of Jack and the Beanstalk*, and *Red: The True Story of Red Riding Hood*. Visit her at www.lieslshurtliff.com.

You talk about the idea for **Rump** *coming to you when you were out running. What advice do you have for young authors to help them come up with ideas for their writing?*

Ideas are a strange, creative concept to me, because I think everyone has good ideas and encounters new ideas every day, and it's not so much a matter of "getting" ideas as paying attention to our thoughts and surroundings and knowing which ideas are worth pursuing and what's the most effective way to execute them. I think practice and experimentation is key. The more you write your ideas down and put them in action, even if you don't think they're all that great, your creative genius will reward you with more ideas, and you'll get better and better at picking out the best ideas to pursue.

When you go back and reread your writing to reflect or revise, what are you listening or looking for?

First, after I complete a draft, I try to give myself as much distance as I can from the project (at least a month) before I come back to it. We tend to get too close to our work and lose objectivity, so it's important to give yourself time to get some fresh perspective. My revision process is much like a funnel. I start with a wide opening, looking mostly at the major plot points and pacing of the story, then gradually narrowing down to aspects of character, setting, dialogue, theme, etc. I do read it out loud to myself during each revision stage, and this definitely brings out areas that are slow or confusing.

Melissa Stewart

Melissa is the award-winning author of more than 150 nonfiction books for children, including *Feathers: Not Just for Flying*; *No Monkeys, No Chocolate*; *Under the Snow*; and *A Place for Butterflies*, and coauthor of *Perfect Pairs: Using Fiction and Nonfiction Picture Books to Teach Life Science*. Melissa maintains the blog *Celebrate Science* (http://celebratescience.blogspot.com) and *Melissa Stewart's Science Clubhouse* (www.melissa-stewart.com).

Many of your nonfiction books have a strong voice. While you convey the information, your writing certainly isn't "dry." How do you go about crafting a book's voice?

Some of my books have a more lively voice (*Animal Grossapedia*), while others have a more lyrical voice (*Feathers: Not Just for Flying*). I know what the voice is going to be before I write my very first word, and before I begin, I read books with a similar voice to put me in the right mindset.

While I was writing *Feathers: Not Just for Flying*, I was struggling to find just the right voice. I can remember asking myself, "How did April Pulley Sayre craft the light, lovely voice of *Vulture View*?" To understand her process, I knew I had to put myself in her shoes, so I typed out the text of the entire book. Seeing the words, phrases, and sentences in manuscript form gave me enormous insight into how language devices can play off one another in books with a strong lyrical voice. As I revise a manuscript, I think carefully about voice and look for ways I can bring it out more strongly if necessary.

Every author I've talked to has been able to identify an area of his or her writing that he or she struggles with. Can you identify an aspect of writing that you are constantly working on?

I often struggle with endings, but luckily I have critique partners who give me wonderful advice. Many of my books end with ideas or even exact wording that they have suggested. I also struggle with structure when writing picture books. Structure is the most critical element of nonfiction, and getting it right can take years. In some ways, Common Core has made this easier by focusing on six nonfiction text structures. Now that I recognize these structures, I can go through them and ask myself: Is this structure right? How about this one? It's still a process of trial and error, but at least I'm no longer reinventing the wheel every single time. It's important for writers to build a toolbox that they can turn to when they are stuck.

Tamra Wight

Tamra is the author of *The Three Grumpies* and the Cooper and Pack-rat series. You will find her—and her stunning wildlife photos—at www.tamrawight.com.

You incorporate a lot of what you study and observe in nature into your writing. What tips do you have for writers to help them incorporate what they notice and know into their own writing?

Our job as writers is to create an image in our readers' minds that is a crisp, clear duplicate of the image in our own when we wrote it. We do this through descriptive writing, and that is my very favorite of all the revisions! You must stand back and silently see the world, not just with your eyes, but with all your senses. How does the wind sound? How does a rainy day smell? When you run your hand along a wooden railing, what does it feel like? Keep a notebook of details, so you can remember details later, or snap photos, which is my medium for research. And, of course, don't forget the library. Not only will you find all the details in the books there, but your librarian is your absolute best resource for research!

What are some tips, techniques, or lessons you could share or teach students to help them with their writing process?

Read—a lot. Read for fun, but also read with an analytical eye. Did you love an action scene because it put you on the edge of your seat and got your heart pumping? Was it a page-turner? Then go back and reread it, not with the words in mind but the sentence structure. Did the sentences get shorter and more powerful to show action or tenseness? Were the chapter endings the kind where they leave you with more questions, rather than answering the ones you already have?

Write often, even if it's just a quick story starter. The more you write, the better a writer you become. Rarely does an author sell their first written piece. And I've never heard of one who sold their first draft of their first story. It takes time. And practice.

This is most important. Don't be afraid to share your work for feedback. No, it's not easy. OK, so it's actually more like run-from-the-room-screaming scary. But putting your words, the ones you've worked so hard on, the words which poured from heart and soul, into someone else's hands is how we become better writers. They will look at your story with different eyes; less critical than our own, sometimes. But beware the critic who only has positive words! Our egos will love it, but the story can't be improved upon unless we know exactly where it gets boring or confusing or where the plot becomes weak. You owe it to yourself and your writing to take this step. Most of all, have fun with it!

Activities for Engaging with Authors

MENTOR MONDAY

- Choose one author to focus on for a week.
- Post the picture and biography of an author, along with any of his or her books you may have.
- Share the questions and responses and discuss how this could help us with our writing.

CLOSE READING

These interviews lend themselves to being used as close reading passages. Make a copy of one and ask the students to

- read the passage slowly and thoughtfully and then reread;
- underline or highlight any comment that attracts their attention or sounds interesting;
- in the left margin, paraphrase "what is the author saying/thinking?"; and
- in the right margin, ask a question or make a connection.

JUST ONE MORE

- Often during an interview or press conference the interviewee is about to wrap things up when they are told, "Just one more question!"
- Invite students to think, if they could ask just one more question, what would it be? Encourage them to try to make it a good one if they only get one!
- Collect these and see whether any can be answered by evidence in their books, on their website, and in interviews online.

ASK AN AUTHOR

- Have students research questions that have been asked of authors (author web pages, YouTube, magazines, etc.). They can use some of the questions from these interviews.

- Create a collection of Ask an Author questions. These could be written on an anchor chart, index cards, or popsicle sticks.

- As a reading response after reading a book (either a read-aloud or independent), pull out one of the questions and invite the students to research the answer that author might give. They can use evidence from the text, websites, and interviews to support their thinking.

CLASSROOM AUTHOR OF THE WEEK

- How would the student answer some of these questions? Interview them with Ask an Author questions as well.

- Find a way to "capture" their response (video, note-taking app on a smartphone, other students take notes on their response).

- Post their interview on a bulletin board or Author of the Day space.

- Remind students that our classroom is filled with authors we can learn from!

TAKE MY ADVICE

- Create a poster or space in your room for a mentor author's advice and leave a space for an author's picture or name. Create a speech bubble that reads in part, Take My Advice.

- Choose a piece of advice from one of the responses that relates to what you are currently working on in writing.

- Post the advice from the author within the speech bubble.

- Perhaps the teacher or students could create a learning target "We can _____" based on the advice.

TWEET ME!

- Many authors are on Twitter or other social media sites. Although students under thirteen years of age should not be, many teachers create classroom accounts.

- Create your own questions for authors (140 characters or less for Twitter) and post them to author websites, Facebook pages, or Twitter accounts.

- Many authors do respond. Take a screenshot of any responses and save these in an anthology of author correspondences or advice.

ADOPT AN AUTHOR

Reach out to authors via their websites or social media and pitch a proposal to "adopt" one for the school year.

- Make your expectations reasonable and clear. Maybe they could do the following:

  - Send one letter or e-mail a month/bimonthly to your class in response to class letters.

  - Skype once a month or a few times a year.

  - Join in on a blog post for your class a few times.

- Authors often have deadlines or busy times of the year, so keep requests simple and flexible. The idea is that students can create a relationship with an author that is deeper than a one-letter activity.

Draft Your Story

Take a moment to reflect on the thoughts and insights of these authors. With some colleagues or on your own, consider the following:

- How could you use these interviews to support your writers?

- What are some common close writing approaches you noticed?

- What authors would you or your students like to interview? What would you like to ask them?

Epilogue

The act of writing this book was the closest writing I have ever done in my life. It reinforced, reminded, and taught me so much about the writing process and about myself. First, it reinforced for me that writing not only reflects thinking but also shapes thinking. I started out to write a book sharing my thoughts on the importance of students closely reading their writing. But I discovered through my work that there is even more our writers needed to be closer to their writing. I began to explore that writing relationship. The more I wrote, the more discoveries surprised me and the deeper my thinking became. Only by writing could that happen.

Second, it reminded me of Donald Graves's belief that the best teachers of writing are teachers who write. The empathy and understanding I acquired for other writers (especially our students) is immeasurable. I can sympathize with young writers facing an empty page and puzzling how to begin or organize ideas. I understand the importance of revision and the thrill in finding the words to express my thoughts so precisely. I can relate to the anticipation of receiving feedback and trying to process what it meant for me and my writing. I have felt the joy and the jitters of finishing a piece of writing and sending it off into the world, not knowing how it will be received. Unless I write, I cannot know these things, not really.

Third, it taught me a lot about nurturing a relationship between the writer and the writing. You can't develop a relationship without some basic elements. Here are some qualities we expect from a relationship. They need to be present in our relationships with our writing as well.

- **Honesty:** Taking an impartial look at our writing through the eyes of our readers as well as ourselves and reflecting on the intended message.

- **Mindfulness:** Being present with our writing and in touch with our ideas and choices. We give it our attention and tend to its needs.

- **Compassion:** Being kind to ourselves as writers and learners. We don't need to be perfect, we need to be purposeful.

- **Communication:** Listening and learning from one another and the writer inside us, we can tap into the strength of many to make our writing stronger.

- **Trust:** When we place trust in the process, we understand that, with effort and support, we will grow as writers and that those around us want us to succeed.

- **Commitment:** When we promise ourselves to write often, give our best effort, and never give up, we will persevere when it gets tough and experience satisfying successes.

- **Acceptance:** Being OK with who we are as writers at this time and knowing that it is not a fixed skill frees us from living up to the image others may have of us. Some things we will be good at and others, not so much … yet!

- **Love:** If we don't love what we do, we won't do it for long. Writers need to find ways to enjoy writing and have some fun. We love what brings us joy and pleasure, if this isn't present in our writing classrooms, our students will never fall in love with writing.

It is my hope that you and your students embrace these aspects and create meaningful relationships with your writing that will enrich your lives far beyond the classroom walls. May you write to express, explore, and discover what is important to you in this life. May you be close writers.

References

Alexander, Lloyd. 1996. *Time Cat: The Remarkable Journeys of Jason and Gareth.* New York: Puffin Books.

Angelillo, Janet. 2002. *A Fresh Approach to Teaching Punctuation: Helping Young Writers Use Conventions with Precision and Purpose.* New York: Scholastic.

Angelou, Maya. 1971. *I Know Why the Caged Bird Sings.* Bantam ed. New York: Bantam Books.

———. 2011. "Maya Angelou on How to Write—and How to Live." *O, The Oprah Magazine. April.* http://www.oprah.com/spirit/How-to-Write-a-Poem-Maya-Angelous-Advice.

Bach, Richard. 1977. *Illusions: The Adventures of a Reluctant Messiah.* New York: Delacorte Press.

Beers, G. Kylene, and Robert E. Probst. 2013. *Notice & Note: Strategies for Close Reading.* Portsmouth, NH: Heinemann.

Boushey, Gail, and Joan Moser. 2006. *The Daily 5: Fostering Literacy Independence in the Elementary Grades.* Portland, ME: Stenhouse.

Brown, Sunni. 2014. *The Doodle Revolution: Unlock the Power to Think Differently.* New York: Penguin Group.

Calkins, Lucy, and Abby Oxenhorn Smith. 2003. *Small Moments: Personal Narrative Writing.* Portsmouth, NH: FirstHand.

Chang, Larry. 2006. *Wisdom for the Soul: Five Millennia of Prescriptions for Spiritual Healing.* Washington, DC: Gnosophia.

Chappius, Jan. 2012. "How Am I Doing? Effective Feedback Helps Students See What They Know and What They Need to Keep Working On." *Educational Leadership* 70 (1): 40.

Cohn, Neil. 2013. "Navigating Comics: An Empirical and Theoretical Approach to Strategies of Reading Comic Page Layouts." *Frontiers in Psychology—Cognitive Science* 4: 1–15. doi:10.3389/fpsyg.2013.00186.

Cornelius, David. 2015. *Let's Do Life.* Bloomington, IN: Author House.

Covey, Stephen. 1989. *The 7 Habits of Highly Effective People: Restoring the Character Ethic.* New York: Simon and Schuster.

Daniels, Harvey, and Elaine Daniels. 2013. *The Best-Kept Teaching Secret: How Written Conversations Engage Kids, Activate Learning, and Grow Fluent Writers.* Thousand Oaks, CA: Corwin Literacy.

DiCamillo, Kate. 2014. "Author Kate DiCamillo Connects with Young Readers." *Washington Post*, December 12. http://www.highbeam.com/doc/1P2-37482788.html?

Dorfman, Lynne R., and Rose Cappelli. 2007. *Mentor Texts: Teaching Writing Through Children's Literature, K–6.* Portland, ME: Stenhouse.

Dweck, Carol S. 2006. *Mindset: The New Psychology of Success.* New York: Random House.

Earl, Lorna M. 2004. *Assessment as Learning: Using Classroom Achievement to Maximize Student Learning.* Experts in Assessment. Thousand Oaks, CA: Corwin.

Fisher, Douglas. 2012, April 3. "Close Reading and the CCSS, Pt. 1." McGraw Hill Education. YouTube video. https://www.youtube.com/watch?v=5w9v6-zUg3Y.

Fletcher, Ralph J. 2011. *Mentor Author, Mentor Texts: Short Texts, Craft Notes, and Practical Classroom Uses.* Portsmouth, NH: Heinemann.

———. 2013. "Keynote." Dublin Literacy Conference. Dublin, Ohio, February 23.

Gaiman, Neil. 2010. "Ten Rules for Writing Fiction." *The Guardian*, February 19. http://www.theguardian.com/books/2010/feb/20/ten-rules-for-writing-fiction-part-one.

Gantos, Jack. 2001. *Joey Pigza Loses Control.* New York: Scholastic.

Graves, Donald. 1995. "Answering Your Questions About Teaching Writing: A Talk with Donald H. Graves." *Instructor Magazine*, November–December.

———. 2004. "What I've Learned from Teachers of Writing." *Language Arts* 82 (2): 88–94.

Harrison, Corbett. *Always Write: Mentor Texts.* http://corbettharrison.com/mentortext.html.

Hunt, Lynda Mullaly. 2012. *One for the Murphys.* New York: Nancy Paulsen Books.

Iso-Ahola, Seppo E., and Charles O. Dotson. 2014. "Psychological Momentum: Why Success Breeds Success." *Review of General Psychology* 18 (1): 19–33.

Johnston, Peter. 2012. "Guiding the Budding Writer." *Educational Leadership* 70 (1): 64–67.

Kristo, Janice V., and Rosemary A. Bamford. 2004. *Nonfiction in Focus: A Comprehensive Framework for Helping Students Become Independent Readers and Writers of Nonfiction, K–6.* New York: Scholastic.

Lamott, Anne. 1995. *Bird by Bird: Some Instructions on Writing and Life.* New York: Anchor Books.

Lehman, Christopher, and Kate Roberts. 2014. *Falling in Love with Close Reading: Lessons for Analyzing Texts and Life.* Portsmouth, NH: Heinemann.

Lewis, C. S., and W. H. Lewis. 1993. *Letters of C. S. Lewis.* Revised and enlarged ed. San Diego, CA: Harcourt Brace.

Messner, Kate. 2011. *Real Revision: Authors' Strategies to Share with Student Writers.* Portland, ME: Stenhouse.

Murray, Donald M. 2012. *The Craft of Revision.* 5th ed. Anniversary ed. Boston: Wadsworth Cengage Learning.

Newkirk, Thomas. 2014. *Minds Made for Stories: How We Really Read and Write Informational and Persuasive Texts.* Portsmouth, NH: Heinemann.

Newton, Sir Isaac. 1676. Letter to Robert Hooke, 15 February (modernized version).

Palacio, R. J. 2012. *Wonder*. New York: Knopf for Young Readers.

Parry, Jo-Ann, and David Hornsby. 1988. *Write On: A Conference Approach to Writing*. Portsmouth, NH: Heinemann.

Phillips, Larry W., ed. 1999. *Ernest Hemingway on Writing*. New York: Simon and Schuster.

Probst, Robert. 1987. *Transactional Theory of the Literary Work: Implications for Research*. Urbana, IL: ERIC Clearinghouse on Reading and Communication Skills (ERIC No. ED284274).

Rief, Linda. 2003. *100 Quickwrites: Fast and Effective Freewriting Exercises That Build Students' Confidence, Develop Their Fluency, and Bring Out the Writer in Every Student*. New York: Scholastic Teaching Resources.

Riordan, Rick. 2005. *The Lightning Thief*. New York: Disney Hyperion Books.

Rosenblatt, Louise, M. 1988. *Writing and Reading: The Transactional Theory*. Technical Report No. 416. New York: New York University, Center for the Study of Reading.

———. 1994. *The Reader, the Text, the Poem: The Transactional Theory of the Literary Work*. Carbondale: Southern Illinois University Press.

Stockton, Nick. 2014. "What's Up with That: Why It's So Hard to Catch Your Own Typos." *Wired*. August 12. http://www.wired.com/2014/08/wuwt-typos/.

Taliaferro, John. 1999. *Tarzan Forever: The Life of Edgar Rice Burroughs, Creator of Tarzan*. New York: Scribner.

Thompson, Lawrance Roger. 1966. *Robert Frost: The Early Years, 1874–1915*. New York: Holt, Rinehart, and Winston.

Trenfor, Alexandra K. The Learning Revolution Project. http://learningrevolution.com/page/great-educational-quotes.

Truss, Lynne. 2004. *Eats, Shoots & Leaves: The Zero Tolerance Approach to Punctuation*. New York: Gotham Books.

Vygotsky, Lev S. 1978. *Mind in Society: The Development of Higher Psychological Processes*. Cambridge, MA: Harvard University Press.

Wiggins, Grant. 2012. "Seven Keys to Effective Feedback." *Educational Leadership* 70 (1): 10–16.

RECOMMENDED RESOURCES

Authors Reading Their Work. http://sqworl.com/8t8v5l and https://www.youtube.com/playlist?list=PLank6fPmAnywqWA-2KJO6q3GoBVw1iUq1.

Burke, Jim. 2009. *Content Area Writing: How to Design Effective Writing Assignments, Teach Students Expository Writing, Assess and Respond to Student Writing*. New York: Scholastic.

Burns, Marilyn. 1995. *Writing in Math Class: A Resource for Grades 2–8*. Sausalito, CA: Math Solutions.

Chappuis, Jan. 2009. *Seven Strategies of Assessment for Learning*. Boston: Allyn & Bacon.

Daniels, Harvey, and Steven Zemelman. 2007. *Content-Area Writing: Every Teacher's Guide*. Portsmouth, NH: Heinemann.

Hattie, John. 2012. *Visible Learning for Teachers: Maximizing Impact on Learning*. London: Routledge.

Heard, Georgia. 2014. *The Revision Toolbox: Teaching Techniques That Work*. 2nd ed. Portsmouth, NH: Heinemann.

Johnston, Peter H. 2004. *Choice Words: How Our Language Affects Children's Learning*. Portland, ME: Stenhouse.

Lane, Barry. 1993. *After the End: Teaching and Learning Creative Revision*. Portsmouth, NH: Heinemann.

———. 1999. *Reviser's Toolbox*. Shoreham, VT: Discover Writing Press.

Lane, Barry, and Miles Bodimeade. 2003. *51 Wacky We-search Reports: Face the Facts with Fun*. Shoreham, VT: Discover Writing.

Marzano, Robert J. 2010. *Formative Assessment & Standards-Based Grading*. Bloomington, IN: Marzano Research Laboratory.

McCloud, Scott. 1999. *Understanding Comics: The Invisible Art*. New York: Turtleback.

McLachlan, Brian. 2013. *Draw Out the Story: Ten Secrets to Creating Your Own Comics*. Toronto, ON: Owlkids.

Messner, Kate. 2011. *Real Revision: Authors' Strategies to Share with Student Writers*. Portland, ME: Stenhouse.

———. 2015. *59 Reasons to Write: Mini-Lessons, Prompts, and Inspiration for Teachers*. Portland, ME: Stenhouse.

———. Teachers Write! http://www.katemessner.com/teachers-write/.

Moss, Connie M., and Susan M. Brookhart. 2012. *Learning Targets: Helping Students Aim for Understanding in Today's Lesson*. Alexandria, VA: ASCD.

Skyping Authors. http://www.katemessner.com/authors-who-skype-with-classes-book-clubs-for-free/.

Tovani, Cris. 2011. *So What Do They Really Know? Assessment That Transforms Teaching and Learning*. Portland, ME: Stenhouse.

Index

Page numbers followed by *f* indicate figures.